# TOWARD A
# THEOLOGY OF
# RADICAL INVOLVEMENT

# TOWARD A THEOLOGY OF RADICAL INVOLVEMENT

*The Theological Legacy of Martin Luther King Jr.*

## LUTHER D. IVORY

Abingdon Press
Nashville

TOWARD A THEOLOGY OF RADICAL INVOLVEMENT:
THE THEOLOGICAL LEGACY OF MARTIN LUTHER KING JR.

*Copyright © 1997 by Abingdon Press*

*This book is printed on recycled, acid-free, elemental-chlorine-free paper.*

**Library of Congress Cataloging-in-Publication Data**

Ivory, Luther D., 1953–
    Toward a theology of radical involvement: the theological legacy
of Martin Luther King Jr./Luther D. Ivory.
        p.   cm.
    Includes bibliographical references.
    ISBN 0-687-01453-0 (alk. paper)
    1.  King, Martin Luther, Jr., 1929–1968.   2.  Theology—
History—20th century.   I.  Title.
BX4827.K53I96   1997
203'61.092—dc21                                                            97-1296
                                                                              CIP

97 98 99 00 01 02 03 04 05 06—10 9 8 7 6 5 4 3 2 1

MANUFACTURED IN THE UNITED STATES OF AMERICA

# CONTENTS

# PART TWO
# THE PRACTICAL APPLICATION OF RADICAL INVOLVEMENT THEOLOGY: TRANSFORMATIVE PRESCRIPTIONS FOR THE SITUATIONAL CONTEXT

# PREFACE

I was fifteen years old when Martin Luther King Jr. was felled by an assassin's bullet while standing on the balcony of the Lorraine Motel in Memphis, Tennessee, 1968. It was that event, and circumstances surrounding it, that proved to be decisive for the direction my own life would take. Paradoxically, the tragic death of Dr. King would serve as the conduit for my personal resurrection moment. It was out of the collective grief and confusion of that painful period in the nation's history that I emerged with a deep commitment to discover and fulfill my destiny. Resultantly, I was propelled toward a search for self-discovery, meaning, and purpose.

To recall the ethos of Memphis at that time is to acknowledge a glaring inconsistency in attitudes and sentiments held by Memphians relative to Dr. King's purpose and presence. The sanitation workers appeared to be genuinely elated about the fact that the "Doc" (a term of both endearment and respect often applied to King) was coming in to lend support, garner public sympathy for, and draw media attention to the strike. The local NAACP, AFSCME (the labor union), and several prominent, local ministers had voiced strong support for King and the movement.

It became increasingly clear to me, however, that a lack of consensus about the wisdom and necessity of the strike as well as King's role in it was prevalent. To be sure, most whites in Memphis (according to polls, newspaper coverage, media interviews, and plain ol' everyday "business as usual" behavior) supported the city against the demands of the sanitation workers, over 90 percent of whom happened to be black. The issue of economic justice had exposed the raw nerve of

7

racism and Jim Crow ethics operating in the social fabric of Memphis life. The sanitation strike had come to serve as the vehicle through which fundamental issues related to both civil and human rights of black folk, such as the exercise of basic, constitutionally guaranteed rights including citizenship and voting; equal access to public facilities as American citizens; the opportunity to enjoy basic social amenities and to be treated with the dignity and respect accorded every human being; the equitable distribution of basic social goods in education, housing, jobs, and income; and the role of blacks in local government could be raised in the public square. In fact, the entire structure of the city's segregated way of life was being challenged, and this resulted in the further overt polarization of the city along racial lines.

It was clear that whites, as a collective sociopolitical force, neither desired nor appreciated King's presence. In fact, whites generally seemed to thoroughly resent his coming. Yet, this response was to be fully expected of whites, I had thought. Indeed, had not the King-led movement threatened to dismantle the very institutional structures as well as the web of tightly constructed social and political networks from which white Memphians had benefited derivatively for so long, and upon which they had come to depend for their livelihood? Certainly one did not have to summon the prophetic powers of Nostradamus to be able to predict the pervasive fears and largely negative reactions of whites to the justice struggle of blacks. Likewise, it did not require a herculean leap in rational thinking to understand why whites would so deeply loathe King's intrusion into those territorial prerogatives that they had considered the domain of whites, and whites alone.

It was another matter altogether, though, to witness the negative reactions to King's arrival by some in the black community of Memphis. This was especially true of many poor blacks whose worldview was linked to certain religious centers prominent on the African American spiritual landscape. Emerging as they did out of the lower socioeconomic levels, these persons exhibited a tenacious loyalty to the many small "storefront" Baptist, Holiness, and Pentecostal churches found in virtually every black neighborhood across America.

The religious perspective that informed these groups tended to focus primarily upon a personal salvation aimed at the interior conversion of the individual psyche. Consequently, the emergent ethical focus concerned itself with the internalization and enforcement of

8

strict behavioral codes designed to influence and guide personal conduct. Much attention was given to the moral content of individual lifestyles and interpersonal relationships. In this way, the private faith of the individual Christian was given central place. The role of religious faith was conceived mainly to convict, restrain, and guide the affairs of the individual Chrstian as private citizen. The task of religion, therefore, was understood primarily as that of nurturing the development of faith in the individual disciple in order to produce morally responsible beings who would, in turn, make better citizens. The moral and social improvement of society was achievable solely through the redemption of the individual soul. The implicit, operating logic seemed readily apparent: if the salvation of enough individuals could be achieved, the society would derivatively, by association, experience a similar transformation.

Of paramount importance, then, was personal sin and redemption, while scant attention was given to an analysis of sin and redemption in powerful corporate structures operating in the culture of the day. As a result, the arena of private faith was severed from the realm of public responsibility. Efforts at promoting the spiritual reformation of the solitary individual had little connection with engaging public debate on social problems or the shaping of public policy. Therefore, adherents of these groups tended to discourage a strong correlation between religious faith and the transformation of social, political, and economic institutions.[1] Consequently, according to the faith perspective of these churches, King's activist spirituality (which viewed religious faith as unavoidably and inseparably connected to the prophetic task of transforming both the individual and the social order) would be considered illegitimate.

My family had been thoroughly immersed in this particular religious persuasion. My parents were representative of a significant segment of the black community who thought King's presence in the city was not only unnecessary and untimely, but dangerously counterproductive, and even un-Christian. They had resented King's presence in Memphis for those reasons alone. In retrospect, my grandparents and parents had feared that the unspoken "gentlemen's agreement" that had existed between the races in Memphis for centuries would crumble under the assault of marching feet and revolutionary rhetoric. This precariously held balance of power amounted to a racial powder keg that they felt was certain to explode under the pressure of nonviolent direct action. My parents had remained convinced that such disruptive activity would leave in its wake irreparable social disintegration and psychological dislocation. Consumed as they were with matters of daily survival, and indoctrinated thoroughly with a brand of privatized religion, my parents, at that time, possessed neither the belief structure of engagement nor the energy of activism required to embrace and support the movement in a public manner.

As our family watched the local evening news, my grandparents and parents would say to us, "That Martin Luther King ought to just stop all this. He ain't thinking 'bout what he's doin'. Comin' in here and just stirrin' up more trouble. We don't need him comin' in here with this mess. We got enough to deal with. This ain't nuthin' to play with. This is dangerous. Somebody gon' end up gettin' hurt. We need to pray. He's a preacher. He ought to know better. Pray, and let God deal with these white folk!" Then they would lay down ironclad parental law. "Ya'll stay away from down there. You ain't lost nuthin' down there at them rallies. So don't be goin' down there for nuthin'."

As any student of human behavior knows, the surest way to incite action of any kind is to forbid it. Such was the intensity of my desire to find out what the strike (and more specifically, the "Doc") was all about that I could barely contain my composure while in my grandparents' and parents' presence. There was a buzz, an excitement, a fever everywhere. It was contagious, and I was hopelessly caught in its grip. I went to the rallies as often as I could. I followed King in the media as he increasingly drew my attention to the plight of black and poor people. I read King's analysis of religion as a force for social revolution as well as personal conversion. I listened to King as he argued that the church had to assume responsibility in challenging injustice and participating in the struggle to transform the society. On the eve of the "Mountaintop" speech, I slipped out of the back window of our house, unawares to my parents, and heard what would become King's swan song. By next evening, King was history. The man who had surreptitiously become my hero now lay dead at my doorstep.

I did not know at that time that I would devote the greater part of my life to trying to understand who King was and what his public ministry entailed. Somehow, I was convinced that in death, King's meaning and legacy would emerge with a clarity in the public square that had eluded him in life. And yet, twenty-nine years after his death, American society remains unclear about the meaning of King for ourselves and for the world. We are perplexed about King's prophetic piety. We do not seem to be able to probe the depth and content of his faith. We are riddled with questions as to the integrity of his character as well as his intellectual depth and ability as a scholar. The culture of America has not yet come to terms with either his humanity or the "larger than life" persona he cast. Well into the 1990s, we continue the struggle to ascertain his relevance and his legacy for contemporary society.

In short, we are caught on the horns of a dilemma—a crisis—relative to the identity of King. Like the citizens of Memphis in 1968 (both black and white), citizens of the nation and the world today harbor multiple, diverse viewpoints and feelings about King. The reason for this state of affairs may be directly attributable to the fact that like them, we are as yet unclear as to who King really was and what he was really attempting to accomplish. The "world house," of which he spoke so poignantly, has not yet resolved its identity crisis with regard to King.[2]

This book grows out of my own desire to gain clarity about the identity and the relevancy of Martin Luther King Jr. for our time. While this project culminated in my doctoral dissertation, I come as a pilgrim, a seeker who has wrestled with King for some twenty-nine years. And yet, I have not journeyed alone. I want to offer gratitude to the many companions who have accompanied me along the way: the Ivory family—my parents (William and Dorothy Ivory), sisters, and brothers—who have nurtured and supported me; the Bungalo Braves, my "homies," who taught me a lot about loyalty and belonging; Mr. Frank Johnson of Johnson's Grocery and "Prof" Nelson Jackson who taught me the value of honesty; and the teachers of Douglass Elementary, Hollywood Jr. High, and Douglass High who introduced me to the world of books, and made me believe that I could not only learn, but also successfully engage in critical thinking. I offer gratitude to First Baptist Mount Olive where I learned the stories of the Bible, developed a love for the black Church, and where the roots of my spiritual awareness lie; to New Harvest Baptist for recognizing and providing the opportunity for me to express and develop my God-given gifts; and to three Presbyterian churches—Bethel, Parkway Gardens, and Emmanuel, all of which loved me and helped me to hear and respond to a call to the ministry of Word and Sacraments.

I want to give a word of special gratitude to Dr. George VanDevate, my philosophy teacher at UT/Knoxville who forced me to read Plato's *Symposium* and Eldridge Cleaver's *Soul On Ice;* to the faculty, support staff, many student-scholars of Union Theological Seminary in Richmond, Virginia, for what they have meant in my development as a man and a scholar; to the School of Theology, Virginia Union, for its unfailing support through difficult times; to Woodville Presbyterian Church for taking me in, and giving me a chance; to Candler School of Theology, Emory, for opening new horizons of thought, and for believing in me; to the members of my doctoral dissertation committee—Don Saliers, Rebecca Chopp, Ted Runyon, and a very special word of thanks to my mentor, friend, and adviser, Noel Erskine; to Gayraud Wilmore, Jose Miguez-Bonino, and Jürgen Moltmann who helped deepen and clarify my understanding of and commitment to the prophetic tradition of religious thought; to Will Coleman, Lester Staton, Daryl White, and Angelo Chatmon who remain friends as well as intellectual playmates; to the Schultzes, my adopted parents—Ben, I miss you, and I wish you were here to witness this day; to my "in-laws" who are the greatest; and my first colleagues in ministry, the "voices of Genesis." To Otis Turner and Thomas McPhatter, friends and colleagues. Thanks for the vocational "challenge" and your continued support during chaotic moments. Thanks also to Bluff City Christian College—may you live long and prosper.

Finally, thanks to the National Black Presbyterian Caucus, the Presbytery of Memphis, and to the steering council and members of New Life Community Presbyterian Church where I serve as organizing pastor. I thank you for believing in me and taking a chance with a nontraditional thinker.

And to my incredible immediate family—Carole, Candice, Donne. I could never have completed this book without the many, unspoken sacrifices you have made over the years and the support you continue to give. You have given up so much in order for me to pursue personal and vocational goals. I want to publicly thank you for not abandoning me at times when, I am certain, my sanity became an issue for serious debate. I am very much in your debt. I could not hope to repay you without God's permission to live another lifetime.

# INTRODUCTION

**M**artin Luther King Jr. ranks as one of the most important and celebrated figures in the twentieth century. On the American scene, a national holiday has been named in his honor and is celebrated by millions each year. Countless scholarships, schools, bridges, streets, libraries, and churches bear his name. Plays, movies, books, and songs have been written about his life and his contribution to the struggle for human and civil rights. On the world scene, his influence extends beyond national boundaries as both his philosophy and method of nonviolent direct action have been embraced in many countries by social philosophers and leaders of protest movements. Without question, as a global figure of mythic-heroic proportions, King's life and thought continue to wield significant influence in struggles for political, economic, and social justice around the globe in the 1990s.

And yet, despite varied and significant efforts aimed at the veneration of King, I am convinced that a clear public understanding of his meaning for us today has not yet been adequately or fully achieved. There has not yet emerged in literature, media, or popular culture a clear and compelling public understanding of King's message and legacy that is true to the full "text" of his life and thought. At the same time, public debate has not yet been seriously engaged with regard to King's alternative social-economic-political vision. As a result, the Kingian legacy has had a rather limited, episodic, and superficial impact on society as regards the shaping of a lasting public policy agenda. Indeed, with the exception of discussions about the practicality of nonviolent social change, both national and international communities seem to identify little else in King's thinking that is worthy of serious, critical, intellectual engagement.

Additionally, mass public confusion about King's life and thought exists in both academia and the public square. Multiple and competing images of King continue to generate ambiguity about his vocational identity. Business entrepreneurs, driven primarily by a desire to achieve the maximization of profit, skilfully employ marketing strategies that subtly co-opt King as a capital-producing icon in the marketplace. Political and ideological detractors devise subtle delegitimation strategies that effectively blunt the radical and prophetic thrust of his legacy. As a result, both academia and the public remain unclear about the identity of King, and ambivalent about his meaning for the world.

No singular, overarching area seems to account for the lack of clarity about the identity of King. Similarly, one cannot point to any one variable as the sole reason for the public's inability to grasp the more profound aspects of King's message or its failure to appreciate the genuinely radical nature of his perspective. However, one particular area, more than any other, requires investigation as a prime factor in the perpetuation of mass public confusion about King. I maintain that the cultural ambiguity surrounding King is fundamentally driven by how little credence he has been given to date as a serious, creative theological thinker. The key to resolving the mass public confusion about the identity, meaning, and relevancy of King lies in uncovering the conceptual underpinning that informed his life and work.

Clearly, academia and the public seem to genuinely recognize King's contributions in the roles of minister and social activist. However, his equally valuable contributions as a structured, innovative theologian have yet to be fully appreciated. He has never been given due credence as a major American theological thinker, nor has he been given equitable consideration on a level with other figures in the pantheon of American theological voices such as Jonathan Edwards, Reinhold Niebuhr, Walter Rauschenbusch, James Cone, or Rosemary Ruether.

The time has come for a long-overdue corrective to the decades of insufficient attention, inadequate focus, and improper treatment of King as a theologian. I am convinced that the current cultural ambiguity and mass public confusion about King are best understood as a collective crisis of identity. This identity crisis has, in turn, fueled the public's distorted conception of his message and meaning. Hence, the public continues to be victimized by truncated analyses of King's perspective and interpretations of his legacy that dilute and minimize his relevancy for our time.

If the nation and the world hope to understand and appreciate the breadth and depth of King's contributions, we must adequately attend to the issue of his vocational identity or human calling. The resolution of the public's identity crisis with regard to King, therefore, lies in its capacity to reconceptualize him as a theologian. Every aspect of his public witness and social activism was undergirded by a solid theological platform. In order to understand the who, what, and why of King's vocational identity, one must begin with the sustained intellectual formulation that informed his public actions. Indeed, it is the theological basis of his activities rather than the social involvement itself that provides the point of departure from which to best understand the man, the message, the mission, and their meaning.

This book examines the vocational identity or human calling of Martin Luther King Jr. primarily as a theologian. To be sure, other scholars and studies have investigated and recognized prominent theological and ethical themes in King's thought. Increasingly, scholars have identified him as a theologian or ethicist who emerged from the black experience in America that involves suffering, survival, and the incessant struggle for freedom and justice. However, neither has research to date been sufficiently attentive to King as a highly structured, imaginative, and serious theological formulator, nor has the central hub of King's theology been identified and delineated in the foci and categories of "traditional" theology. This has contributed substantially to the public's continued lack of clarity about King's identity, message, meaning, and legacy.

In this text, I argue that King is best understood as a creative theological thinker who offered a theology of radical involvement. King's theological perspective sought to raise permanent, generative tensions for the culture of his day. At the same time, it sought to resolve those tensions in light of a radical, Christian vision that was thoroughly informed by a notion of "the radicality of involved love." King's social activism was based upon an ethic of community, and this ethic was informed by structured theological formulation on how love radically involves itself in the affairs of human history. In this way, I intend to establish a critical correlation between King's highly visible patterns of proactive public engagement and his less visible, underlying framework of theological thought.

Each chapter of this book seeks to contribute to a clearer public understanding of King by examining some aspect of the book's main thesis as stated above. Chapter 1 explores the personal crisis of vocational identity that King himself struggled to resolve throughout his life from his early years up to the moment of destiny in Memphis. In so doing, it examines the family history and the black religious tradition from which King emerged. That history and tradition had provided some important clues that assisted King in his search to discover and come to terms with his ethnic and religious identity. However, it had also raised some rather problematic concerns about his pursuit of a vocation. King's personal crisis of vocational identity deepened as his formal education exposed him to other traditions of faith, protest, and intellectual debate. As these diverse traditions vied for recognition and allegiance, King was faced with a quandary about how these myriad strands of thought might be made compatible with his family history and religious tradition in order to form a coherent faith perspective. Of major importance is how the resolution of his personal crisis of vocational identity relates to King's simultaneous quest to obtain definitive answers, and hence clarity, about the nature and reality of God. This discussion illuminates both the nature and resolution of King's personal crisis of vocational identity. As such, it provides vital clues for how contemporary culture must resolve its own mass public confusion about the identity and relevancy of King.

Chapters 2 and 3 identify the content of King's resolution to his personal crisis of vocational identity. Of major significance is a presentation of those theological claims and convictions that served as the bedrock upon which King built his vocational self-understanding. King struggled to arrive at those conceptions of God, church, Christ, humanity, and history that would provide clarity about vocational identity. Of major significance is the extent to which King's doctrinal and vocational struggles took place at the intersection where both thought and action meet in history.

Chapters 2 and 3 are primarily archaeological in nature. That is to say they present data unearthed from King's voluminous writings. These chapters are important as they demonstrate how King's emphatic linkage of doctrine and vocation, leads to an emergent theological focus on radical involvement which, in turn, becomes the driving force in King's perspective. These chapters also establish and build definitive support for the contention that King is best understood as a theologian: his activist rhetoric and emancipatory social action were thoroughly informed and profoundly driven by a particular understanding of God and God's intentions for history and humanity.

Chapter 4 offers a summary of the results of the discussion in the previous chapters. The primary focus of this chapter is an examination of the nature, content, and aim of King's theology of radical involvement. In probing the basic contours of radical involvement, the undeniably more radical and prophetic foci emerge prominently in King's theology. Therefore, careful attention is given to King's persistent concern with critical analysis and prophetic critique of concrete human situations. Further, significant attention is devoted to the way King's theology leads to emancipatory praxis aimed at comprehensive societal transformation. In fact, this chapter may be read as a public conversation about how King's theology relates to the world. The discussion of radical involvement serves as a bridge between Parts I and II of the book.

In chapter 5, the focus shifts to King's ethical perspective. It demonstrates the ease with which King was able to move between (what was for him) the partially permeable boundary between theology and ethics. Not only is King's ethic derivative of his theology, his ethic is basically an extension of his theology. King's theology of radical involvement led to an emergent ethical focus on community, which had as its basic agenda the creation of a society where justice is normatively established in interpersonal, cross-cultural, and structural forms. King's ethic begins with the human situation, and deals primarily with what he called the "triple evils" of racism, war, and poverty. These represent the corridors of theological-ethical struggle through which King called the nation to pass.

King's ethic of community may be seen as part of an active, concrete, vocational response to the demands of a theology of radical involvement. The proactive nature of King's theology sponsors a variety of resistance efforts designed to activate struggle against institutional arrangements that perpetuate injustice in society. As King understands the doctrinal content of Christian religious faith and responds vocationally to it, he is able to demonstrate in thought, word, and deed the lifestyle mandated by his theological commitment. King comes to view his very life as a means by which *to be* and *to do* the vocation of theologian. In demonstrating the inseparability of King's

17

theology and ethic and how that ethic operated in the context of a racist, militaristic, class-oriented market culture, we will better understand how King's theology and ethic may speak to us today.

Chapter 6 assesses the relevancy of King's life and thought for contemporary society. It suggests that King's theology of radical involvement can be "read" in light of how certain tensions emerge as permanent features of his approach. As a result, King emerges as a much more "radical" thinker in view of the prophetic critique and challenge as well as the transformative vision he offers society. This chapter explores, in preliminary fashion, several generative tensions that King's theology acutely raises for the modern-day theologian and the contemporary church. Further, King's theological and ethical program makes a rather convincing case for the argument that the crises of postmodern society are, at bottom, accompanied by tensions that ought to be viewed as permanent features of life. Collectively, we, like each preceding and successive generation, cannot hope to avoid them, but rather must face and resolve them. The focus will turn to three areas of generative tension in King's thought—values (identity), personal lifestyle (ethics), and societal ordering (hope for a viable future).

After laying out the various crises and tensions that King's theology raises, the discussion will focus briefly on two specific aspects of American society—the issue of class and the problem of violence. The various crises and tensions that attend these issues are explored in light of King's theological program. The findings suggest that a theology of radical involvement and a derivative ethic of community will be relevant to public policy issues, debate, and the shaping of legislative agendas. King's perspective may provide helpful insights in efforts aimed at the democratization of social and political structures and the humanization of economic institutional forces operating in a market culture.

A word needs to be said about the outline of the book. As these chapters unfold, a pattern naturally emerges out of the methodology used to investigate and write this text. King's method for doing theology involved a two-step movement and this serves as the blueprint for the structure of this book: one from lived experience to text and back to lived experience in the manner of current liberation theologies. King's first step takes the situation of lived existence seriously and begins with situational analysis. The second step in

18

King's method of doing theology moves toward a reflective-active response—social action aimed at situational transformation.

Like King's approach, the argument of this text follows a two-step movement. Chapters 1, 2, 3, and 4 represent the first movement of the dialogue. They are concerned with an analysis of King's historical situation and textual utterances (both written and oral) for purposes of theoretical construction. They might best be identified as analytical-descriptive in nature. Chapters 5, and 6 represent the second movement of the dialogue. They are concerned with the practical implications of those analytical categories developed and described in the first movement. As such, they point toward situational transformation and deal with the practicalities involved in applying thought and action to the contemporary situation. They might best be identified as constructive-prescriptive in nature.

A word also needs to be said about the sources used in the research for this book. I am in basic agreement with Lewis Baldwin's contention that there are no significant discrepancies between King's published essays, speeches, and books and his unpublished sermons, speeches, personal correspondence, and interviews.[1] Therefore, I have relied upon primary sources—namely King's books, articles, interviews, sermons, and speeches. In addition, I have made full use of secondary historical sources—biographical material, historical documents that chronicle the period of King's public witness, and interpretive analyses and social commentary on the 1960s era.

Finally, this work does not claim to be definitive or exhaustive. My primary objective is to advance public discussion on King by calling attention to the inadequacy of our current understandings of him and by offering a new way of envisioning him. I hope to promote in both academia and the public a revisitation of his life, work, and thought by convincing readers of the absolute necessity of engaging in a critical rereading of King. Perhaps, King will be given due credence for the profound level of critical analysis he articulated as well as the revolutionary challenge and bold vision he embraced. In so doing, we might be able to appropriate King's thought for our time. A secondary objective is to generate a new discussion about King's importance as an intellectual. King's significance as a theological thinker certainly merits further attention by scholars. Perhaps a deeper appreciation of the contributions he made as a theologian will finally be forthcoming.

## PART ONE

# THE EMERGENCE OF
# RADICAL INVOLVEMENT THEOLOGY:
# ANALYSIS AND DESCRIPTION
# OF THE SITUATIONAL CONTEXT

# CHAPTER 1

# MARTIN LUTHER KING JR. AND THE CRISIS OF VOCATIONAL IDENTITY

One has only to look to the writings of Joseph Washington and Albert Cleage to encounter a provocative entry point into a discussion about the identity of King. Washington and Cleage represent two theologians who fail to discern the more profound theological bases of King's thought and action.[1] Cleage appreciates the contributions King has made in identifying the liberation of the poor as central to the gospel, but sees the bankruptcy of the remainder of King's theological program.[2] Washington denies any significant theological understanding in King. Examining his nonviolent strategy, Washington sees King not as a theologian, but rather as a syncretistic philosopher who was undisciplined by a community of theological thinkers.[3]

In the view of these two thinkers, King is entitled to wear many hats—ethicist, civil rights leader, philosopher, and Baptist preacher. However, King's donning of the theological cap is problematic for both. For Cleage, King is deserving of the cap, but it does not fit too well. King's theology lacks the radical thrust necessary to sustain movements of liberation by black and poor in situations of oppression around the globe. For Washington, King is undeserving of the cap since he was certainly *not* a theologian. Therefore, we may *not* look to King as a contributor of any substance or weight in the theological realm.

The assertions of Cleage and Washington concerning both black religion and King were met powerfully and successfully by black religious intellectuals and others writing in the early, rudimentary stages of black theology in the 1960s and 1970s. Indeed, black religious intellectuals continue to clarify the sources, norms, methods, tasks, and aims of theology in the 1980s and 1990s.[4] While the responses of black theologians and ethicists continue to build support for and foster a greater appreciation of King's legacy, he is yet denied the place he has merited in the theological circle of honor. There remains a current and persisting failure to recognize King as the uniquely innovative religious intellectual he, in fact, was. Among both the general populace and many scholars in academia, the early viewpoints of Washington and Cleage continue to hold sway. Hence, King is implicitly and civilly invalidated as a theologian. Viewed primarily as a social activist, his significant theological intellectual productivity is discredited.

Unquestionably, King has had a profound impact upon American life and culture. While we may debate the nature of the difference, it seems unarguably clear that we are living in a society that is fundamentally different from what it might or would have been had King not lived. Since King holds such an apparently hallowed, symbolic, and heroic role in American society, we are thereby constrained to identify King's relevancy and legacy for the nation and the world. Consequently, these quintessential queries are implicitly raised: Who was Dr. Martin Luther King Jr.? What did he think, say, and do? How is it important for us today?

Answers to these questions, however, reveal a lack of consensus and clarity. King, as currently understood in public consciousness, is caught in a crisis of identity. Tragically, there exists a lack of clarity about his identity. This, in turn, has diminished the public's capacity to grasp and acknowledge the creativity and radicality of his thought. Hence, the full scope and potential of his program for the contemporary situation remain largely untapped.

A multitude of scholars, journalists, biographers, and social commentators have sought to provide definitive answers to questions regarding King's identity. The result has been the rapid, indiscriminate interjection into both comprehensive American culture and the worldwide community of a multiplicity of "images" of King. Many of these competing "images" represent analyses of King that have been helpful in gaining clarity about many facets of King's life and thought, but they have also tended to obscure the issue of King's identity, and further cloud the public mind.[5]

To examine the literature and media records is to be struck with the diversity and multiplicity of images available for popular consumption. Some "image" King as a "prophet" as opposed to a systematic theologian.[6] Others, in contradistinction to Washington's thesis, argue that he was a creative theologian.[7] Still others appear to situate King almost entirely within the domain of social ethics.[8] These scholars attempt to extract from King's life and work valuable moral-ethical resources with which to address contemporary social problems. Still others tend to view King as a great social strategist;[9] an apostle of nonviolence;[10] a communist;[11] a guardian of white values;[12] an American loyalist;[13] a militant or conservative militant;[14] or a humanist.[15] Much to the misfortune of a vulnerable and often unsuspecting populace, such multi-imaging of King tends to promote ambiguity rather than clarity about King's identity.

The proliferation of interpretive frameworks has led to confusion in the public arena. The fact that many of these images are incompatible and even conflictual in nature (e.g., communist *v.* American loyalist) exacerbates the problem. Multiple, competing images of King, while providing some clues, have heightened the sense of ambiguity surrounding him, and have failed to clearly tell us who, in fact, King really was.

Moreover, the number and variety of images of King offered for public consumption continue to mushroom. Recent biographical research focusing on King's life and times has given us yet additional images of King as a modern day Joshua[16]; a symbol of ideological conflict and social upheaval;[17] a cross-bearer;[18] a field general-tactician;[19] and a modern Joseph figure.[20] Given the steady proliferation of "King literature," it is predictable that additional images of King will invade the academy as well as the marketplace.[21] This does not bode well in terms of the possibility for a clear resolution of the identity crisis surrounding the public understanding of King. The powerful currents of discourse about him constantly shift according to the latest image holding sway in the public mind. Until these images are scrutinized, tested, exposed, and debated, it is unrealistic to expect clarity in the public domain with regard to the identity of King.

Fortunately, King himself was no stranger to the dilemma of crisis. The primary shortcoming with many of the prevailing images of King is that few take into account how King himself understood and wrestled with his personal crisis of identity.[22] In light of this, we may raise several pertinent questions: In what way(s) did King experience a crisis of identity?[23] How did he resolve this crisis? Does his mode of

25

resolution provide clues for how we may resolve our own public crisis of identity with regard to King?

At several points in King's life, major struggles and decision-making opportunites emerged. While these were inevitably centered around King's understanding of the nature, purpose, and direction of his call to public servanthood, King also faced the necessity of hammering out a clear self-definition.[24] These "moments of decision making" represented crucial, "kairotic events" during which King faced "live options" regarding his sense of historical individuality and personal destiny.[25] How King affirms or denies that individuality becomes crucial for his emergent self-understanding, and substantially influences his sense of mission and vocation.

What were these moments of decision making in King's life that are indicative of his personal crisis of identity? I suggest there were three, which, when viewed together, illumine the nature of that crisis as primarily vocational. King's resolution of the crisis took on the character of a vocational response.


## THE DILEMMA OF SELF-IDENTIFICATION

First, King experienced a crisis of self-identification over against other personalities and societal structures that attempted to define him according to specifications external to himself. King's comments on nonconformity as well as his language in reference to extremist personality are instructive in this case. Early in his life, King was noted for his stubborness.[26] He had resented and resisted external control of his life by others, including the significant others of his immediate family. At the same time, he often exhibited a tendency toward quiet acceptance and aquiescence in the face of authority. King's self-analysis revealed that his was a personality that carried within it a tension between two strains of introversion and extroversion. His childhood involved a process of working out this tension so that by the time he was an adult, he had begun to think of himself as an ambivert.[27] Nuances of King's crisis of identity began to emerge further at the very point where his encounter with segregation had first begun. The shoe store episode where King and his father had been refused service for sitting in chairs reserved for white patrons is but one in a series of incidents through which King's crisis of self-identification (as a black person over against the system of segregation) was precipitated,[28] forcing the young boy King to ask, "Who am I?" and "Why am I being treated as I am?"[29]

The crisis of racial identity would resurface while King was a student at Crozer Theological Seminary. His blackness, so visible and conspicuously high-profile in a predominantly white situation, made King extremely self-conscious with regard to his racial identity. How would he respond to the challenge of "living black" in an atmosphere where black culture was so marginalized? King reached back and appropriated strands of elemental puritanism from his religious and cultural background. This puritanist strain tended to stress a rather uncompromisingly conservative code of personal ethics. Along with strict prohibitions against smoking, drinking, dancing, gambling, and such, it harbored a predisposition toward Manichaean thinking that emphasized rigidly demarcated ethical behavior—either/or, black/white, right/wrong. This view failed to appreciate or tolerate any sense of moral ambiguity or give consideration to the subtleties and complexities involved in the process of living.

As one might imagine, this puritanist strain often lent itself to fostering an ethic that placed inordinate emphasis on natural limitations, a legalistic concern for "rightness" in personal discipline, and "propriety" in social ordering. It often provided support for those who favored cooperation with "things as they were." At times, in both private and public spheres, it led to a conservative stress on the primacy of preserving the status quo ordering of society.[30]

The personal and social ethic inherent in this puritanist strain did, in fact, help King. It provided him with clear guidelines for personal behavior. At the same time, the internal contradictions inherent in the puritanist strain tended to make the resolution of King's crisis of racial identity more difficult. As a member of a definite numerical minority in a predominantly white academic institution in the 1950s, King also had to face head-on those implicitly held assumptions regarding the "proper place" of blacks in the social order.

Operating in the collective psyche and ethos of a racist culture, these assumptions brought with them criteria for judging appropriate and inappropriate modes of behavior. Blacks faced the burden of having to weigh virtually every decision or action in light of how it might be interpreted or judged by whites. In situations where a group is in a pronounced numerical disadvantage, the numerically advan-

27

taged group tends to view each member of the minority group as a psychic prism. Each individual's actions often serve as the basis upon which every other member of that group is prejudicially judged.

As a black man, King faced this dilemma while a student at both Crozer Seminary and Boston University. Would he stay in his socially prescribed "place" and allow his behavior to be controlled by rigid, preset notions of what was socially acceptable for blacks? Or would he attempt to break out of old racial proscriptions and experiment with new behavioral norms and new forms of relating to others that cut across race, class, and religion? The critical appropriation of the puritanist strain of his religious tradition both helped and hindered King's efforts to resolve his personal crisis of identity. Although King resented that emphasis on strict personal morality and rigid, austere conduct in private affairs, he was willing to decide "for" it in this particular situation. While a student at Crozer during the 1950s, King experienced the racist ravings of a white classmate who had been the victim of a harmless prank. His response was based, in large part, on a sense that being black and Christian had thrust upon him a certain responsibility to act soberly and moderately at all times. Further, King became a stickler for promptness, immaculate dress, cleanliness, and class preparation, and was excessively concerned with presenting a positive image of blackness.[31]

It was the puritan ethic operating in the psyche of King that drove his concern with personal conduct and self-presentation in the Crozer situation. Here King's crisis of racial identity became linked to a broader conflict related to a choice for the conservative and rigid elements or the more progressive and permissive elements in the puritan ethic. This conflict was evidenced in choices regarding personal identity and conduct, racial politics, religious orientation, and the degree to which he would be open to influence by diverse intellectual traditions.

Moreover, King experienced several incidents that made choice for or against his historical individuality and personal destiny both unavoidable and necessary. In this case, King struggled to assert his individuality against those proscriptions of race that impeded his ability to exercise freedom in personal decision making. While a student at Crozer, a racial incident in a local cafe made it necessary for King to affirm his right as a black human being to be served with the same dignity and respectability accorded any other member of the human community.[32] At the same time, King found himself attracted to a white woman and appeared unyielding in his determination to marry her, despite the protestations of friends. Immediately, a crisis of individual freedom and choice over against the history and reality of racial estrangement in America presented itself for resolution. The choice he eventually made demonstrates that although King opted for an affirmation of blackness, it was not without a struggle to break free of oppressive structures, customs, and mores.

King not only experienced a crisis of self-identification with regard to his racial self, he also faced this crisis regarding his existential self. Here the crisis emerged through King's self-assertiveness over against the operative force and compulsivity of his father, "Daddy King" who was prone to domineering and dictatorial excesses.[33] The tension in this crisis is evidenced in several pivotal decisions King had to make, each one forcing a confrontation of wills between himself and Daddy King.[34] These important decisions included Martin's choice of Crozer Seminary and Boston University to complete his graduate education; his choice of marriage to Coretta Scott over against the elder's wishes; King's role in the movement at several points, especially Montgomery and Birmingham; and his choice of the Dexter Avenue pastorate, to name a few.[35] Daddy King had sought to rule with an iron hand and force Martin to make choices of the elder King's liking. Martin, without excessive argumentation, managed to stand his ground and win the day in each case, much to the elder King's chagrin.[36]

W. E. B. DuBois, the astute social critic and historian, observed that the identity crisis in black existence represents a historical dilemma. It is a history of strife and "longing to attain self-conscious manhood, to merge [one's] double self into a better and truer self."[37] As a black man, King faced this history and its attendant crisis of self-identification in a society that sought to invalidate black existence as a genuine expression of the human experience. In the context of racism and autocratic parental guidance, King struggled to achieve racial self-identification and self-assertion on one hand and personal agency on the other hand. On both counts these struggles represented facets of a larger arena of tension and became symptomatic of King's crisis of vocational identity.

## THE CRISIS OF FAITH

The second arena of tension is found in King's crisis of faith. James W. McClendon is essentially correct when he points out that a key to an accurate understanding and interpretation of King lies in acknowledging the centrality of his religious faith.[38] King's faith emerged from the context of the black church, within whose bosom he had been nurtured since childhhood. The basic elements and thematics of this faith perspective will be presented in greater detail later in this chapter. For now, it is important to point out that King initially rejected the very faith perspective that would one day provide him nurture and sustenance during moments of crisis and demanding choice. Interestingly, although thoroughly immersed in its ethos, King as a young man found himself somewhat repulsed by the idiom and style of worship and preaching he had seen demonstrated in the black religious tradition.[39] This had deep implications for whether King might resolve the vocational crisis in favor of law, medicine, or the ministry. Further, when King did decide for the ministry, his critical view of black religion would provide the motivation for him to remain open to the perspectives of other religious and intellectual traditions. At any rate, King had to decide for or against the faith of the black religious tradition.

It was also the case that King's crisis of faith persisted throughout his public life. His decision for the faith does not render him immune to the ongoing crisis of faith. That is to say, at several points in his life, King faced a kairotic moment of destiny that forced him to examine the role that religious faith would play in his life. And yet, in the crucibles of personal and emancipatory struggle, his faith acted as a powerful existential adhesive that held him together.[40] It was a strong religious faith that enabled King to weather the threats of death in Montgomery. From his first public speech in Montgomery, faith sustained him during his arrests, court apearances, and death threats. In fact, at the precipice of despair and hopelessness, an encounter with the presence of God in the "kitchen experience" in Montgomery helped King face his fears, and gave him courage to proceed with the boycott.[41]

It was this faith that King would call upon again in the Birmingham jail, and of which he spoke at the March on Washington in 1963.[42] When mounting pressures tempted him to leave the movement, or when he became cynical and pessimistic in his outlook, King's faith in God gave him a certain hope in the future and the courage to continue the struggle. By the time King stood amid the rubble of the Sixteenth Street Baptist Church in Birmingham lamenting the death of four little girls, his faith had made two things abundantly clear. First, it convinced him of the absolute futility of trying to leave the movement. He had been called to a vocation of public service, a destiny from which he could not hope to escape. The Zeitgeist had tracked him down, and he accepted the fact that he was in for the long haul, regardless of the outcome. Second, faith had provided the assurance that God was with him, and would never leave him alone in the struggle against forces of evil and injustice.

King would rely upon that faith time and time again. Near the end of his life, when he began to speak out more vociferously against Vietnam and poverty, his popularity began to wane significantly. His continued insistence on nonviolence was likewise ill-received. Yet an unshakable faith in God guided King through the frightful and turbulent tensions between the options of violence versus nonviolence, hope versus despair, love versus hate, and action versus apathy. King's faith sustained his belief in the power of agapeistic love to convert enemies into friends.[43] King's faith relied strongly on biblical themes of Exodus and communal liberation, the tradition of prophetic utterance, and cross and resurrection events. This allowed him to promote a belief in the coresponsibility of both God and human beings to work toward the realization of justice within history. Further, the tradition of black religious dissent provided existential and empirical grounding for a belief that purposive divine and human activity were both necessary to achieve progress in human history.[44]

King's crisis of faith also involved a decision about the centrality of the gospel for his own life. He experienced this crisis continuously and acutely amid the forces of racism, classism, militarism, consumerism, nihilism, fatalism, conservatism, and the general cultural chaos and psychic disintegration of his day. At the point of each major personal and public decision, it was King's faith that was also undeniably at issue—to embrace hope or give in to despair; to embrace nonviolence as an absolute strategy or concede the merits of tactical violence as a possible strategy in the freedom struggle; to be an apathetic spectator or an active participant in the unfolding drama of liberative action and revolutionary ferment, to name a few.

31

King's crisis of faith was heightened when he decisively entered the liberation struggle in the context of America. From the "kitchen experience" of Montgomery in 1956, to the alienation experienced in the wake of his public critique of the Vietnam War in 1967, to the sense of exasperation felt in organizing the Poor People's Campaign in 1968, to the severe bouts of depression during the last year of his life, to the haunting and ominous somberness in the final "Mountain-top" speech in 1968, King's religious faith is repeatedly placed on the witness stand. The events of his life required that his private self be constantly exposed to intense public scrutiny. In coping with this crisis of faith in a public as well as a private forum, King arrives at a clear understanding of himself as a person of deep and abiding faith—faith in the God of radical agape love. This self-description had important implications not only for how King resolved the crisis of faith, but also for his vocational self-understanding as well.

## THE CONFLICT OF INTELLECTUAL TRADITIONS

The third arena of tension in King's life was related to his exposure to those myriad traditions and histories of critical social, philosophical, and religious inquiry. In the intellectual development of King, one becomes acutely aware of the manner in which diverse traditions, ideas, and streams of perspective act to shape the individual as they compete for recognition and loyalty. At the point of exposure, these traditions become adamantly and perpetually insistent that we make a choice for or against them. That very insistence creates a crisis within as we try to decide how various traditions of thought will inform and guide our own developing perspective.

King's difficult and ultimate challenge was to arrange various philosophical, theological, and ethical interpretive frameworks into some kind of integrative schema. The construction of that schema would take place within the crucible of his quest to arrive at vocational clarity and integrity. The undertaking of this effort meant that a battle among diverse intellectual currents was now being waged within the psyche of King. It amounted to a battle for the very heart, mind, and soul of the man. In his quest to discover and apply viable content and methodology in the vocation of the ministry (especially as it related to the struggle for freedom, justice, and equality), King was forced to decide for or against alternative modes of thought.

It would be impossible to trace and locate successfully all of the many strands of ideas that influence an individual's thinking. This was certainly true of King.[45] King himself, though, provides solid clues as to those traditions that decisively shaped his own thought in his account of the Montgomery struggle in *Stride Toward Freedom.*

King admitted that the heritage of black struggle against segregation in the South had provided him with the conviction that racism could neither be explained on rational grounds nor justified on moral grounds.[46] This heritage of dissent had been introduced to him through the witness of the black community and the black church. By the time King arrived at Morehouse College at the tender age of fifteen, he had developed a substantive concern for both racial and economic justice.[47] King lacked serious intellectual foundation, and Morehouse provided him with the rudimentary elements. It was here that the black religious tradition was exonerated and made efficacious for King. Through the teaching and example of Walter Chivers, George Kelsey, and Benjamin Mays, the vocation of ministry, the symbolic role of the black preacher/scholar, and the emphases on prophetic critique, social justice, and radical dissent were elevated. The black religious tradition had gained respectability in King's viewpoint.[48]

And yet, his "serious intellectual quest for a method to eliminate social evil . . ." led King to pursue further study at Crozer and Boston where he encountered many other diverse intellectual traditions.[49] It was here that he first read Walter Rauschenbusch's conception of a social gospel. He read social philosphy and ethics of Plato, Aristotle, Rousseau, Hobbes, Bentham, Mill, and Locke. He was further stimulated to read in the area of communism, and was challenged by the economic theories of Karl Marx. Marx shook King, and forced him to deal with the conception and role of God in the construction of society. King would ultimately reject communism, and later write a sermon dealing with the relationship between Christianity and communism.[50] King's faith would also be severely tested by the scathing critique of Christianity found in the writings of Friedrich Nietzsche.[51]

King was baptized in a torrent of exposure to liberal theological thought. At Crozer, King finally arrived at the intellectual satisfaction that religious fundamentalism had never been able to provide. That intellectual peace affected him so deeply, he claimed, that he "almost fell into the trap of accepting uncritically everything it encompassed."[52] Reinhold Niebuhr's Christian realism; Paul Tillich's philosophical, apologetic theology; the pacifist viewpoints of A. J. Muste, Allen Knight Chalmers, and Walter Muelder; Mohandas K. Gandhi's methodology of nonviolent resistance; Hegel's conception of history; the personalist philosophical theology of Edgar Brightman and L. Harold DeWolf,[53] all represented a diverse intellectual perspective, the merits of which King had to weigh critically and carefully.

With so many powerful intellectual traditions competing for King's allegiance, the profound nature of the crisis he underwent is readily apparent. The completion of his formal academic study was marked by a dissertation in which King dealt with the nature and reality of God. King argued with conceptions of God in the thinking of Paul Tillich and Henry Nelson Wieman.[54] That King focused his analysis on God is instructive, for throughout his life, as we shall see, King searched for God—to know God, and to discern God's will for him vocationally.[55] We also find demonstrable evidence of King's approach to critical thinking in the dissertation. King read thinkers in a dialectical fashion, looking for both the yes and no in each person's argument.[56] King appropriated this approach from both the philosopher Hegel and from the black abolitionist thinker and freedom fighter Frederick Douglass. Ultimately, dialectical thinking led King to look for the element of truth in every tradition while recognizing that no one tradition had obtained a monopoly on the whole of the truth.[57]

The use of this method of critical thinking resulted in King's emergence as one who was, in the words of Washington, "not an intellectual in the usual sense of this term."[58] King is to be viewed as a great synthesizer of thought cut in the mold of an Aquinas. The exposure to variants of thought shook him, but they did not deracinate him intellectually. He was able to borrow eclectically from each tradition and to synthesize them into a schema by which to interpret reality and to guide vocational choice. It is this methodological bent in critical thinking that has led Cornel West to refer to King as ". . . the most significant and successful organic intellectual in American history." "Never before in our past," says West, "has a figure outside of elected public office linked the life of the mind to social change with such moral persuasiveness and political effectiveness."[59]

34

# FOUR SOURCES OF KING'S THOUGHT

King resolved the crisis of competing traditions synthetically. While all these forces of thought have some influence, West is most on target when he identifies four *major* prophetic sources in King's thought: the black church/religious tradition, liberal Christianity, the Gandhian method of nonviolent social change, and American civil religion.[60] These sources helped to organize much that King thought, said, and did, and they enable us to better see how King's self-descriptions helped to illuminate and resolve his crisis of vocational identity.

## The Black Church/Religious Tradition

Without question the prophetic black church tradition, or the black religious tradition of radical dissent, decisively shaped King's thinking. In fact, although King never lost his capacity to critique it, it was the tradition within which King was most thoroughly grounded.[61] An area of King's thinking that has long been neglected,[62] this tradition provided King with the initial and basic orientation to prophetic oration; emphasis on biblical thematics of justice, deliverance, and liberation; a sustaining faith; and what may be appropriately labeled a "dissenting tradition" or a "tradition of radical protest."[63]

This tradition is responsible, in large measure, for what makes King a man of faith. Because he made choices that did not sever him from his ties in this tradition, King was rescued from the type of "Americanity" that so often besets the black intellectual.[64] In a real sense, it was the black religious tradition that "saved" King. As he immersed himself in the liberal, Euro-American thought of northern white institutions, he was in imminent danger of losing touch with the roots of black culture. One must not overlook the possibility of King's thorough assimilation into Anglo-American culture. Yet, King never forgot the culture or the religious perspective that gave birth to him. He never abandoned the rhythms, cadences, thematics, and foci of the black religious tradition. His nurture in it, and his return to it, provided him with the centering, critical mass of beliefs, ideals, and ideas about God, sin, history, self, humanity, and society from which to weigh alternative traditions. This tradition gave King a faith that never allowed him to forget the necessity of a deliberate activistic thrust on behalf of justice. It never allowed him to embrace despair and pessimism. When King entered the stage of world history, he

35

carried with him an oratorical style and bent of personality that had already been thoroughly influenced by and nurtured in the faith of the black church. In fact, the tradition of black religious faith proved central to King's development into the distinctive oratorical genius and creative theological thinker that he became.

### The Tradition of Liberal Christianity

And yet thematics, principles, ideas, and ideals in other traditions of thinking served to expand, qualify, and deepen the rudiments of that faith. Through study and exposure to prophetic liberal theological thinking, King was eventually able to describe himself as an "evangelical liberal" without exhibiting the slightest anxiety about oxymoronic incongruity.[65] This tradition of liberal thought provided King with a qualified optimism with regard to the liberal doctrine of the basic goodness of humankind;[66] an understanding of the gospel as having to do with both the formation of individual virtues and character as well as societal reconstruction; an emphasis on shaping public conscience and striving for progressive moral improvement in social life; the relevance of the gospel to social and political issues engendering a dual emphasis on the sacredness of the person and unavoidable social responsibility; an unshakable belief in the redeemability of society, the benevolence of God, and the basic goodness not only of humans but of all of creation; metaphysical grounding for the idea of a personal God, and the inherent dignity and worth of all humanity.[67]

### The Tradition of Gandhian Nonviolent Social Change

Prophetic Gandhian nonviolent methodology for social change gave King further intellectual and experiential bases for the notion of noncooperation or civil resistance that King had extracted from Thoreau during his days at Morehouse. Gandhi's life and teachings, however, made a moral claim on King's life in a way that no other theoretician, tactician, social philosopher, or social activist was able to do. Gandhi rescued King from the devasting critiques by Marx and Nietzsche that stressed the hopelessness of the power of Christian love to solve social problems.[68] Gandhi decisively demonstrated for King that the agapeistic love ethic of Jesus Christ embodied a transformative power that could operate on a social as well as an interpersonal level.[69]

King had found the method for social reform that he had been seeking, and in the process had come to embrace the principle of love through nonviolent action as the only viable option available to agents of liberative struggle that was both morally correct and practically sound. King was acutely aware of the attractiveness of Gandhi's Hindu method as a faith system. He argued that a choice for Gandhi's method did not amount to a choice against loyalty to the Jesus of Christianity. King never became a convinced adherent of Hindu doctrine. Thus, he could say that while Gandhi furnished the method in Montgomery, it was Christ who furnished the spirit and motivation of the movement. Love exemplified by Jesus Christ provided the regulating ideal. Nonviolence as exemplified by Gandhi served as the technique.[70]

### The Tradition of American Civil Religion

Finally, prophetic American civil religion's influence on King demonstrates how in King's resolution of competing traditions, he was able to build bridges between diverse and seemingly incompatible cultures. As a product of southern culture, black culture, black church, and the northern white academy, King was able to bridge both church and society as well as black and white culture through the appropriation of a language that allowed common public discourse.[71]

West aptly defines American civil religion as ". . . that complex web of religious ideals of deliverance and salvation and political ideals of freedom, democracy, and equality that constitute the evolving collective self-definition of America."[72] King was able to tap into a cluster of shared values, concepts, and ideals, both religious and political, floating in public consciousness, to which he could make immediate appeal. In this regard, civil religion provided King with a language appropriate for public discourse about equality, justice, and freedom. The foundational documents of the nation became a seminal source of King's public witness to America.[73]

The convergence of these four sources of King's thinking, (along with strands of other thinking traditions), is reflective of a crisis that occurred when (inundated by a plethora of perspectives) King was forced to choose either for or against them. Intent upon living with maximal vocational integrity, he sought to clearly define his vocational identity. How King eventually chose from among this competing mass of ideas is testament to the role each played in shaping his sense of vocational calling. And yet, in the final analysis, King's intellectual journey of crisis and tension raised conundrums that were answered by King only through struggle and practical action.[74]

# THE CRISIS OF VOCATIONAL IDENTITY

Together, these three areas of tension in King's life—self-identification, faith, and tradition—are indicative of his intense, personal crisis of identity. What they clearly reveal is that King's crisis presented itself primarily as a crisis of vocational identity. That is to say, King's crisis of identity revolved precisely around the axis of decision making with regard to a "... sense of being called to perform some special task, carry some burden, [or] play some significant role . . ." in the drama of human history.[75] From the very beginning of King's wrestling with the choice of vocation as to law, medicine, or religion, much more was involved than the achievement of personal career objectives or the acquisition of money, prestige, and power. The vocational dilemma involved for King (as it must for every human being) a struggle to move beyond a fixation with job-ism (work that is done in return for wages) or career-ism (work that is done to enhance one's individual position in the corporate world or in society). The vocational dilemma forces the individual to look outward toward the needs of others rather than solely or even primarily at one's personal needs, objectives, and desires. As the early Protestant reformers understood it, *vocatio* was inseparably connected to a notion of human calling, and involved a sense of the proper stewardship of one's time, talents, and resources in service to God and humanity. In this sense the notion of vocation stressed the moral accountability of human beings to both God and the human community. Further, vocation stressed a sense of responsibility for the well-being of the created order. Utlimately, vocation meant a commitment to worship God, and to serve God by working to advance God's kingdom in history. God had assigned every human being a specific purpose at birth. It was that individual's task to discover that calling, embrace it, commit one's life to it, and seek self-development in order that one might perform that vocation to the best of one's ability.

At stake, then, is a decision about how King will accept the call and challenge to join God in the struggle for freedom. The vocational crisis forced King to decide how he might best serve God, his people, and the world in the ongoing quest to obtain justice. To be sure, King did not slight or deny the rightness and propriety of working toward the achievement of personal goals and interests. King maintained a respect for what he referred to as "rational self-interest" or "concern for the self."[76] King's endorsement, however, amounts to a qualified one. He viewed rational self-interest as valid *only* when held in dialectical tension with what he called "concern for the other." Through the vocational dilemma, the tension between personal goal and social responsibility was precipitated. As King wrestled with the nature of his vocational calling—what it meant and the direction his life must take—he gradually became certain that "life's most persistent question is what am I doing for others?"[77] The issue of public moral agency, so central to an understanding of vocation, was acutely raised in King's mind.

King admitted that his life has been consumed by a constant and incessant search for a method by which to achieve equality for blacks.[78] It is in the context of his quest to discover this liberationist methodology that King's decision for the ministry must be understood. And yet contrary, perhaps to King's own expectations, the vocational choice of ministry did *not* bring a definite end to the crisis. Instead, King's life was marked by further vocational tension. Again, he was caught at the point of decision about the nature and direction of ministry that would best achieve the goals of freedom and justice. This led to King's critique of black religion and the black church even as he embraced both. The crisis in vocational identity forced him to decide what type of minister he would be, what type of church he would support and help to build, what type of faith he would nurture, what understanding of God, faith, and the gospel he would promote.[79]

King's vocational resolution of the crisis of vocational identity led him to a particular self-understanding as a servant of God to the people. He saw himself first and foremost as a Baptist preacher.[80] However, this self-description represents a code word, for King undersood it to mean much more than mere exhortatory vocal presentation. King's self-understanding as minister of the gospel of Jesus Christ had everything to do with his affirmation and confirmation of a vocational call to place the entirety of his existential selfhood in the struggle for justice. His decision to prepare theologically; to accept the leadership of the bus boycott; his beliefs about the nature, aim, and direction the boycott should take, all point to and are derivative of his sense of vocation. There is more content to King's phraseology of "Baptist preacher" than is apparent at first glance, and the *more* has to do with King's further self-description as a "Drum major for justice, peace, and righteousness."[81] In this self-understanding lies the clue to the meaning of his servanthood ethic and his sponsorship of a theology that mandated courageous, radical involvement aimed at both personal and social transformation.

## SUMMARY

To summarize, King's crisis of vocational identity manifested itself as tension in the three areas of personal self-identification, faith, and tradition. King would resolve this crisis vocationally by deciding for the ministry against law and medicine. This decision did not mean that King would enjoy a life free of other vocation-related tensions and contradictions. On the contrary, tensions derivative of the very vocational choices he made became a constant feature of his life. Each time King made a decision for or against one reality, that very choice provided the aperture through which other tensions would subsequently emerge. Such tensions would haunt King at various points throughout his life: the choice for a privatistic as opposed to a public faith; the appeal to blacks only as opposed to a wider public audience; whether to seek support from Christian religious organizations alone or risk sacrificing his focus by seeking the support of other religious and/or secular organizations; how to maintain a proper sense of sinfulness with a freedom found in forgiveness; how to deal with a sense of both guilt and thankfulness for a privileged lifestyle; how to combine militancy and nonviolence simultaneously; the embrace and critique, love and disappointment of both church and society; how to hold realism and idealism in fruitful tension and balance.

As we have said previously, King did not necessarily view crisis in a negative sense thanks to DuBois, Douglass, and Hegel. These three had taught him that growth comes only through struggle and tension. A crisis also represented an opportunity for growth, transformation, and reconstruction. There was a positive side to crisis.[82] To be sure, crisis was often accompanied by anxiety and fear. And yet, it was not crisis as such, but rather one's response to crisis that mattered most.[83] In a sense, King felt such crisis and tension necessary for coming of age.

In this vein, these questions are broached: How did King resolve the crisis of vocational identity? In what way(s) did he ultimately respond to those tensions of self-definition, faith, and competing traditions? The answer is to be found in King's vocational self-understanding as a Christian minister. In the efforts to acquire a method for the alleviation of social evil, King found answers to the questions of God, Christ, self, church, and society. Although King never hammered out doctrinal positions on these categories in systematic fashion, he did arrive at positions that are both implicitly and explicitly stated in his writings, speeches, sermons, and interviews. His answers provided a theological platform from which King could interpret and understand his vocational identity. Therefore, an inspection of that theological platform will prove illuminative for clarity on King's vocational self-understanding. It is to that perspective that we now turn.

# CHAPTER 2

# THE THEOLOGICAL ROOTS OF KING'S VOCATIONAL RESPONSE:

## God and Humanity

K ing responded to the nagging vocational crisis by choosing to undergo formal academic as well as on-the-job training in the areas of ordained pastoral ministry, philosophy of religion, and systematic theology. This choice of vocation brought with it an accompanying challenge to gain conceptual clarity about guiding vocational beliefs, values, loyalties, and commitments. King struggled to hammer out those foundational theological claims and convictions upon which to build a vocational self-understanding.

The quest to achieve doctrinal clarity as a minister of the Christian gospel stimulated, concomitantly, a serious engagement into philosophical and theological inquiry. Hence, King's vocational response raised important questions about the nature of God, the person and work of Jesus Christ, the content and requirements of the gospel, the church and its role in society, and the nature of the human enterprise. In responding to the crisis of vocational identity through a commitment to the Christian ministry, King was, at the same time, making a choice for the vocation of theologian. As a developing theologian, King sought intelligibility in the expression of his faith and struggled to dispel ambiguity about the nature and requirements of the vocational call to ordained ministry. In the quest to know and come to terms with God, self, and world, King-the-theologian provided purpose and direction for King-the-minister-and-public-servant.

And yet, King's method of "doing theology" represented a paradigm shift in the way theological formulation had been conceptualized. Indeed, the very way in which King understood and approached the aim and tasks of the theological vocation was markedly different from the prevailing models of academia. It is instructive that King's

43

theological discourse, either followed or was articulated in the midst of public "campaigns" aimed at societal change.[1] It was public utterance responsive to the urgent crises of particular situations. Consequently, King's speech may be characterized as sustained reflection upon concrete, social action in light of a commitment to a specific theological vision. In this sense, King's method of "doing theology" was driven by what contemporary liberation theologians refer to as "liberative praxis."[2]

# VOCATIONAL RESPONSE

Use of the action-reflection model also placed restrictions on the way King's perspective was "packaged" and presented for public consumption. His theological formulation took place within the arena of public discourse and was aimed at (initially) regional and (later) national audiences (in essence, the collective American conscience). Given the imperatives of both the context and purpose (societal conversion), the discursive method was, in a sense, *pre* determined. The situational context proscribed the employment of theological-ethical dialogic encounter in the marketplace of ideas. Indeed, the arena of the public square demanded the use of a rhetorical style driven by the passion of persuasive argumentation rather than the systematic, rationalistically ordered speech so characteristic of academia.

Fortunately, the strong emphasis on preaching in the black religious tradition prepared King to use language with a deep appreciation for its persuasive power to convict and reform. Thus, King's evocative oration emerged as a form of oral theologizing. Shaped by the prevailing cross currents and dynamics of social, political, and economic crises, King's speech was concerned to a much greater extent with the pragmatics of societal change rather than the demands of rational conviction and formal systematization.[3]

In addition to his speeches and sermons, King's theology is explicated implicitly through his books, interviews, and essays. It is not neatly or systematically presented in the doctrinal categories of classical theology, nor is it explicitly delineated in a singular magnum opus. Rather, King's theology represents a "systemic" mode of thinking emergent from, informed by, and in critical dialogue with a public context of liberative struggle.

And yet, King was in fact, a Christian minister, preacher, and theologian who also was exposed to formal studies at some of the nation's most prestigious institutions of higher learning. As a formally trained, systematic theologian who wrote numerous research papers, King demonstrated a solid familiarity with doctrinal terms of classical theological discourse. His writings, speeches, and sermons reflect this training. Therefore, what is implicitly stated in King's thought can be made explicit in the terminology, categories, and foci of classical theological discourse—Christology, ecclesiology, anthropology, Christian discipleship, eschatology, and so forth.

Yet, the intent here is not to "prove" that King was a theologian by demonstrating how his thinking can be stated in the terminology of classical theology. Admittedly, King was not a theologian in the traditional sense of the term. That is to say, he did not "theologize" in the traditional, normative format of structured, rationalistic discourse typical of scholars. It was the street rather than the library that delineated the primary contours of his research laboratory. It was the concrete fulfillment of justice rather than polished, published treatises that defined the aim and focus of his program. King's basic theological concern centered on the "lived practice" or involvement of theology in human affairs (orthopraxy). At issue was the relevance of religion for the modern sojourner. Therefore, he wanted to ascertain and tap into the liberative potential of theology for reshaping the conduct of human beings in the daily affairs of living. In this sense, King defies rigid, traditional, Western characterizations. His theology represents a significant departure from the "norm" of classical theology, which historically has evidenced more concern with systematic formulation of doctrine (orthodoxy).

And yet, King certainly had solid grounding in the conceptual framework of classical, Western theology. Certainly, King decisively reshaped this tradition of theological discourse. In so doing, he demonstrated remarkable intellectual and tactical dexterity as well as discursive improvisation. Nevertheless, he had maintained a critical linkage to it. It must be remembered that King was a black Christian theologian, and it was as such that he spoke to the public parish, and that his distinctive contribution to the nation and the world must be understood. So King's thought can be made intelligible to the Christian community and the broader culture in the terms of classic theology and since this *can* be done, it *ought* to be done as a first step. As a second step, we may demonstrate how King's thought represents a divergent shift in the nature, focus, and method of theology. In this way, the unique innovations in King's program may be recognized, and more fully appreciated.

In light of these assertions, we may ask: What constituted the elemental threads of King's theological perspective? How did King come to understand God, the gospel, Jesus Christ, the church, humanity, sin, and eschatology? In what way(s) did King's developing doctrinal positions help to definitively resolve those prevailing ambiguities, tensions, and contradictions that fueled his crisis of vocational identity? We now turn to an exploration of the theological roots of King's response.

To present the material in a manageable format, this chapter will deal with King's conceptions of God and humanity, while the following chapter will present his understanding of Christ, church, and the future.

# KING'S UNDERSTANDING OF
# THE INVOLVED GOD

Central to King's vocational understanding is a conception of God as a cosmic liberator and reconciler who is radically and inextricably involved in the affairs of human history. King conceived of God as a proactive, Divine Personality working ceaselessly within the drama of human experience to create a beloved community where the virtues of love, justice, and peace become normative for every conceivable relationship. This conception of God represents the axis upon which King's theological program turns. All subsequent doctrinal understandings of Christ, the gospel, humanity, sin, and eschatology are, in fact, derivative of King's view of God.

## Divine Love as Divine Involvement

King's conception of God as "Love-in-Action" proved to be the linchpin to his theological framework.[4] A belief in God's unfathomable and immutable love for humanity provided the basis for King's imaging of a parent God who cares for us; who would not abandon us to despair in our crises; who would provide guidance, sustenance, and companionship in the trials and tribulations of life.[5] Personal experiences of life and faith, a reading of the biblical narrative, and a study of personalist theistic philosophy had convinced King that God was personal, loving, and immanently at work in the unfolding drama of history to create moral value and to redeem the human community.[6]

King argued that love was the essence of God. Love was the life-creating force at work in the cosmos. Love was the redemptive process actively overcoming forces of alienation and fragmentation through radical acts of Divine Self-giving.[7] Love provided the conceptual clue for ascertaining the nature and purposes of God, and derivatively, the meaning and end of life.

King posited the primacy and potency of love as the most powerful and durable force in the universe. In consonance with this position, he identified love as the basis of freedom, responsibility, and genuine community.[8] Love was foundational for King's understanding of the Christian life as a discipleship commitment to a type of socially active Christianity.[9] At the same time, love provided conceptual grounding for a notion of Divine-human coresponsibility—the infinite and the finite working together in history to effect the transformation of *de* humanizing laws, institutional structures, policies, and acts. In the triadic interrelationship between love, power, and justice, love served as the principal, catalytic force. Love motivates humanity to make choices for justice and against compromises with injustice. Love is the only force capable of transforming estranged interpersonal relationships into reconciled friendships.[10]

For King, love represented the heart of the nonviolent movement for justice.[11] In King's view, it was the love ethic of Jesus that provided the spirit of the movement, guided its methodology, and determined its primary objectives. This love was expressive of a radicality that manifested itself in a caring God, acting in human history to bring about deliverance and justice to the oppressed. King's God was the cosmic incarnation of "radical love in action"—Divine Personality placing itself in harm's way in order to effect the redemption of the human community.[12]

The Bible, along with Greek metaphysics, provided key insights from which King developed an understanding of God as the embodiment of radical agapeistic love. To articulate the content of this love,

King turned to the writings of Anders Nygren, Paul Ramsey, Paul Tillich, Howard Thurman, and others.[13] Appropriating the interrelated concepts of eros, philia, and agape, King focused on distinctions between each to explicate the content and meaning of love in the freedom movement.

> At the center of our movement stood the philosophy of love. The attitude that the only way to ultimately change humanity and make for the society that we all long for is to keep love at the center of our lives. . . . The Greek language uses three words for love. Eros is a sort of aesthetic love . . . a sort of romantic love . . . philia and this sort of reciprocal love between personal friends . . . But when we talk of loving those who oppose you and those who seek to defeat you we are not talking about eros or philia. The Greek language comes out with another word and it is agape. Agape is understanding, creative, redemptive good will for all men [sic]. Biblical theologians would say it is the love of God working in the minds of men [sic]. It is an overflowing love which seeks nothing in return. And when you come to love on this level you begin to love men [sic] not because they are likeable . . . but because God loves them.[14]

As the basis of reconciliation, agape was the operative force actively engaging the powers of disintegration, working for the restoration of the human community.

> Agape is not a weak, passive love. It is love in action. Agape is love seeking to preserve and create community. It is insistence on community even when one seeks to break it. Agape is a willingness to go to any length to restore community.[15]

Because radical agape love represented the fundamental being of God and the central cosmic principle, King believed he had discovered humanity's highest good: love. And yet, God was coterminous with radical agape love. This point is crucial in that it allowed King to avoid the dangers of cosmic dualism that understood God and love as two distinct, cosmic realities.[16] In such a view, God and love may, at least theoretically, be in opposition. King categorically rejected this notion. Since love represented the "essence" of God (not one of many "attributes"), the ends of love and God remain perpetually in harmony. What love demands is precisely what God demands. Radical

48

agape love acting in history always seeks the realization of objectives that are fully compatible with Divine intention.

In this sense, King spoke of a personal God who values human personality, is concerned with the establishment of just relationships in the created order, and who is actively at work in the cosmic order and in human history seeking to restore relational harmony. Love is courageously confrontational and, upon occasion, radically disruptive in its pursuit of peace and its demand for justice. Likewise, God immanently engages in cosmic redemption, is "love in action" working to overcome hate-producing fears, confronting forces of darkness, defeating evil, converting enemies into friends, and creating the beloved community.[17]

As radical agape love in action, the God we come to know in Jesus Christ has not deistically withdrawn to a detached, transcendent, other worldly relationship with the created order. Rather, God participates throughout the universe and within human history in community-creating projects where justice, peace, love, and hope are assigned normative status. In this respect, King believed that God was a creative force of power and love, always at work in the universe working to restore harmony to the disconnected fragments of history. Because God's power was limitless and God's love inexhaustible, King maintained a steadfast hope in God's ability to ultimately prevail victoriously against the forces of injustice.[18]

King was careful to acknowledge the pervasive, intransigent, and intractable nature of sin and evil in the universe. He admitted how the goodness and power of God are problematical for the theist in light of the cruelty of nature, the unmerited suffering of the innocent, racism, disease, poverty, war, and famine. Only the most superficial optimist would fail to take evil seriously as a reality in nature and history.[19]

And yet, King held to a belief in God's ability to reign triumphant over any force that threatens to thwart God's divine purpose. He rejected the notion that God was limited in power or capacity, expressed in the doctrine of theistic finitism advanced by Nicholas Berdyaev, John Stuart Mill, and his mentor, Edgar S. Brightman. While taking seriously both physical and moral evil, King argued that a satisfactory solution to the problem of evil must offer a conception of God that holds in balance both the goodness and the power of God. This solution, he warned, was not accessible by intellectual assent.

Rather, the solution was spiritual, requiring a leap into the darkness of faith that led not to despair but to hope.[20]

For King, God possessed the goodness to care, and the power to act in the face of massive dislocation and universal suffering. In the final analysis, it was King's spirituality that led him to believe in the ultimate defeat of evil and the eventual victory of the forces of good.

### The Personal God Who Structures the Cosmos through Divine Law

As radical agape love in action, God is also the Great Lawgiver. In part, God uses divine law instrumentally to structure the cosmic order. Bostonian personalism had provided King with a philosophical grounding for the view that the proper ordering of the universe necessitated the operation of certain fixed, immutable, unbreakable laws. It is through these laws, set in motion by God, that the universe is continually governed and sustained.[21] While these laws are important for King's understanding of humanity, the positing of their existence lent credence to King's assertions about God's community-creating activity in history. As loving Personality, God wills the operation of the universe as a coherent unity of just and harmonious relationships between and among God, humanity, and the remainder of the created order.

To achieve this end, God set a multiplicity of laws in operation to ensure the perpetuation of what King refered to as the *moral foundation of the universe*. Personalism formulated a moral law system, rooted in God, upon which universal order rested. As supreme mind and Creator of the universal moral order, God sustains the basic justice of the cosmic process through objective moral law.[22] The influence of personalism on King's thinking led him to affirm the reality of absolute moral values. These fixed, immutable moral principles placed in the structure of the universe served as the basis for moral choice. As moral agents, humans must make ethical choices consistent with the basic morality of the cosmos. Since the content of moral law is justice, choices that promote injustice are disharmonious with the cosmic moral framework. Unjust laws, practices, and structures are in rebellion against God. King argued that just as the physical world was governed by silent, invisible laws, so too was the moral world. The moral order was structured by moral law in such a way that life would work only in a certain manner. God had woven into the fabric of the universe certain fixed, absolute moral laws. To defy and disobey them was to risk great peril for self and society.[23]

Personalists argued that reality was constituted of a multiplicity of moral laws operating in the universe cementing it into a single unity. This *Moral Law System* consisted of five sets of laws.

The first set of *Moral Laws* consisted of the Logical Law that stressed the consistency of values and moral choices, and the Law of Autonomy that stressed the necessity of self-imposed ideals as opposed to uncritical acceptance of the ideals of others.

The second set of *Axiological Laws* stressed a need for the moral-ethical coherence of held values. This cluster included the Axiological Law, the Law of Consequences, the Law of the Best Possible, the Law of Specification, the Law of the Most Inclusive End, and the Law of Ideal Control.

A third set of *Personalistic Laws* dealt with the nature of human personality and included the Law of Individualism, the Law of Altruism, and the Law of the Ideal of Personality.

The fourth set of *Communitarian Laws* focused on the social basis of human personality. It was made up of the Law of Cooperation, the Law of Social Devotion, and the Law of the Ideal of Community.

The fifth set of laws identified as the *Laws of Praxis* attempted to offer guides for daily conduct in the construction of human community. The Law of Conflict and Reconciliation, the Law of Fallibility and Corrigibility, and the Metaphysical Law made up this set.[24] Love, for the personalists, was affirmed as the fundamental principle of the moral order and ideal. Love, or God, was the unifying thread that wove together these moral laws into a coherent system that structured the created order.[25]

These moral laws helped King expose the internal contradictions in both segregation and tokenism, and assisted in providing the basis for King's ethical response to the nation's (and the world's) moral ills. Further, they gave King metaphysical grounding for one of his most confident convictions: that in the cosmic struggle between justice and injustice, both God and the universe were on the side of justice.[26] The implications for humanity were clear. Human choice must lead to actions that reflect harmony with cosmic moral law. Drawing upon distinctions of law found in Aquinas, Augustine, and others, King argued that human law was inevitably subordinate to a higher moral law that reflected divine purpose for cosmic existence.

51

In fact, moral law was the standard by which the justice, legitimacy, and authority of all human law must ultimately be measured.[27] The belief in the moral foundation of reality was used effectively by King to mount a moral appeal to engage in acts of civil resistance that required breaking legal statutes and disobeying court injunctions.

For King, the moral structure of reality placed unavoidable ethical demands upon the moral agent to work for the establishment of justice in the human community. Liberative acts and resistance efforts against injustice were in line with God's moral law. At the same time, the engagement of justice-oriented action meant that one had "cosmic companionship." The struggle for justice and community did not take place in cosmic isolation. As both radical agape love in action and architect of a just moral order, God was a responsible "coworker" cooperating with humans to realize divine purpose in history.[28]

God was just, personal, and caring, maintaining the basic justice of the universe through a framework of absolute moral values, moving the trajectory of history inexorably toward a morally just end—the beloved community. Consequently, King rejected the notion that history was irrelevant, meaningless, and devoid of purpose. History was the theater of God's radical love acting to bring healing to a broken world. Although moral progress was slow and evil seemingly intractable, King believed that a salvific narrative was being played out on the stage of history. God's love for a humanity made in God's image, and for a world that God had pronounced good, was proof that God would not abandon the world in its struggle to redeem its history. King believed that the great moral, political, and social changes that were taking place at that time were indicative of God's redemptive activity in history. That redemption would take place within the context of a liberation drama set in, not apart from, history. God would speak history's final, triumphant word about love, justice, and peace.[29] For this reason, King repeatedly made the bold claim that although the moral arc of the universe was certainly long, the bend of that arc was, without question, in the direction of cosmic justice.[30]

## The Biblical God: Divine Love and Power Effecting Cosmic Justice

As a Christian minister, King relied upon the Bible as the primary source of the revelation of God's nature. The pages of the Old and New Testaments served as a window through which King acquired epistemological certitude about God's being as well as God's radical engagement with the world. King turned to the central, authoritative text of his faith in an effort to discover, in narrative and symbolic forms, the concrete manifestations of God's proactive involvement in the redemption of history. It was there, in the biblical narrative account of God's ways with God's people, that King identified the theological key that unlocked the essential meaning of the gospel.

Of course, King did not come to the text without carrying the weight of his own presuppositions. King knew firsthand the black experiential plight of suffering, oppression, and disenfranchisement. He was also a product of a black religious tradition that regarded the Scripture as the most important lens through which to interpret reality.[31] A progressive, liberal Protestant approach to the Scripture combined with King's lived black experience and faith orientation gave him the critical interpretive framework within which to engage in a "political reading" of the biblical text. Methodologically, this "political exegesis" supplied the operative interpretive principle by which King came to make sense of God and the gospel.[32]

The gospel as "good news" pointed to King's discovery that the entire drama of the biblical *Heilsgeschichte* (salvation history), revealed a God who was concerned about those counted as "least" in the borders of the nation-state. In the pages of the Scripture, King read of the God of the Exodus, the sender of the Prophets, and the triumphant Christ. This God came to be understood as a *Liberator God* who not only hears the anguished cries of marginalized, oppressed children, but who also cares for and acts decisively on their behalf.

For King, *freedom* emerged as the operative interpretive principle. The Bible contained a gospel of freedom that chronicled the mighty deeds of a God of justice whose radical love expressed itself in continuous, liberative activity to free God's children from dehumanizing powers.[33] Consequently, when read in light of the black experience in America, King came to see the Bible as highly relevant to the sociopolitics of the present.

In his book of sermons, King articulates the nature, purpose, and will of God as radically involved love actively pursuing the restoration of the shalomic community of love, justice, and peace.[34] The Old Testament Exodus and the New Testament Christ events represent concrete historical embodiments of God as radical agape love in action, seeking the freedom of the children of God. The sermon "The Death of Evil Upon the Seashore" demonstrates King's use of the

Exodus liberation drama of the Bible as a paradigmatic model for how God operates within human history. Divine love and power act to protect and deliver those who are least able to defend themselves in the face of raw, naked power in any of its forms—political, social, military, economic. For King, the story is a symbol of the triumph of good over evil. It is important in that it reminds us that in the very nature of the universe, God is actively working on the side of justice, redeeming human history in the struggle for freedom.[35]

The Christ event of the New Testament pointed to a God whose radical love will go to any lengths to restore justice in human community. Indeed, the Cross and the Resurrection represented a divine willingness to struggle and suffer in the pursuit of cosmic redemption.[36] For King, the Cross was clear evidence that God was willing to take extraordinary measures to restore broken community. A more detailed investigation of King's understanding of Jesus Christ is presented in the next chapter. For now, it is enough to say that Jesus Christ was the embodiment of a personality and lifestyle commensurate with a total commitment to live in radical obedience to God's will. King saw Jesus as the radically involved personality, motivated by a strong God-consciousness, striving to live in harmony with divine will, exhibiting sacrifical love in personal conduct, and working to achieve redemption in interpersonal and communal relationships. Jesus Christ is important for King, in part, because Jesus reveals God's decisive incarnational involvement in history, and dispels the deistic misconception of God as "detached Other." In Christ lies definitive proof of God's willingness and ability to achieve divine purpose. The blessed assurance at the center of the Christian faith was that in the struggle between good and evil, God was not a neutral spectator. God was standing alongside the forces of truth and justice.[37]

Both the conception of a morally structured cosmic order and a biblical God of freedom and liberative justice provided grounds for the construction of a faith that was secure in its belief that God was concerned with the establishment of justice and community. It was the Bible, especially, which served as the source of King's assurance that God was on the side of justice, at work overcoming forces of alienation, restoring a fragmented and broken world.[38]

*Summary*

King was convinced that God was in firm control of the universe and that God was a companion to those who struggled for justice. More than any other thematic, King's theological perspective was shaped by an understanding of God as radical agape love in action. He believed in a personal God who was radically active—structuring justice in the cosmic order through moral laws, involved in history working to bring about justice, engaging the forces of evil, overcoming estrangement, and redeeming creation.

It was a radical faith in the Liberator God of the Bible and experience that catalyzed the movement at its inception in Montgomery. Faith in this same God provided King with the inner spiritual and moral resources to persist for twelve agonizing years of public service, joining God in the struggle for justice.[39] Faith in this God gave King the courage and tenacity to maintain a paradoxical hope about the final outcome of the freedom struggle.

King's conception of God as radical agape love in action served as the hub from which King developed a subsequent understanding of humanity.

# THE INVOLVED HUMAN BEING: HUMAN RESPONSIBILITY AND THE DIVINE MANDATE FOR RADICAL HISTORICAL PARTICIPATION

King's conception of God as radical agape love in action had direct implications for both his anthropological assumptions and his understanding of human responsibility. The creative, governing, and redeeming activity of God in human history had deputized human beings as stewards of nature and culture. For King, these divine custodial and caretaking functions pointed to an inescapable moral obligation—a divinely assigned, human task.

Drawing primarily from biblical revelation, the philosophical anthropology of personalism, and the social sciences, King established a critical correlation between divine sovereignty and human responsibility. Consequently, he had little tolerance for any approach in personal lifestyle or social strategy that induced apathy in the face of the crises of human existence. King argued, on theological grounds, that postures of complacency, creative avoidance, or indifference to the vexing problems of personal and communal living constituted sin.

King viewed life as a dynamic theater of interactive forces: sacred and profane, divine and human, personal and social, life and death, justice and injustice, integration and disintegration, reconciliation and fragmentation. The interplay between and among these often-times conflictual vectors generated permanent tensions, demanding hard choices as those tensions became localized in competing claims, commitments, loyalties, values, and interests. Human beings must manage conflicting realities and guide them toward morally positive ends. Life was not a sphere of static relations, perpetually fixed, requiring minimal human intervention. Rather, life was an arena of potentiality, ripe with possibilities for either anarchy or order, chaos or community. The form of particular societal arrangements and the quality of life they engendered would ultimately be determined by the nature and extent of purposive human activity.

King believed that the struggle for justice was, at bottom, an attempt to resolve the tension between conflicting cosmic forces. In this sense, the times were "revolutionary." That is to say, antithetical cosmic forces had converged in a particular historical moment, heightening the intensity of the conflict beyond normal limits. The revolutionary situation pointed to a heightened sense of conflictual forces. God never intended life to become a spectator sport for onlookers or bystanders, and the urgency characteristic of revolution-ary times demanded revolutionary responses.

King's anthropology was derived from his understanding of God. His main concern was to identify who we are as human beings (identity issue), and what God requires us to be and to do (ethical issue). King's resolution of these two issues moved through his epistemological claims about God. As our knowledge of God in-creases, we arrive at a deeper knowledge of God's will for human community. In that knowledge lies a clear discernment of ethical prescriptions for guiding conduct in daily affairs. For King, proactive involvement with the world constituted the only legitimate response to God's redemptive activity in the unfolding drama of history. Only in the process of actively engaging the permanent, generative ten-sions of life in harmony with divine purpose may humans achieve freedom, maturity, and completeness.

## King's Understanding of the *Imago Dei*

Like John Calvin, King began with the epistemological question: Who is God? To know God and what God was about in the world was at the same time to know one's self.[40] Consequently, King's conception of God became pivotal for his view of humanity. King credited personalism for giving him "metaphysical and philosophical grounding" not only for the idea of a personal God, but also for asserting the inherent dignity and worth of all persons.[41]

For a black man who had experienced the absurdities of racism, a critical, positive self-affirmation was an important element in the resolution of the identity issue. Covert and overt socialization patterns effectively communicated the powerful negative message that blackness was a badge of shame and dishonor, a mark of innate inferiority and nobodiness. King used the notion of the *imago Dei* to counter the cultural devaluation of black worth and to assert notions of black dignity and equality. This image of God provided the conceptual basis for an understanding of humanity as the familyhood of God and enabled King to understand racism as more than a sociological issue, thereby establishing the grounds upon which to identify racism as essentially a theological-moral problem.[42]

As the authoritative text of the black church tradition, the Bible was central to King's understanding of humanity. Nurtured in the biblical faith of black Christianity, King had been exposed to a tradition of religious interpretation that had always understood the *imago Dei* in light of its broader, sociopolitical implications. Personalism merely provided the supplemental, metaphysical basis for the notion of the *imago Dei*. Theologically, the *imago Dei* functioned as the interpretive prism through which King articulated his basic anthropological assumptions.

King insisted that God was the source of all life, and that all human beings were created in the image of God. In other words, all human beings bore the stamp or imprint of God's essence, each meriting recognition as a child of God. As such, the sanctity and sacredness of all human life must be acknowledged. Every person, regardless of race, nationality, creed, or gender, was to be valued and treated with respect and dignity. Every person, regardless of social position, economic status, or education, was somebody. The labeling of other persons as human nobodies was oxymoronic.[43] Since the *imago Dei* was innately shared in equal measure by all humans, King believed that

57

every person had inherent worth and was deserving of the highest respect. The sacredness of all human personality rendered graded evaluations of people's worth as good, bad, better, and worse as both meaningless and idolatrous. With regard to racial diversity, no moral justification existed for asserting the divine right of one race over another. For King, the Christian ethic was unequivocal: all humans were deserving of respect and dignity because all humans were equally loved, respected, and valued by God. Human worth was intrinsic, based on the relatedness of each person to God. Therefore, matters of intellect, racial origin, social position, or biophysiological makeup were improperly viewed as determinants of human worth.[44]

The genuine worth of humans was to be measured by a standard other than human. Consequently, King used the *imago Dei* to appeal to the white conscience. He urged whites, on theological grounds, to acknowledge the sacredness of black beings and the humanity and equal worth of black folk as brothers and sisters in the one, large family of God. King also used the *imago Dei* to issue appeals to blacks to overcome a sense of nobodiness and to develop a healthy self-love and a sense of somebodiness. King argued that this change in racial self-perception represented, perhaps, the movement's greatest achievement.[45]

The *imago Dei* provided a basis for King's critique of various social, political, and economic structural arrangements. King rejected communism because it placed humans in the service of the state and reduced them to instrumentalities or "things" with which to achieve the ends of the state.[46] On similar moral-theological grounds, King attacked the structural edifice of segregation. Appropriating terminology from the Jewish theologian Martin Buber, King viewed segregation as a sociocultural framework that substituted "I-It" for "I-Thou" relationships. Segregation reduced persons to the status of "things," scarred the soul, and degraded the personality, effectively blocking the development of black (and ultimately white) potential.[47]

The *imago Dei* enabled King to critique the ideology and ethos of racism on moral grounds and thereby raise the issue of race as a theological issue. King appealed to the nation (as a self-described Judeo-Christian people) to see racism not merely as an unsound social policy or politically unfeasible. Reconciliation in race relations could be achieved only when racial discrimination had been approached as a serious moral-spiritual problem of idolatry.[48]

The *imago Dei* also provided a conceptual basis from which King made public appeals to embrace nonviolence as the *only* viable method available for oppressed persons struggling to achieve freedom. Violence of any type amounted to a fundamental denial of the sanctity of human life in its denial of or injury to the image of God in all persons. In this regard, even in the legitimate struggle for justice, violence constituted not only an impractical, but also an immoral response to collective evil.[49]

In addition to providing a basis for a belief in the inherent worth and dignity of human personality, the *imago Dei* led King to affirm two other convictions. First, the "unity of all humanity," and second, that "life demands freedom."[50] Because all life was interrelated through the One God, the deliberate exclusion of persons or groups from membership in the human community could not be morally justified. The image of God in every person meant that there could be no such thing as an "outsider" or "nonresident" in the human enterprise. King considered this point as axiomatic truth.

King comunicated this belief through the phrase "sociality of human life."[51] He was convinced that God's moral ordering of the universe, God's image in human personality, and God's active work in history, when viewed together, revealed God's ultimate goal for humanity to be that of *community*. God had structured reality in such a way that full human development became an existential impossibility apart from living in community with others. The image of God catalyzed the gregarious instinct in human nature. The development of human speech, character, intellectual growth, values, conscience, took place *not* in isolation, but in relationship with other members of the human family. The moral principle of interrelatedness or interdependence took precedence over the principle of self-reliance in King's thinking and had serious import for his ethical perspective. Communities based upon segregation could not be accepted or tolerated since they violated the interdependent, social character of existence. Genuine community must concretely reflect, in its institutional structures, the principle of interdependence. Therefore, integration, not segregation, emerged as both content and method to achieve the beloved community.[52]

To be made in God's image also meant that "life demands freedom."[53] No human being could be justifiably denied the basic God-given freedom to deliberate and weigh alternatives, choose what was right and good, and participate in making decisions that affected one's life. Of course, there remained recognizable, legitimate limits to freedom. The flawed nature of human reason placed constraints upon the ability to know and decide with perfection. The plurality of personal interests and pursuits involved in determining notions of the good in society made the adjudication of multiple ends into a larger, common good highly problematical. Finally, the empirically verifiable evidence of sin meant that humans often fail to choose the good even when they know it. In light of what appeared to be superlative moral alternatives, humans might yet choose that which was clearly morally bankrupt.[54]

And yet, the image of God in human personality had not been completely obliterated by sin. Therefore, humans did possess the capacity to choose for God, justice, peace, and love, and against hatred, injustice, and violence. Divine sovereignty neither negated nor overrode human responsibility. Within the human personality was found a dual potential for both good and evil. Humans possessed the power to consider moral options and make correct moral choices. King seized every opportunity to place the necessity of informed and prayerful moral and political choice before both the individual and national conscience.[55]

Clearly, the *imago Dei* and other related concepts in King's understanding of humanity were more than abstract concepts. This gave his view of humanity specific, concrete content relating qualities of personality such as consciousness, imagination, rational capacity, choice, and conscience to compassion for and responsibility toward others. When King raised the question "What is man?"[56] the concept of the *imago Dei* led him to a discovery of freedom as the essence of humanity. God intended that all humans live as free beings.

The evils of social alienation, political oppression, economic exploitation and deprivation, and psychological deracination and denudation amounted, at bottom, to a denial of freedom to blacks and the poor. The denial of freedom was an attempt to play God by defacing the image of God, and making another person over in one's own image. This, for King, represented the supreme theological problem—idolatry or godlessness, establishing one's own relative perspective as absolute, and in the process trying to put God out of business. Linking the denial of freedom with the idolatrous defacement of the *imago Dei*, King launched a powerful and incisive critique of the white church.[57] He also made an appeal to the black church to avoid the danger of becoming the very reality that it sought to transcend. King was concerned that the black church not be seduced into embracing and modeling the idolatry for which it had rightly criticized the white church.[58]

In summary, the *imago Dei* provided moral grounds for asserting a notion of freedom, the content of which was defined in concrete, sociopolitical terms. King was able to make a direct link between moral considerations of human worth and dignity and the issue of Constitutionally guaranteed political, economic, and social justice (jobs, housing, education, voting, and so forth).[59] In this way, King was able to establish a permanent dialectical tension between morality and politics. Consequently, societal structures and institutional arrangements must be critiqued in light of their harmony with the divine moral order as well as their affirmation or denial of the inherently sacred worth of all human beings.

## Sociopolitical Implications of King's Anthropology

Viewed in light of black suffering and oppression, massive poverty, and rampant militarism, King's understanding of humanity led to some important implications for responses to collective evil. First came a moral obligation to weigh alternatives and to decide for the good, the right, and the just. Second came the moral necessity to act responsibly on behalf of freedom, challenging attitudinal perspectives or institutional arrangements that degraded human personality. King believed that the social, political, and economic structuring of society was ultimately determined by one's understanding of humanity.[60]

Recognizing three distinct components of humanity (biological, spiritual, and sinful), King acknowledged the body as both sacred and significant. Any program aimed at spiritual and moral redemption must also be concerned with the physical well-being of the body, including the material conditions within which physical existence takes place. Anthropology became linked to morally responsible, active engagement in the world on behalf of freedom and justice. Since King acknowledged no clear separation between body and soul, mind and matter, identity and ethics became linked. The resolution of the identity issue was linked to notions of the *imago Dei,* inherent human dignity and worth, sacredness of personality, interrelatedness of all life, and the sociality of human life. These assertions carried important consequences for the ethical question "What ought I to be and to do?" For King, to be human carried an inherent, inescapable ethical obligation to seek the development of a complete, integrative life. This life was marked by three components: a right relationship with God, a proper concern for self, and a compassionate concern for others.[61]

A discussion of moral conscience relative to King's notion of the integrative life is fruitful for an understanding of the sociopolitical implications of his anthropology. For the individual, the development of moral conscience is vital to formation of the integrative life. The integrative life is internally guided by a trialectic focus on God-consciousness, self-attunement, and communal responsibility. King identifies these tripolar realities as length, breadth, and height, respectively.[62] A complete, integrative life has equal focus on all three. In essence, it is a life guided by a conscience that is in tune with the moral demands of the universe. This is what King meant by living in right relationship with God. The seeds of conscience (though dulled by the effects of sin) are present in the human psyche by virtue of the image of God. The task is to awaken and develop the conscience so that it will be responsive to moral appeal. Indeed, the aim of moral education and spiritual formation is to awaken the conscience to a proper sense of God and the cosmic moral structure.

This relates directly to the focus on self-attunement. In the awakened conscience, the individual strives for inner harmony and a commitment to a lifestyle in consonance with particular moral values: justice, peace, love, self-control, patience, forgiveness, rational self-interest, and so forth. Because the image of God is never totally obliterated, human beings are not doomed to live lives of total depravity. Rather, human nature always contains a kernel of conscience that can be awakened so that human beings can respond to goodness, and choose what is morally just.[63]

Further, a proper focus on self-attunement in the integrative life involved the development of a positive self-concept. Self-affirmation was a form of psychological freedom and an important part of the process of healthy identity formation. King's anthropology, with notions of inherent dignity, self-worth, and sacredness aided psychological emancipation. The sociopolitical payoff was that as levels of self-love and self-esteem rose, new definitions of self would emerge resulting in the arousal of personal conscience. Conscience would operate in these positive conceptions of personal and group identity, significantly lowering the incidence of costly acts of self-denigration— abuse, addiction, violence, rape, and crime. King applied this analysis primarily to blacks, but believed this would prove beneficial to other groups and the nation as well.

In addition to God-consciousness and self-attunement, awakened conscience operated in the integrative life to generate a notion of communal responsibility. King's anthropological belief in the social and interdependent character of human existence worked with conscience to affirm the moral obligation to be concerned with the plight of others. King felt that too many private consciences in America had been co-opted by an overemphasis on individual achievement and an underemphasis on communal consciousness and social responsibility. In King's own case, an awakened conscience converged with a heightened sense of communal responsibility as he wrestled with moral convictions that led eventually to his unpopular stands on the Vietnam War, poverty, conspicuous consumerism, and capitalist values.[64]

The focus on communal responsibility and concern for the welfare of others also had a significant sociopolitical payoff. Conscience, combined with King's notion of the interdependence and sociality of all humanity, to promote a sensitivity to suffering and the misfortunes of others. It generated a sense of restlessness in the face of injustice, and a felt moral obligation to join in proactive solidarity with those committed to the struggle for justice. In this way, the individual experienced an inability to remain apathetic in the revolutionary situation.[65] Instead, the person undertook courageous risk in a life of commitment to the transformation of society, and the realization of justice in human community.

In national life, King coupled a notion of collective conscience with his anthropological assumptions to speak to the nation's social ills. In his critique of America, King accused the nation of living a disintegrative collective lifestyle. First, America was out of harmony with moral law. The nation had buried its national conscience underneath the capitalistic principle of profit maximization. In so doing, America had fallen victim to bad anthropology that allowed her to embrace a false body-soul dualism with regard to blacks and the poor. The bodies of black and poor folk had been commodified and sacrificed for the benefit of others. The national conscience was morally bankrupt and suffering from misguided values and misplaced priorities.[66] Focusing on God-consciousness and harmony with the moral demands of the universe, King accused America of moral hypocrisy.

Second, King accused America of having a schizophrenic personality. The collective moral conscience of America had been compromised to the point that the nation stood tragically divided against its own better self. King pointed to the contradiction between America's profession of the democratic ideal and practices that represented the very opposite of democratic principles.[67]

Finally, King accused America of having a blunted social consciousness. King believed that this was evident in America's treatment of the "least of these." The anthropological notions of the inherent worth and dignity of all human personality, and the sacredness of all human life should have operated in a Judeo-Christian context to awaken the collective American conscience. America should have been sensitized to the plight of the marginalized poor and disfranchised minorities.

King initially believed that the national conscience was disturbed by practices within that violated the sanctity of human life. He had felt that the nation sought peace within itself and the capacity to live with its conscience. King believed that the conscience of white America was open to moral appeals concerning the demands of justice. In fact, King described the black-led freedom movement as the troubled conscience of America.[68] Therefore, King had sought to effect a "coalition of conscience." Blacks and whites with a developed sense of social responsibility would join forces to transform power relations, institutional structures, moral values, and sociopolitical priorities of the nation through radical, nonviolent social action, legislation, and public policy initiatives.

However, America had made a too easy peace with her conscience with regard to those in her midst who were denied basic subsistence necessities. By 1967, King's optimism had altered significantly about the capacity of the collective white conscience to be awakened and the nation's soul to be redeemed.[69] In the case of white America, Reinhold Niebuhr's anthropological assertion had proved to be correct. In the long run, groups tend to behave in significantly less moral and just ways than individuals. Focusing on communal consciousness, King accused the nation of moral irresponsibility. In both individual and national life, King's notion of the integrative life combined with his anthropological assumptions had important sociopolitical implications.

## Summary

King's understanding of humanity amounts to a belief in the involved human being. God as radical agape love in action is the source from which all life is derived. Human beings are made in the image of God and hold the essence of radical love. All human beings had inherent worth and dignity, and the sanctity of life was upheld. The social and interdependent character of human existence and the unity of all life meant that humans were one single family of God.

But the human being assumed inescapable moral obligation to become a responsible coworker with God, joining radical agape love's struggle to defeat evil, establish justice, and restore human community in history. Although King took seriously the flawed character of human existence, he nevertheless held that doctrines of human nature must not overstress the corruption of humanity. Human beings, as moral agents and agents of social change, possessed the power to make positive moral choices and engage in liberative action aimed at the transformation of society in accordance with the moral norm of justice.[70]

The central focus of King's understanding of humanity is the nature of human involvement in the drama of God's redemption of history. Therefore, the emphasis is placed on human participation through radical, emancipatory action. King rejected any understanding of humanity that severed the tension between divine sovereignty and human responsibility. The basic task of human beings was to develop the integrative life of proactive engagement with God, world, flesh, and devil. Consequently, all forms of gradualism, detachment, or passivity in the face of justice's urgent demands constituted inadequate and immoral human responses.[71]

# INVOLVEMENT AS "MARK" OF THE CHRISTIAN LIFE

King was a Christian theologian and an ordained minister of the Progressive Black Baptist denomination. His religious faith exerted a profound impact upon his social activism. It is important to consider the way in which King's view of God and humanity significantly influenced (and was influenced by) his conception of the essential meaning and relevance of the gospel. In turn, this gospel perspective provided the basis for a doctrine of Christian discipleship.

To be sure, the birth, life, ministry, teachings, death, and the resurrection of Jesus Christ were the linchpin in King's view of the Christian life (see section on Christology). The gospel of Jesus Christ, when read in light of the nature of God and the nature of humanity, reinforced King's notion of the involved human being. The gospel established more specifically divine expectations for humanity. The Christian, confessing the lordship of Christ, knows in a concrete human personality what it means to live a life of complete integration. Christ demonstrates what it means to be genuinely human. Thus, for the Christian, Christ becomes illuminative as a paradigmatic model of the integrative life.

To be made in God's image and to know God through Jesus Christ of the Gospel narratives provide clarity about God's purposes for humanity. At the same time, one comes to know what human responsibility demands in light of God's restorative action. Knowledge of God's will and work in the world informs what we actually do—how we structure social life; the prioritization of values on the public agenda; the establishment of proximate loyalites; and the exercise of purposive human activity. Through the Gospel narratives of Christ, commitment to the Christian faith provided certainty that the God we came to know in Jesus Christ modeled a discipleship of radical obedience. This radical obedience in turn led to a witness of radical involvement in solidarity with God's restorative action in the world, on behalf of the concrete, historical realization of freedom, justice, and peace in the beloved community.

The notion of the involved human being was further clarified and deepened for the Christian, in King's view, as a mandate for a radical Christian discipleship that modeled a radical involvement that sought to proactively join the God we know in Jesus Christ in the perennial struggle to create the shalomic community. The Christ of the Gospels demonstrates this type of radical historical participation. Indeed, a "mark" of the Christian life was the capacity to commit one's life in totality to the cause of freedom, justice, and community—a cause that extended well beyond the contours of one's personal interests.

Throughout his life of public service, King never wavered from the maxim he considered to be axiomatic: that "other-preservation"—the capacity to imagine one's own destiny as inseparably interconnected with that of others—was "the first law of life."[72] In this way, King's view of the Christian life became coterminous with a socially active lifestyle that avoided both the privatization and the interiorization of spirituality.

## NEIGHBOR-LOVE AND JUSTICE-ORIENTED PRAXIS

King categorically rejected the notion that authentic human life was possible or desirable apart from community. Life, in its completeness, was understood as a *tridimensional* enterprise. Along with concern for one's personal welfare or rational self-interest (length), and concern for the nurturance of a faith relationship with God (height), one other dimension was required. King argued that humans needed to develop the capacity to transcend narrowly circumscribed, individualistic, sectional, racial, and class interests. These interests, while legitimate, inclined the personality to become inordinately egocentric unless balanced by sufficient attention to and involvement of the self with the plight of others. King refered to this dimension as breadth—an involvement of the particular individual in the universal concerns of humanity.

Several tenets of King's anthropological framework converged to provide the content of "neighbor-love": the interrelated structure of all reality; the sociality of all human life; the unity of humanity; the image of God in all human personality; the operation of community-creating agape love in the cosmic order as well as the human heart. These conceptual threads buttressed King's adamantly-held view that individual human development was irreparably damaged when persons were forcibly consigned to live in an ethos driven by egocentrism, excessive individualism, alienation, apathy, and disinterestedness in the plight of the "other."

Again, agape love was the basis of the community. King's emphasis on love gave him grounding for a way of seeing the "other" not as enemy, but as friend and neighbor.[73] Further, this dimension of breadth (concern for the other based upon agape love) led King to argue that the Christian life of obedience to the God we know in Jesus Christ mandated a proactive, radical involvement on behalf of concretized justice in society.

Concern for the conditions and existential plight of others acknowledged the unity of humanity. It demonstrated movement toward the realization of an integrative personality. Concern for the "other" was in harmony with the paradigmatic narrative of Jesus Christ. Finally, it led to activity aimed at establishing the just, human community.

The confession that "Jesus is Lord of life," by its very nature, imposed on the believer a moral obligation to actively participate in God's work of renewal in a fragmented and broken world. For King, commitment to the Christian life was a privilege that also brought an inescapable responsibility. In this way, King linked the contemplative life of inner spiritual development with the activistic life of outer prophetic social transformation.

The critical link between faith and action was agapeistic neighbor-love. It affirmed the interrelatedness, mutuality, and interdependence of humanity. Relying on the content of neighbor-love, King consistently stressed the themes of unity, sociality, and interdependence of human life. Arguing against segregation statutes, King asserted the common destiny of all humanity.[74] Neighbor-love insisted that we see our own well-being in light of the well-being of others. The interdependent nature of human life meant that each person was part of the other, diminished or enlarged by the plight of the other. King often paraphrased John Donne in support of the interdependence principle.[75]

Interdependence meant common destiny on every level of human relationship—interpersonal, group, national, and international. King argued that the basis of his involvement in Birmingham was his recognition of the interrelatedness of all human community. For this reason, he could not remain in Atlanta unconcerned and unaffected by the events in Birmingham.[76] In the famous "I Have a Dream" speech at the 1963 March on Washington, King asserted that whites must, likewise, come to see that their destiny was linked to the destiny of blacks, and that the freedom of whites was inextricably tied to the freedom of blacks. America as a nation must come to realize the interdependent basis of its existence. Its very livelihood depended upon the mutual sharing of resources and goods with other nations.[77]

After a visit to India in 1957, where he had witnessed stark, grim, massive poverty, hunger, suffering, and dislocation, King argued for American economic aid and food relief. Stressing the common destiny of all nations in the single neighborhood that the world had become, King sought to persuade America to develop a global concern for the plight of other nations.

We are tied together in the single garment of destiny, caught in an inescapable network of mutuality, and whatever affects one directly affects all indirectly. For some strange reason I can never be what I ought to be until you are what you ought to be. And you can never be what you ought to be until I am what I ought to be. This is the way God's universe is made; this is the way it is structured.[78]

Agape love saw the "other" as interdependent *neighbor*. The world, for King, became one large parish, one great neighborhood, a world house, a cosmic community.[79] The conception of human being as neighbor, motivated by neighbor-love, was used frequently to describe the involved human personality. King found the concept of this neighbor-love explicated paradigmatically in Jesus' parable of the good Samaritan. The main character of this story risked personal safety and comfort, and broke with the restrictive religious and cultural traditions of the day in order to come to the aid of a human in need.

Agape is disinterested love. It is a love in which the individual seeks not his own good, but the good of his neighbor (1 Cor. 10:24). Agape does not begin by discriminating between worthy and unworthy people. . . . It is an entirely "neighbor-regarding concern for others." . . . Therefore, agape makes no distinction between friend and enemy; it is directed toward both.[80]

This type of love was necessary for the creation of right relationships in the single world community or neighborhood. Concern for others was of paramount importance in one's efforts to live a life of authenticity, integrity, and completeness as a human being made in the image of God.

The good Samaritan modeled, in King's view, a "creative altruism" that was basic to all genuine human living. It was expressed in actions that were universal, dangerous, and excessive.[81] The universality of the Samaritan's actions did not allow the incidental criteria of race, religion, or nationality to prevent him from recognizing and responding to another human being in need. He was able to look beyond the "external accidents" and see the true humanity of persons. He was able to identify the neighbor as anyone, regardless of race, creed, color, or station, who is in need.[82] In the face of poverty, discrimination, exploitation, or injustice, neighbor-love seeks relief for those in need.

The good Samaritan also demonstrated "dangerous altruism" in that he was willing to undertake courageous moral action to alleviate the pain and suffering of another. He placed his body in harm's way, risking life and limb to rescue a neighbor in need. His concern for the neighbor outdistanced his consideration of the dangers involved, as he promoted a "risked mode lifestyle" in which personal safety was ancillary to a concern for justice.

King consistently modeled this dangerous altruism in a similar lifestyle of personal risk taking. Whether he was in Birmingham, Chicago, or Memphis, he felt a moral duty to risk his life in pursuit of freedom, justice, and dignity for the neighbor. Personal comfort and safety were subordinated to the needs of the suffering victims of injustice.[83] King held that times of comfort and convenience failed to adequately measure a person's true character. Rather, it was only during moments of great challenge and controversy that an individual's ultimate measure could be taken. The true neighbor risked safety, position, and even death for the welfare of others. [84]

The Samaritan also exhibited an "excessive altruism." He went beyond the normal bounds of charitable obligation to help the neighbor. He exceeded the expectations mandated by the situation. King felt that white America needed to develop this kind of attitudinal perspective. White America was fixated on notions of pity, feeling sorry for someone. What was required was empathy, feeling sorry with someone, sharing their pain and burdens. King believed that until the white majority felt the ache of daily black existence, the problems of racial discrimination and poverty would never be solved.

All humans, as children of God and members of the human community, need to assume a responsibility to exhaust every energy and resource to alleviate the suffering of others and to restore community. For King, this type of altruism was not an impossible ideal.

However, it did mean that acts of pity were inadequate. The comprehensive restructuring of economic life was required.[85]

Excessive altruism ultimately called for a type of involvement aimed at the radical restructuring of personal and social values, institutional arrangements, laws, economic, and political systems. Activity of this kind may move well beyond the normal expectations of living and may place well-being in jeopardy. Jesus modeled this lifestyle. As the parable makes clear, the goodness of the Samaritan lies in his capacity to see concern for others as the first law of life.[86] For King, modern-day disciples are called to a similar posture of engagement with the world.[87] Until a person rises above narrow individual concerns to broader issues affecting the human community, maturation has not progressed to the point where genuine human living is occurring.

## SUFFERING AS "INVOLVEMENT IN EXTREMIS": NEIGHBOR-LOVE AND THE CALL TO RADICAL DISCIPLESHIP

Creative altruism placed heavy stress upon a communitarian ethic of care and responsibility that transcended boundaries of race and class. King's appropriation of neighbor-love led him to challenge the apathetic personality. The demands of love in the revolutionary situation brought a moral obligation for noncooperation with the evils of injustice and cooperation with good. In the context of American socioeconomics, King leveled devastating critiques against the apathetic disinterestedness of the affluent toward the poor. Communal responsibility was an inescapable moral requirement, and the individual could not ignore injustice without becoming an accomplice to it.[88] The unity and interrelatedness of all life meant that no person could enjoy genuine freedom, health, or economic stability as long as masses of folk were affected by poverty, sickness, and injustice. More important, for King, the content of neighbor-love was to be found in divine self-giving as witnessed to in the narratives of the Scripture. The biblical content of neighbor-love found especially in the Gospels led King to conclude that suffering was an unavoidable moral necessity in the struggle to achieve freedom.

King held that each individual, as a child of God and a member of the human community or world neighborhood (whether confessing

Christian or not), must commit to a lifestyle of sacrificial self-giving that involved personal suffering in the struggle to achieve justice. Driven by a powerful sense of vocation, he believed that when undertaken in pursuit of a greater cause of justice, righteousness, and community, suffering was unmerited, and therefore, redemptive in nature.[89] In the context of liberative struggle, suffering in the service of justice was tantamount to a vocational calling. Consequently, King argued for the necessity of a particular type of involvement that he identified as radical or extremist.[90] As he studied the lives of Christ, Gandhi, and other exemplars of the freedom struggle, he discovered this "extremist" behavior as the common element in their personal lifestyles.[91]

Throughout his own public ministry, King insisted that the extremism of personal sacrifice and suffering was morally necessary in the struggle to redeem the human community. In fact, a major strength of nonviolent resistance lay in its capacity to generate an existential openness to engage in sacrificial suffering in the battle against forces of evil and injustice. Nonviolent resistance demanded that the freedom fighter willingly accept suffering without retaliating against the moral opponent. If violence emerged as a prominent feature of the justice struggle, the nonviolent resister was prepared to accept, but never to inflict it.[92]

Sacrificial suffering was also necessary to arouse and awaken the oppressor's moral conscience. Risking life nonviolently as a witness to truth, King believed, induced moral shame in the opponent. Especially in the early stages of his public ministry, he was optimistic about the power of sacrificial, nonviolent love to morally disarm whites.

Further, sacrificial suffering on behalf of freedom operated cryptically in the nonviolent resister's inner psyche to elevate estimations of intrinsic self-worth. King witnessed this in Montgomery blacks who had placed their bodies on the line daily in service to justice during the bus boycott. King commented that their willingness to suffer and make great personal sacrifice for freedom actually gave them a new sense of self-dignity and worth.[93]

At the end of the boycott, King was convinced of the moral necessity of sacrificial suffering in efforts to achieve the beloved community.[94] Montgomery had provided empirical verification that the capacity to suffer in the struggle for justice, without resorting to violent aggression, was the method to eliminate social evil that King had been searching for since his early days at Crozer. King was convinced that blacks must adapt this method strategically in the struggle for freedom and equality in America.

King felt strongly that the Christian (ministers especially) must, by example, suffer courageously in the freedom struggle. The gospel emphatically rejected any discontinuity between faith and action. Subsequently, there could be no separation of soul and body, nor disconnection between principle and practice, creed and deed. Professed loyalty to the values of freedom, love, justice, hope, and community required a radical sacrifice in pursuit of their historical realization. For the Christian specifically, this meant a moral obligation to a life of self-denial, cross-bearing, and walking the way of Christ. King identified redemptive suffering as central to this moral obligation for the Christian.[95]

And yet, he also understood it as an unavoidable, moral obligation facing every person in the struggle to humanize the sociopolitical and economic order.[96] Undeniably, the pursuit of justice would exact a heavy cost. King felt the cross was something that each person must bear. Inevitably, the cross would lead to death. In bearing his personal cross, King said that he had experienced death of popularity, financial assistance, moral support, and public empathy. Nevertheless, he felt an unavoidable moral obligation to bear it, and publicly declared his commitment to the way of redemptive suffering through the cross.

The willingness to endure suffering and persecution for truth, justice, and righteousness was the essence of the Christian way. Whether it meant jail or even physical death, King argued that nothing could be more redemptive or Christian than paying the price of physical death to free others from psychological, social, political, and economic death. This point he made clear from the very beginning in Montgomery.[97]

King felt that the requirement for the Christian lifestyle (self-denial, self-sacrifice, and cross-bearing in the face of situations of injustice) was incompatible with the egocentric values of self-sufficiency, self-reliance, hedonistic individualism, and narcissism. The promotion of these values in a culture driven by excessive consumerism must be counteracted by a scale of values informed by the concept of neighbor-love. The Christian especially, must live a life for others. For the black Christian, living for others implied radical emancipatory action in solidarity with oppressed and marginalized blacks and the poor. Cross-bearing was necessary to achieve freedom for those to whom justice had been denied.[98] For the white Christian, to take up this cross in solidarity with those struggling for justice was an act of faith in God and the future. It was the only route to personal and social salvation.[99]

Of course, the "Christian," like others in society, was caught in between the powerful pull of the yes and the no. In this sense, the individual faced constantly the knife-edge of decision—for or against God, truth, and justice. The moral choice was unavoidable—disintegregation or integration, withdrawal or participation, conformity or transformation, apathy or involvement, violence or nonviolence, chaos or community, self-aggrandizement or social responsibility, egoism or altruism.

> Every man must decide whether he will walk in the light of creative altruism or the darkness of destructive selfishness. This is the judgement. Life's most persistent and urgent question is "What are you doing for others?"[100]

The necessity of voluntary suffering in the freedom struggle received its justification in the certain knowledge that such suffering was salvific or redemptive in nature. The interpretation of King's personal trials led him to affirm the virtue and value of unmerited suffering, although he was always concerned about avoiding the pitfalls of unconsciously nurturing a martyr complex. Nevertheless, through the interpretive lens of the cross of Christ, King appropriated the theology of Paul and asserted that, "I bear in my body the marks of the Lord Jesus." Through suffering he had come to experience God in a more personal way, and in the process had strengthened his belief in the redemptive nature of unmerited suffering.[101]

King applied this perspective on suffering to the freedom movement. Speaking in Montgomery, he extolled the great possibilities of unearned suffering to educate and transform. Suffering, he felt, was more powerful than retaliation for conversion of the moral opponent. Nothing that is of fundamental importance can be achieved solely by reason. Rather, suffering of some type was necessary for growth.

King appealed to the redemptive value of unearned suffering in every circumstance of brutality, violence, and hostility.[102] In eulogizing the four martyred children in Birmingham in 1963, King argued that the unmerited and unwarranted deaths along with the suffering of loved ones had "something to say" to every human being. To all who would compromise their moral values by passively accepting injustice and segregation, remain dangerously silent and apathetic in the face of brutality, or opt for personal security amid the revolutionary call for struggle, the message was clear and unequivocal. God redeems through undeserved suffering. Therefore, the girls did not die in vain. God would somehow use the senseless tragedy to fulfill divine purposes. For this reason, King comforted the mourners not to lose hope.[103]

Gratuitous, sacrificial suffering was not to be engaged in indiscriminately. The aim was not to romanticize suffering. Suffering was not to become an end in itself, but rather a means to a greater end. In fact, the presence and experience of unmerited suffering in and of itself was insufficient to facilitate redemption for the dispossessed. King was quick to point out that freedom was not achievable by passively accepting suffering, but by a struggle against suffering.[104] King rejected efforts to sensationalize suffering and struggled to avoid the glorification of what Dorothy Soelle identified as "Christian sadomasochism."[105]

At the same time, King wanted to encourage a type of extremist, radical involvement in the freedom struggle that would invalidate responses characterized by apathy, passivity, and complacency. Humankind was to be actively, radically involved in the creation of the just society. In harmony with divine purpose, the human being (especially the Christian) was to be radically involved in the struggle for justice, and willing to suffer courageously for the redemption of the human community. In this regard, King advocated the development of a specific type of *personality* as expressive of the complete, integrative human life.

## ORIENTATIONAL PERSPECTIVE OF THE RADICALLY INVOLVED HUMAN BEING

King tried to nurture a perspectival orientation and lifestyle in accord with the purposes of the God he knew as radical agape love in action. God continually sought the liberation and reconciliation of the cosmic order. To be made in God's image and to live in harmony with the imperatives of God required radical participation in historical projects aimed at bringing about justice and peace on earth. This kind of engagement called for an awareness of personal responsibility to God, self, and "other" to undertake radical involvement in the struggle to eliminate social evil and establish the beloved community. This orientational perspective functions critically to provide a running critique of the apathetic, nonparticipant in the drama of historical liberative activity.

For King, the radically involved human being represented a personality type. This personality—persuaded of the inseparable connection between faith and practice, truth and duty—is best described as a maladjusted personality, characterized by a pronounced dissatisfaction with the current institutional-structural arrangements of power that tended to perpetuate unjust and inequitable distributions of basic social, political, and economic goods of society.[106] For King, maladjustment suggested a restless determination to see justice prevail. It also suggested the nurturance of an intolerant attitude in the face of certain realities—discrimination, segregation, inequality, poverty, violence, and war. When King searched for historical examples of this maladjusted personality, he found the prophet Amos, Abraham Lincoln, Thomas Jefferson, and Jesus Christ.

King believed that society was in desperate need of personalities who modeled this type of orientation in their styles of living. Maladjustment meant a refusal to hate, injure, or kill, or to "let evildoers rest."[107] It meant demonstrating an unwavering commitment to the struggle for justice, love, and peace. The maladjusted person might be described as an "extremist," a "creative dissenter," a "transformed nonconformist" living in harmony with the demands of a higher moral law, one who harbored a "dangerous unselfishness" that concerned itself with the existential plight of others.[108]

In his classic epistolary response to the white clergymen of Birmingham in 1963, King spoke of the "extremism" of the maladjusted personality. Expressing gratitude for their identification of his nonviolent action as extremist, King asked whether or not Jesus Christ, Paul, Martin Luther, and John Bunyan could be considered extremists. In the struggle for justice, love, and peace, he argues, extremist behavior is a moral necessity. The only issue is whether one's extremism will be on behalf of love or hatred, justice or injustice.[109]

King was convinced of the urgent need for a "colony of dissenters," radical resisters who challenged the status quo and sought radical structural change. He felt that creative, generative tension that elevates personality and advances moral good was necessary for growth. The society was in need of such "nonviolent gadflies" to create positive tension by confronting injustice. Radical dissent, for King, must not be confused with "wanting in" or "buying into" existing values and arrangements. Rather, radical dissenters worked to create new values and institutions that were more humane, just, and compassionate than the old order perpetuated. Ultimately, this was the purpose of the movement.[110]

It was the Christian especially, who must answer the call to a lifestyle of prophetic dissent. King reminded listeners of the temptation to choose paths of least resistance. And yet, the Christian had a mandate, an unavoidable duty, to say no to the voices of conformity. In fact, the hope for a new world order was to be found in the dedicated cadre of disciplined, transformed nonconformists. The salvation of the world depended on those few nonconformists who courageously remained creatively maladjusted in a world of complacent, well-adjusted, conformists.[111]

King held that the chief end of life ("to do the will of God, come what may") required a specific orientation and lifestyle. To be sure, this perspective involved a high cost of personal risk and sacrificial suffering. Yet, King remained convinced that, in the final analysis, the nonapathetic, radically involved, sacrificially suffering, creatively maladjusted, nonconformist personality was coterminous with the complete, integrative life. As King consistently reminded his listeners and followers, this lifestyle perspective was ultimately concerned with the quality of one's life rather than the quantity of years lived.[112]

# CHAPTER 3

# THE THEOLOGICAL ROOTS OF KING'S VOCATIONAL RESPONSE:

*Christ, Church, and the Future*

## CHRISTOLOGY: THE RADICALLY INVOLVED CHRIST

As a minister of the Christian gospel, King held firmly to a profound and enduring faith in Jesus Christ as Savior of the world. As early as 1950, during the first year at Crozer Seminary, his conviction was that an understanding of Jesus Christ was central to the Christian faith. Without an adequate Christology, he argued, solid theological formulation could not be done.[1] Regarding his personhood, King described Jesus as a Jew, a popular teacher of religion, and the most influential character of his day. Regarding his significance and meaning, King credited Jesus with achieving unity with God and humanity. Jesus Christ, in person and work, effected the reconciliation between the human and the divine.[2]

King believed that Jesus Christ had profound relevance for the modern age. The main dilemma was how to make the message and meaning of Christ intelligible to the modern mind. King raised an important and profound christological issue: Who is Jesus Christ, and what does Christ mean for us today? His christological formulation emerged from the context of massive suffering, social dislocation, and existential alienation. The problem of evil, concretely manifested in racism, poverty, and war set the terms of King's theological emphasis. Like the black religious tradition within which he stood, the primary interest lay not in gaining clarity about christological definitions found in the orthodox statements of Nicea and Chalcedon. Rather, King's main concern centered on how the personality of Jesus could provide clues for our own efforts to achieve moral improvement.[3]

What had Jesus said and done about the intransigence and radicality of sin and evil? How had he responded to those concrete manifestations of social, political, and economic injustice prominent in the culture of his day? How might he assess the contemporary black-led struggle for freedom, justice, and equality in America?

The importance of Jesus in King's thinking emerges with force and abruptness during his first public speech of the Montgomery bus boycott. Here King referred to God, Christianity, or Jesus some sixteen times.[4] In Jesus of the Gospels, King discovered a lifestyle, a spirit, a message, and a composite personality that were decisively illuminative for his own vocational self-understanding. It was a faith in Christ's exemplary moral example that led him to delegitimate and to assess as morally irresponsible any form of apathy, complacency, or withdrawal in the face of systemic evil and structural injustice. It was faith in Christ that inspired King's pastoral and prophetic ministry of active engagement in the struggle for justice. By his own public admission, all that he said and did could be directly attributed to an unshakable faith in God and a commitment to the gospel of Jesus Christ.

King credited Jesus with providing the "spirit" of the Montgomery movement. He admitted to an initial skepticism concerning the utility of Jesus' love ethic beyond the level of interpersonal relationships. Mohandas K. Gandhi enabled him to see the applicability of Jesus' love ethic at the level of social reform. Gandhi's method of nonviolent resistance became paradigmatic for King and the black-led freedom movement, though Jesus remained the movement's primary motivating force.[5]

King reasoned that the same agape-driven Spirit that had captivated the early church, had now seized Montgomery's blacks. This accounted for their heightened concern for societal transformation.[6] It was a revolutionary spirit, inspiring sacrificial self-giving, noncooperation with unjust social arrangements, radical obedience to God's will for justice and community, and service to humanity. Jesus was the "bearer par excellence" of revolutionary consciousness.[7] Critiquing the culture of his day, Jesus' revolutionary love worked proactively toward the transformation of personal and social values. He reordered public and private priorities, shattering outmoded, prevailing norms of success, service, and greatness. The revolution of values and reordering of priorities embodied in the spirit of Christ brought with it a mandate for emancipatory praxis aimed at the radical, comprehensive restructuring of society. Jesus' unique God-consciousness and revolutionary spirit embodied radical, agape love in action. Although he had been labeled the "Moses" of his day, King desired to emulate Jesus in his lifestyle. Following Jesus' spirit, King sought to affirm the social as well as the personal relevance of the gospel.[8]

For King, Jesus articulated a new vision of redemption and restoration in the world.[9] Jesus stressed forgiveness,[10] love,[11] peace,[12] self-sacrifice,[13] and ultimate trust in and obedience to God.[14] Jesus' basic message and mode of living demonstrated not only the nature of God, but God's intention for human community.[15]

> Where do we find God? In a test tube? No. Where else except in Jesus Christ, the Lord of our lives? By knowing Him we know God. Christ is not only Godlike, but God is Christ-like. Christ is the word made flesh. He is the language of eternity translated in the words of time. If we are to know what God is like and understand his purposes for mankind, we must turn to Christ. By committing ourselves absolutely to Christ and his way, we will participate in that marvelous act of faith that will bring us to the true knowledge of God.[16]

Jesus marched to the cadences of a rhythm different from the prevailing cultural ethos of his day. In Jesus, King saw a "transformed nonconformist" who had rejected the moribund values of the status quo.[17] Jesus was guided by a higher moral law that took precedence over the flawed codifications of human jurisprudence. In this way, Jesus embodied and articulated a radical gospel of freedom aimed at both personal and corporate redemption.[18]

The ministry of Jesus and the gospel he preached significantly influenced King's emphasis on political and social action in his first pastorate at Dexter Avenue Baptist Church in Montgomery, Alabama.[19] It also increased King's awareness of the important connection between the gospel and service in the cause of justice. Although the issue of Jesus' race or color had been raised in light of the black consciousness movement, it remained a peripheral issue for King. Instead, King emphasized the central importance of Jesus' personality. Biology had little or no bearing on the intrinsic value of one's personality. King saw the significance of Jesus in his unique God-consciousness, spiritual commitment, and his willingness to surrender his agenda to the will of God for his life.[20]

The important focus for King was the love ethic, revolutionary spirit, and gospel of freedom that Jesus embodied. King argued that Jesus did not merely verbalize a love ethic. Jesus matched his message of love and freedom with a commensurate lifestyle. In Jesus, King found no inconsistency between the principles he professed and those he practiced, a perfect alignment between word and action. Jesus' emphasis on the inseparability of love of God and love of neighbor mutually reinforced his faith in God and his revolutionary consciousness. As the incarnation of radical agape love in action, Jesus crossed conventional boundaries of custom, nationality, and race, reaching out to the neighbor in need. Like the good Samaritan, Jesus' love ethic operated beyond the prescriptive norms of culture, leading him to willingly suffer and to risk his life for the victims of immoral power. In so doing, Jesus modeled the power of revolutionary love responding faithfully to the demands of the revolutionary situation. King believed that a commitment to this kind of radical involvement made Jesus the quintessential rabble-rouser, revolutionary, and extremist for love and justice.[21] King pointed out that the Crucifixion on Calvary must be ultimately viewed as a statement against extremist criminal behavior. Three men were executed for the same crime— extremism. Unlike Jesus, two were immoral extremists, violators of God's moral law. Jesus, however, was a moral extremist whose crime was sharing God's law of love, truth, and goodness in an immoral environment.[22]

It was Jesus' example that led King to redefine and reinvest the notion of extremism with new content and meaning. In light of the witness of Jesus, extremist activity aimed at the realization of justice in the revolutionary situation was to be looked upon with honor rather than shame. Jesus was the prototypical maladjusted, nonconformist.[23] His love ethic was inextricably bound to a sense of justice-oriented praxis. This connection made Jesus' love much more publicly confrontational than privately emotional. King felt that this kind of revolutionary spirit (characterized by nonconformity and maladjustedness) was necessary for the conversion of a society that had adjusted all too well to alienation, injustice, poverty, and violence. Following the example of Christ, King sought to remain maladjusted toward the dehumanizing religious, sociopolitical, and economic policies and practices of his time.[24]

In Jesus Christ, King also came to see the extent of God's involvement in the redemption of history and the length to which God was willing to go to restore broken community. In the suffering and death of Jesus Christ, the sacrificial love of God was made manifest. The Cross was a symbol of God's great act of sacrificial self-giving—the willing offering of one's life for another.[25] It also symbolized the high cost exacted on those persons who would join God's work of transformation in the world. The Cross was a vivid reminder of the necessity of suffering in the struggle for justice. King established an inseparable linkage between Jesus' crucifixion on the cross and the Resurrection event. Paradoxically, the tragic nature of the Cross led him to maintain an optimism about the future of human history. In the victory of good over evil at Calvary, unearned suffering in the struggle against injustice was ultimately redemptive.[26]

Finally, for King, Jesus was the teacher par excellence. In both message and lifestyle, Jesus demonstrated how God had intended human life to be genuinely lived. Jesus also functioned, in King's Christology, as a moral exemplar. His revolutionary consciousness held in balance mental toughness with a compassionate heart. Jesus was mature enough to be cognizant of moral-spiritual and intellectual blindness of humanity. At the same time, affirming the inherent worth and sacredness of all persons, Jesus modeled a compassionate attentiveness to the needs of the "least of these." He cast his lot with the poor, dispossessed, and powerless masses.[27]

Jesus' concern for the whole person—body, soul, and mind—provided the basis for a notion of holistic ministry that addressed the totality of human need. He demonstrated that biological needs were as important as spiritual or psychological ones. Concrete survival and safety needs such as food, clothing, warmth, shelter, and health could not be overlooked. The gospel must minister to the whole person. Jesus also demonstrated that in the revolutionary situation of redemptive struggle, the militant and the moderate must be combined. In both personal and social living, the extremes of apathy and violence were morally bankrupt and strategically unsound.[28]

## Summary

King's christological assertions provided grounding for a radical faith characterized by a revolutionary spirit that urged radical involvement. Jesus, the Son of God and the Savior of the world was at the same time Jesus the extremist, the nonconformist, the agitator, the rabble-rouser, and the maladjusted personality. By message and example, Jesus demonstrated love of God and love of neighbor through acts of radical obedience and sacrificial self-giving. For King, Jesus represented God's most powerful and definitive statement against alienation, apathy, and violence. In Jesus, King saw evidence of the radical and extensive nature of divine sacrificial love, as God acted in history to restore broken human community. Jesus Christ was the concrete embodiment of revolutionary consciousness and the articulator of a gospel of freedom. The life, ministry, death, and resurrection of Jesus Christ revealed the nature and the intent of God's will for humanity. At the same time, the Christ event defined the basic nature and content of God's gospel of freedom—the mandate for a socially active Christianity, a type of radical involvement in the world.[29]

## ECCLESIOLOGY: CHURCH AS RADICALLY INVOLVED COMMUNITY OF FAITH

King's conception of the nature and task of the church in the world was derived from his understanding of the Christian gospel. As we have already seen, King's perspective on the Christian gospel was filtered through the prisms of the black experience and the black Christian religious tradition. His formal studies of liberal Protestantism, (especially Walter Rauschenbusch and the social gospel movement) provided key elements in his developing theological framework. King's understanding of the gospel both affirmed and promoted the moral necessity of a socially active Christianity. The church, for King, emerged as the custodial community of an activist spirituality. The church was made of those who had pledged unwavering loyalty to the gospel of Jesus Christ. Its primary task was to bear witness to the truth and to remain faithful to its mission, that being to articulate in word and to model in action commitment to a gospel of moral and social redemption, and to embody that commitment in a world dominated by the "superpersonal forces of evil."[30]

This commitment to the gospel of Jesus Christ provided the basis for what King felt was a clear moral mandate to the church. It must seek a radical involvement in the struggle against evil in interpersonal relationships and in corporate structures. The church, embodying the spirit of Christ, inherited an escapable moral obligation to work proactively toward the establishment of justice in human community. King appropriated this ecclesial understanding to deliver devastating critiques of both black and white institutional churches relative to the liberative praxis found in each. He was concerned that the church be true to its moral and social responsibility to radically participate in the redemption and transformation of both individuals and the society into a beloved community.

## The Gospel as Freedom

Fundamental to King's ecclesiology was a conception of the gospel as essentially a manifesto for freedom.[31] The content of freedom was to be understood in programmatically concrete political, economic, social, psychological, and spiritual terms. King's view of the gospel complemented an important element of his understanding of humanity. In both, King affirmed freedom as the most fundamental human requirement. Life, in its most profound and cosmic dimensions, demanded the unencumbered exercise of freedom.[32] Ultimately, King grounded freedom in the actions of a radically involved God who works in and through history to effect the restoration of love, justice, and peace in human community. Essentially, King understood freedom, justice, and equality in terms of the biblical notion of shalom.

Through the message of the gospel, King heard the voice of freedom speak with remarkable power and clarity. The inherent moral demand was unmistakable and urgent. Nothing is as important as the eternal value of freedom.[33] This "freedom gospel" provided additional motivation for King's socially active spirituality. In the famous "Letter from a Birmingham Jail," King compared himself to the prophets of the eighth century and the apostle Paul. He stated that he, like them, had also felt the compelling urge to carry the gospel of freedom beyond the borders of his own hometown.[34]

In the Prophetic literature and Exodus narratives of the Old Testament as well as the Gospels and the early church record in Acts of the New Testament, King discovered a clear emphasis on a radical and decisive confrontation with ideological perspectives and institutional-structural arrangements that operated to perpetuate either the diminution or denial of freedom. From the perspective of the biblical faith, Christian discipleship was inseparably linked to the yearnings of the oppressed for freedom. Freedom, for King, represented the very essence of the gospel.

## The Relevance of Religion: Social and Political Implications of the Gospel of Freedom

For King, the gospel of freedom was intimately and critically linked to structural transformation. He accepted and affirmed the thesis that the content of freedom relative to the gospel was, in the final analysis, a call to radical discipleship—emancipatory praxis aimed at the establishment of political, social, and economic justice in concrete terms.[35] Consequently, the gospel was highly relevant in a societal context marked by massive unemployment, poverty, economic and social injustice, social disintegration, cultural chaos, and psychic dislocation.

We may recall that King emerged from the context of the black religious experience that has always promoted a strong ethical concern with the issues of both personal salvation and social transformation. Black religion has historically affirmed the close connection between religion and life, faith and action, theology and ethics, church and world, gospel and sociopolitical context.[36] This religious tradition had nurtured in King an uncompromising belief in the applicability of the gospel and the Christian faith to matters of public policy. Utilizing a "political exegesis" of the Scripture, King emerged with a sharpened awareness of the sociopolitical implications of the Christian religion. As a result, he possessed an activist spirituality that had an intense concern for sociopolitical and economic justice. King approached the issues of racism, poverty, militarism, materialism, and consumerism not only as social and political concerns, but also as fundamentally moral-theological crises.

Rauschenbusch, DeWolf, and other liberal Protestant thinkers had further assisted King in developing a theological basis for his ethical concerns. In so doing, they had helped him to avoid the inadequacies of a one-dimensional religious preoccupation with personal salvation.

Speaking of Rauschenbusch's influence upon his conceptualization of religion as a relevant social and political force, King said Rauschenbusch gave to American Protestantism a sense of social responsibility that it should never lose.

> The gospel deals with the whole man, not only his soul, but his body; not only his spiritual well-being, but his material well-being . . . any religion which professes to be concerned about the souls of men and is not concerned about the social and economic conditions that scar the soul, is a spiritually moribund religion only waiting for the day to be buried.[37]

True religion, driven by a gospel of freedom, was inevitably concerned with the totality of life, refusing the facile compartmentalization of life into neat, unrelated, realms—sacred and secular, spiritual and political. For King, the human lives in two realms—internal and external. The internal marks the realm of spiritual ends (moral values, faith, and such). The external marks the realm of material ends (physical, social, political, economic needs). He charged that religion that failed to see the interrelatedness of spiritual and material was an irrelevent religion. As long as the basic needs of human living are not met, the soul cannot flourish. Again, King pointed to the gospel emphasis of the religion of Jesus to advocate that human beings were more than dogs. They required food, clothing, shelter, *as well as* a self-esteem enhancement and spiritual guidance. Religion must attend to both the economic and spiritual well-being of humanity simultaneously.[38]

The gospel of Jesus and its religious focus became a paradigmatic model. King had discovered a prophetic religious consciousness that expressed equal concern for both soul and body, spiritual and material aspects of humanity. Since the content of the gospel was freedom, Jesus' religion promoted a preferential moral concern for those most in need of social and political deliverance—the marginalized and disfranchised poor in society. In so doing, it established and affirmed the critical linkage between soul and body, public and private, spiritual and material, internal and external realities.

King employed this understanding of religion to bring a moral critique upon the church and its leadership with regard to its passive indifference to and compliance with structural injustice. In his description of the apathy of many black ministers in Montgomery prior to the bus boycott, King placed the blame on a false conception of religion. Too many ministers had failed to see that religion was social as well as personal, this worldly as well as other worldly in focus. Too many ministers had failed to understand that religion deals with both heaven and earth, and that the Christian gospel seeks to change both the souls of human beings and the environmental conditions within which people live. King said that this faulty understanding of religion and the gospel had resulted in many ministers turning away from the moral and social responsibility to address the economic, social, and political conditions of human beings. This religion, King argued, amounted to little more than a narcotic, a tranquilizer that effectively drugged people into a passive acceptance of their plight.[39]

This viewpoint was tested in the Montgomery situation when a segment of its white political and religious leadership questioned the legitimacy of his role in the bus boycott. Arguing that the vocation of a Christian minister had no connection to social and political issues, they sought to delegitimate King's participation in the struggle for social reform. In response, King counterargued that the essence of the gospel of Jesus Christ represented a critical, inseparable linkage between faith and action, personal piety and social transformation. In fact, there is no conflict between a personal devotion to the religion of Jesus Christ and the struggle for freedom in social living. The gospel of freedom is social as well as personal.[40]

King maintained this view of the gospel throughout twelve years of public witness. Speaking to a crowd of striking sanitation workers and their supporters in Memphis on the eve of his assassination, King again stressed the gospel's moral requirement to engage in a socially active ministry that was relevant to human needs. For King, the other worldly concern with peace and joy "over yonder" in heaven must be balanced with an equal concern for love and justice "down here" on earth. Talk about the new Jerusalem of the future had no relevance apart from discussions about the new Atlanta, New York, Los Angeles, Philadelphia, and Memphis of the present.[41]

*The Church as Bearer and Embodiment
of Prophetic, Revolutionary Religion*

Convinced of the social and political relevance of the gospel of the Christian religion, King challenged individual Christians to become passionately committed to the struggle for justice.[42] This would require a recovery of the revolutionary gospel of Jesus Christ that the early Christians embraced and used to boldly challenge a hostile status quo. As modern Christians, we must recapture and bear witness to the revolutionary spirit of Christ for the purposes of constructing a genuinely Christian world.

King believed that as custodians of the gospel and followers of the faith, the church represented the one community in the world where commitment to freedom was total and absolute. The church was the sign and symbol of the revolutionary gospel of Christ working actively in history to effect personal and social transformation. As such, it was the concrete expression, the embodiment of socially active Christianity. The church inherited an inescapable moral mandate to model justice, love, and peace in its relationships. And yet, as the locus of a revolutionary spirit, the church must also take seriously the divine imperative to become radically involved in communal praxis *against* individual and corporate evil and *on behalf of* social, political, and economic justice. Any instance of unjust treatment of the poor was itself enough to prompt and morally justify radical corrective action. The Christian church should be challenged by any protest against evil. It must assume the moral and social responsibility inherent in Jesus' injunction to allow the revolutionary spirit to provoke it to radical emancipatory activity on behalf of those who are least able to either defend themselves or to fend for themselves in society.[43]

King's ecclesiological perspective was heavily influenced by and based upon a prophetic model of religion. The prophetic model understood the gospel as essentially social in nature. It stressed a public, corporate concern of religion as a necessary counterbalance to the excessively privatistic focus predominant in culture.[44] For King, as bearer and embodiment of a prophetic, revolutionary consciousness emergent from the gospel of freedom, the church's task was to become the moral guardian and social factor of salvation. As moral guardian, the church assumed the unenviable task of serving as an uncompromising corporate conscience. Its concern was the development of morally sound personal and social values. Therefore, as a first step, the church must seize the initiative to combat spiritual poverty and moral laxity. The church must strive to convince human beings of the moral rightness of affirming and developing the virtues of kindheartedness, conscientiousness, compassion, intelligence, and responsibility in society.[45]

Of paramount concern was the church's willingness and capacity to combat "intellectual and moral blindness," which, for King, led inevitably to tragic misuses and abuses of freedom on both interpersonal and societal levels. King believed that all reality was ultimately based on moral foundations, and that sociopolitical evils were, in the final analysis, theological-moral issues. Therefore, the church, as custodian of moral values, assumed a heavy moral responsibility to conscientize the populace, to challenge the old order, and even to disobey the rules of social custom and convention when necessary. Through religious education, the church must expose the ideological roots of race hatred, help mitigate irrational phobias with regard to racial intermarriage, and keep the principles of brotherhood, love, justice, equality, and freedom at the center of the faith. It must promote the vision of the beloved community as a divine imperative that takes precedence over practical human considerations.[46] It assumed an inevitable moral obligation to give prophetic voice against the immoralities in living, and to lead the way in the attempt to effect a revolution of moral values with regard to the triple evils of racism, poverty, and war.[47]

As the social factor of salvation, King felt that more was required of the church than to merely speak out against evil. As a second step, the church also assumed a moral obligation to actively resist and confront collective evil. A critical prophetic voice must be accompanied by confrontational prophetic action. In a revolutionary situation, the church should be launching out into the arena of social action.[48] The church should be assuming the leadership position in efforts directed toward social reform.[49] The church could never be content to merely address itself to social reality at the theoretical level. Espousing ideas about what *ought* to be done was not enough. Rather, King argued, the church must actively seek the realization of those ideas and ideals at the practical application level of radical, prophetic social action. There must be no inconsistency between the church's creeds and its deeds.

In the areas of housing, police protection, politics, education, economics, the church must exert its influence in an effort to eliminate glaring injustices. Christian ministers were challenged to model the gospel of freedom in their individual lives and to encourage

90

similar commitments of lifestyle in their collective organizations.[50] King insisted that the church must attend to the totality of needs of those broken lives it encountered. The spiritual and the material were inseparably linked in the church's ministry. On one hand, the church must feed spiritually hungry souls the bread of faith, hope, and love.[51] On the other hand, the church must go farther in its response to the question, What is God calling us to do? For King, the answer was simple. The church must feed those who are hungry, work for the economic security of those who are poor, provide clothing for those who are naked, provide shelter for those who are homeless, educate those who are illiterate, comfort those who are distressed, heal those who are sick, and seek the deliverance of those who are oppressed.

In times of acute moral crisis, and in the face of revolutionary urgency, the church must become the molder and shaper of public consciousness.[52] As a community shaped by a revolutionary prophetic consciousness, the church must answer the divine imperative to become "coworkers with God," actively participating in God's efforts to establish justice in human history. In this way, the church could avoid the apathy and nihilistic fatalism that had characterized much of its approach to moral and social problems throughout its history.

### King's Critique of the Institutional Church: Disillusionment, Disappointment, and Cautious Optimism

King's belief in the radical demands of the gospel and the roots of social activism inherent in the Christian religion provided grounds for a substantive, continuous, and at times scathing critique of both black and white churches in America. In King's assessment, the institutional church in America was dangerously close to becoming a powerless and irrelevant force in society. For King, this represented a significant difference from the fervor and activism of the early church. The Sunday religion of the contemporary church was irrelevant to the realities of Monday morning. The church had painted over social club values with religious exuberance. King felt the church needed to recapture the revolutionary spirit of the early Christians. Like the early church of the New Testament, King had wanted the church's witness to disturb the power structure, and usher in a spirit of revolt against status quo systems of immorality and injustice.[53]

By contrast, the white church's failure to assume its public role as moral guardian and social factor of salvation was obvious and clearly demonstrable. In the cause of justice and freedom, the white church was not only a nonfactor, it was an accomplice to the forces of evil and injustice. King boldly and repeatedly spoke of the shocking hypocritical record of the white church's duplicitous relationship with the slavocracy, Jim Crow segregation, and contemporary structural-institutional racism. The white church had provided the sophisticated theological rationalizations for slavery and racism. Moreover, it had been conspicuously silent and lax in the face of its moral obligation to actively resist and confront the forces of collective evil and injustice in society.[54] It was guilty of the basest levels of conformity to the prevailing values and practices of an unjust status quo. Repeatedly, it had demonstrated cowardice with regard to its moral-spiritual leadership in society. It had too closely aligned itself with the privileged classes and was too quick to defend the status quo.[55]

King identified the church as the most segregated major institution in American society. It harbored a chasmic internal division in its soul that simply had to be closed. This moral schizophrenia caused the church to lag woefully far behind the Supreme Court, trade unions, factories, schools, department stores, athletic gatherings, and virtually every other social organization in terms of integrating its own body. King issued a pointed challenge to the white church to remove segregation from its own midst as a way of demonstrating its commitment to the gospel of freedom and the struggle for justice.[56]

King candidly admitted that at one time he had been rather optimistic and hopeful about the white church's capacity to involve itself in the quest for dignity and equality. However, in light of appalling empirical evidence to the contrary, he had become greatly disappointed with the white church, its ministerial leadership, and its laity. While he could point to some notable exceptions, generally the white church had been "weighed in the balance and found wanting" through a gross abdication of its moral responsibility. It had withheld its solidarity with a movement that sought a public confrontation with collective evil. It had allied itself with the wrong side of truth and pledged its support to immoral uses of power. Responding to the criticisms of several white clergymen regarding his involvement in the Birmingham Campaign, King stated that the white moderate and the white church and its leadership had become his greatest disappointments over the years. While he hoped they would give suppport to the freedom struggle, they had remained content to write creedal affirmations and ecclesial resolutions supporting justice, but in theory only. They had remained apathetic in the face of great social issues, ignoring the moral demands of responsible social action in the revolutionary situation. Separating the gospel from social concerns, they had withdrawn from the emphases of socially active Christianity.

However, King points out a deeper disappointment with the white church—its loyalty to a spirit of conformity to the social mores and norms of the day. Speaking of the white church's social neglect and her fear of being viewed as nonconformists, King accused that body of being an archdefender of the status quo and a sanctioning agent for society. King stated that such moral laxity and apathetic silence made him weep because he was witnessing firsthand the white church's loss of prophetic spirit. Hence, it was no longer a disturber, but rather a consoler of the operating power structure.[57]

In the final year of his life in 1967, King felt that the white church had made some progressive strides toward critical social reflection. However, it yet remained captive to a ministry marked by moral trepidation and an uncritical acceptance of the dominant values of an exploitative, dehumanizing consumer culture. The white church had not yet escaped the imminent danger of God's judgment for its shameful behavior. It must publicly acknowledge its guilt through silence, apathy, and weak support of the gospel's servanthood ethic of justice. Further, it must obey God's call to participate in God's moral and social redemption of human history. King warned that anything less than this would mean that the white church would forever lose its revolutionary zeal. In so doing, it would amount to little more than a community without moral and spiritual authority and become an irrelevant social club.[58]

King challenged the church to provide spiritual sustenance, moral guidance, and social vision. With the early church as the paradigmatic model, King had hoped that the present-day church would become "an active partner in the struggle for freedom," a "thermostat that transformed the mores of society," an "outside agitator," and a "disturber of the peace."[59]

King's maturing faith also enabled him to avoid a sentimental romanticization and an uncritical valorization of the black church.

King delivered a specific and sharp critique of the black church for its laxity in the areas of moral and social reform. In a sermon entitled "A Knock at Midnight," King made a bold indictment against the failure of many black churches to provide sustenance to oppressed exiles struggling to survive in the wilderness of America's "sick" society. Midnight was the metaphor King used to describe the present situation. It represented the hour of a person's or group's greatest need. He identified two types of "Negro" churches that had left persons disappointed at "midnight." One type burned with emotional zeal. It reduced worship to entertainment. It often confused spirituality with muscularity. The other type froze from lack of passion and had an inordinate concern with classism. It was exclusive in its concerns for others, rendering its focus only on those who met certain "professional" criteria.[60]

King also leveled criticisms at some black churches and their ministers for the glaring apathy and complacency in the freedom struggle. Nevertheless, King generally lauded the black church as the institution in America most committed to a proactive engagement in the nonviolent struggle for justice.[61] He pointed out that the black church had exercised a major influence in nonviolence's central place in the black-led struggle for freedom and justice. King acknowledged the movement's reliance upon the black church as the main center of revolutionary activity.[62] In this way, King pointed to a fundamental difference between black and white churches' responses to the movement. In contradistinction to the white church (with some exceptions), the black church had made major contributions to the nonviolent freedom struggle in America.

*Summary*

King's criticisms of the church were based upon a conception of the church as the radically involved community of faith. In adherence to a gospel of freedom that generated a prophetic, revolutionary model of religion, the church was obligated to work toward the realization of the beloved community. The religion of Christ had profound social and political implications. As bearer and embodiment of that prophetic, revolutionary religious consciousness, the church was called to a socially active Christianity that sought the radical transformation of both individual psyches and societal structures. To be sure, King felt that, for the most part, the church had failed to live up to this responsibility. However, he remained dimly hopeful that the church could rediscover its true identity, recapture its prophetic spirit, and carry out its moral and social mission.[63]

## ESCHATOLOGY: VISION AND HOPE INSPIRING RADICAL INVOLVEMENT IN A RADICAL FUTURE

As a vital component of his radical faith, King's eschatological perspective provided both an ideal vision and a paradoxical hope in God's radical future. In so doing, it served as the inspiration and motivating force for King's unswerving commitment to the struggle to create a more just social order. For King, eschatology had less to do with a doctrine of the final end of things than with an attitudinal perspective about the ultimate trajectory of the future. The central question was, "In light of my faith in God, what am I to hope for with regard to the future?"

A careful analysis of King's life and thought reveals a remarkable capacity to image and sustain hope in the possibilities of a future that was qualitatively different from the present.[64] King's understanding of history as fundamentally conflictual allowed him to be open to the transient nature of reality. Consequently, one detects a prominent emphasis on conflict resolution in his thought. At the very heart of the universe, he believed, the superpersonal forces of good and evil were perpetually locked in a perennial struggle for cosmic control.

And yet, a strong faith in an able, loving God and the justice of the universe sustained King's belief that ultimately the forces of good and justice would emerge triumphant over the forces of evil and injustice. For King, the destiny of history, despite its chaotic and turbulent nature, remained subject to the controlling purpose of a loving God.[65] King was certain of God's active participation in the universe and throughout history to bring about the restoration of broken community. Because God's will could be preempted by neither evil forces nor sinful human activity, King asserted with bold confidence that although truth may be temporarily defeated, it will ultimately triumph victoriously over evil.[66] It was faith in a God of radical love and unmatched power that provided King with the inner spiritual and moral resources to face the difficulties of life. It gave him a quiet courage to face an uncertain future with the hope that wrongs would be righted and justice would be realized. To paraphrase a popular saying in black religion, King may not have known what the future held, but he certainly knew who held the future. The certitude of his faith in God motivated King to vigorously pursue a historical agenda for the moral, social, political, and economic improvement of the world.

This unshakable faith and confidence in God's radical involvement in and beyond history infused King's hope in the future.[67] Consequently, King was rather optimistic about prospects for the historical realization of his "dream" of the just, loving, and peaceful human community. In collaboration with God, the cosmic companion, humanity possessed the capacity to bring the vision of a just social order to full historical fruition.[68] It was, in actuality, God's future. King believed that the future was, literally, divine vision and act radically breaking in upon human history with a subpoena to co-labor on behalf of the beloved community. As such, the future represented radical alternatives—possibilities for renewed personal lives and restructured interpersonal and institutional relations. Indeed, the future, stamped with God's own guarantee had profound implications for thought and action in the present order.

At this point, it is important to note that King's understanding of the future was not in terms of a temporally distant and idealized Utopia. Rather, he conceived it as God's unbounded, compelling, proleptic presence, exerting a powerful, magnetic "pull" force on the present. In King's thinking, the historical moments of past, present, and future were chronologically distinct only in human understanding. From the divine perspective, these moments were coextensive and symbiotically related in both time and space. Therefore, the "radical new" of the future placed unavoidable ethical demands upon the "stagnant old" of the past and present. God's future brought with it a nonnegotiable "moral ought" that impacted decisively upon the present "as is" condition. Hence, it was a radical future, bringing with it the mandate for a revolution of values and priorities—a deep and pervasive transformation in the dynamics of institutional power and the politics of institutional morality. The future represented the potential for a new humanity, a new social order, simultaneously "already" and "not yet fully" realized in human existence.[69]

Despite its radical demands, God's future contained a remarkable power to activate and inspire hope within and among those who struggled to make the future vision a present reality. King claimed that the movement was sustained primarily through a hope in the triumph of a vision for the future. This vision was, in fact, God's will for humanity. While we must await the complete fulfillment of the vision at some point in the future, we could rest assured that it was, nonetheless, God's future. Therefore, King was guided by a powerful sense of the inevitability of victory relative to the achievement of that vision in human history. Resident in his faith was a belief that someday in the future, justice would triumph, the beloved community would be concretely realized in history, and God would have the final word in the universe.[70] While the forces of evil remained recalcitrant, the outcome was certain. Injustice would be decisively defeated. Justice would definitively prevail. Even in the midst of the Vietnam holocaust, a declining personal popularity, and a waning national consensus on civil rights, King clung tenaciously to this faith and hope. King believed that the final word in reality would be uttered not by deception and hatred, but by unarmed truth and unconditional love. To be sure, violence and war dominated the national and global landscapes. And yet, though wounded, justice would rise up and reign supreme in the public square. Because all humanity would one day bow before the altar of God, King believed that love and nonviolent redemption would still overcome some day.[71]

To actively pursue justice, love, and peace was, at the same time, to be in full harmony with God's will for the future of humankind.[72] Fatalism and despair, while problematic, were negated to a large extent because of King's strong faith claim that God had provided cosmic companionship in the struggle against injustice. Consequently, hope in the inevitable triumph of the future was positively promoted. After twelve years of public ministry, King remained optimistic about the outcome of the struggle.[73] In 1967, he was a self-described optimist. He acknowledged that his voice was, perhaps, discordant with the prevailing national mood of pessimism. As he listed the numerous experiences that might have made him a grim and desperate man, he argued that his faith in both God and humanity gave him a strength that was incomprehensible to others. It was through the challenge of embracing struggle, he said, that his hope was affirmed. Admitting that his trust might falter in weak moments,

97

King held resolute to the belief that God loved humanity, and had not designed and executed a program for human failure.

At the same time, King was acutely aware of the dangers of blind, naive hope. Experience had tempered his excesses in this regard and helped him to avoid an unwarranted optimism that remained oblivious to the real crises and difficulties that lay ahead.[74] In the effort to avoid naive idealism, King did not want to become victimized by debilitating pessimism. Therefore, he altered his self-description. Avoiding the extremes of superficial optimism and crippling pessimism, he described himself as an "optimistic realist" or "realistic optimist." Although sin makes human improvement precarious, real social progress was possible, within limits.[75]

King charged that he had personally been the victim of shattered dreams. Therefore, he could understand the difficulty in trying to maintain hope in the midst of despairing circumstances. The solution, however, did not lie in the perpetuation of bitterness and resentment. Neither did it lie in the adoption of a fatalistic philosophy and lifestyle of detached resignation. Rather, the answer was in one's capacity to be both realistic enough to accept temporary setbacks and optimistic enough to hold on to eternal hope. When dreams are shattered and disappointments are many, one's faith in God as radical love in action was the determinative factor of hope. Only faith in God—the custodial guarantor of a radical future—could provide the inner strength required to deal with despairing circumstances without falling victim to despair.[76]

King continued to believe that humans could make significant improvement in individual and social life. His faith in God's power to historically concretize the agenda of a radical future vision had given him a hopeful bent. Nevertheless, King's hope rapidly amounted to a "cautious optimism" after the Selma Campaign for Voting Rights in 1965. An acknowledgment of the persistence and intransigence of pernicious evil led him to significantly qualify the nature of his optimism. The brutal validation of sin, witnessed in the powers of the state—namely police, military, and budgetary—meant that King could no longer ignore the extent to which institutions and groups were able and willing to wield raw, naked power to perpetuate private ends and to ensure corporate survival. And yet, because it was based upon an unshakable faith in God, King's hope in the power and inevitable triumph of the future was never completely diminished. Indeed, it was present in Montgomery of 1958,[77] Birmingham of

1963,[78] the Nobel Prize acceptance speech of 1964,[79] Selma of 1965,[80] and the final "Mountaintop" speech in Memphis of 1968.[81]

For King, the proposition that it is despair, not oppression, that ultimately defeats a people became axiomatic. He saw hopelessness as the great archenemy of revolutionary spirit and action. Therefore, he was concerned about maintaining a high "hope index."[82] Hope, not frustration, was the key to both survival and revolution.

## KING'S ESCHATOLOGICAL VISION: RADICAL TENSION BETWEEN PRESENT AND FUTURE

King was oriented, motivated, and guided by an eschatological vision of a future human community characterized by inclusivity, justice, love, and peace. When asking himself, "What am I to hope for?" King answered with the future vision of the beloved community. It was this radical vision that generated hope and inspired optimism in the future.

King admitted that the premier voice among the social gospelers in America, Walter Rauschenbusch, had also exerted considerable influence on his eschatological perspective. Rauschenbusch had helped him to see that religion demanded accompanying sociopolitical action relative to the particularity of the conditions one faced.[83] King knew that such action must be guided by a clearly understood and articulated goal or vision. Herein lay the problem. How was he to define the content of such a goal? What were its parameters? How could he "image" abstract conceptions of justice, love, peace, and inclusivity in terms that were intelligible and compelling to both church and society? In wrestling with this dilemma, King was able to critically appropriate two important concepts from Rauschenbusch that enabled him to arrive at significant conceptual clarity. Rauschenbusch's notion of the "beloved community" subsumed under his broader conceptual motif of the "kingdom of God" helped King to envision and articulate an eschatological goal with historical concreteness and specificity.[84] Rauschenbusch defined the kingdom of God as "humanity organized according to the will of God." Further, it was understood as the "organized fellowship of humanity acting under the impulse of love."[85] Rauschenbusch's biblically based motifs were further anchored by a millennial hope that such a society of justice and love, while not fully achievable in a utopian sense, was at least partially realizable within human history.[86]

King combined these conceptions with other eschatological notions to both describe and proscribe a tranformed, new society characterized by just and loving relationships on both interpersonal and social levels. In juxtaposition to the status quo, the "beloved community" as a future goal was markedly different in ethos, character, and aim. It was both continuous and discontinuous with the present social order. It represented an unshakable belief in the future historical establishment of a fully integrated society where inclusivity, justice, love, and peace became concretely and normatively embodied in human relationships. In King's theological and ethical perspective, the "beloved community" was both sign and symbol of the reign of God's kingdom. That is to say, it both *pointed to* and *participated in* the realization of God's radical future.

King reconstructed and articulated this eschatological vision for public consumption. Through a masterful use of the "dream" motif, he made the radical future vision intelligible and compelling for both religionist and secularist alike. On the occasion of the 1963 March on Washington, in the midst of the Birmingham Campaign, King articulated with power, clarity, and concreteness the contours and content of "the dream." It was a future moment in history where the nation's creedal affirmations matched perfectly with the nation's deeds. It was a time when racial harmony became rule rather than exception, and a higher premium was placed on moral character than on skin color. It was similar to Isaiah's biblical vision of national peace and equity, and would be concretely embodied in the nation's southern states where justice was most visibly absent.[87]

In fact, King had already developed the predominant threads of the "dream" long before 1963 while serving as pastor of Dexter Avenue Baptist Church in Montgomery, Alabama, in the late 1950s. Further, King had made public presentations of the "dream" in several speeches prior to 1963.[88] In each instance, the "dream" is described in concrete social, political, and economic terms. The dream was about equal opportunity, the equitable distribution of privileges and property. It was about a time when gifts and resources are publicly shared, the dignity and worth of all persons are affirmed, where decision-making responsibilities are publicly shared.[89]

King's dream was fueled by the biblical prophetic model of the Old Testament coupled with a deeply held belief that the dream was compatible with the best values of the American libertarian tradition. In essence, the dream was coterminous with the "American dream."[90] On one hand, King's dream—a metaphysical, moral vision with implications for interpersonal, intergroup, national, and international relations—was virtually identical in content and orientation to the biblical prophetic moral-social vision of the shalomic community. Here, *mishpat* (social justice) and *sedaka* (right relationality in concrete sociopolitical and economic terms) took on the character of normative prescriptions. Like the Old Testament prophets, King believed that this type of ordered community represented a partially realizable eschatology, which would materialize in several flawed institutional arrangements at some future point in human history.

And yet, King argued that the "dream" was "deeply rooted in the American dream." King's description of the "American dream" focused on an inclusive community marked by a diversity and high degree of acceptance and toleration for ethnic, religious, creedal, nationalistic, and class diversities. The "American dream" promoted the full participation of all citizenry to pursue the basic, inherently God-given rights to life, liberty, and the pursuit of happiness. Within this framework, King expressed hope and realistic optimism that the movement's goal of freedom would be ultimately met. In the dream, the movement's goal received both divine and national approval. God's will for human community and the nation's heritage of freedom were integral components of the struggle for freedom, justice, and equality.[91]

King's "dream," in the final analysis, juxtaposed the historical moments of present and future. Consequently, King was able to seize upon the inherent generative tensions involved in the dialogic encounter between the "isness" of current sociopolitical realities and the "oughtness" of future moral ideals. King challenged the collective will and disposition to imagine a radical future, fundamentally different from and oppositionally related to the present. In this challenge, he sharpened the focus on certain polar dynamics that, by their very nature, presented the nation with unavoidable tensions—old versus new, already versus not yet, staticity versus dynamism, chaos versus community, progression versus regression, sickness versus health, and fragmentation versus integration. If the national character were to be whole, the tensions raised so acutely through these polarities required urgent attention.

King's analyses of the "as is" condition of the present situation pointed to one definitive conclusion: things must somehow change. By presenting a compelling vision of the future, he was able to provide both a goal and a pathway to a different, more improved society. King's dream of a "like it to be" future state was situated in glaring contradistinction to "the way things were." In this way, the dream brought with it an unresolved tension between the "now" of the present and the "later" of the future.

The power of King's eschatological vision generated the unavoidable necessity of choice. ·Its descriptive contours brought with it normative and prescriptive demands. Like Paul Tillich's "kairotic moment" and William James's "live option," King's "dream" took on the character of an active spirit of a tomorrow breaking in upon the "today" of lived existence. That in-breaking did more than inspire a tenacious hope that resisted any form of fatalism and resignation. It also confronted every reality that was disharmonious with God's community of love, justice, and peace. In so doing, it pronounced a judgment upon the sociocultural status quo of the day. In the light of existential actualities of racism, poverty, and militarism, both individual and social-structural change were mandated.

This transformation required a decision for or against love, justice, community, peace, and inclusivity. That same decision, in King's mind, was tantamount to a choice between adjustment to the cultural chaos of the present and empowerment by and for the "dream" of a beloved community of the future. For King, to be a human, a Christian, an American, was at the same time to know ourselves to be grasped by the power of a "dream" that denounced racial, social, and class determinism on both personal and corporate levels. The "dream" as a radical future vision simultaneously announced the "gospel" of moral and social improvement. It was hope in God's radical future that convinced King that individuals and the nation could make significant moral and social progress. To be grasped by the "dream" was to be seized by a revolutionary urgency to act, to participate in the grand collective experience of grappling with the resolution of those polarities generated by the perpetual tension between present and future.[92]

# FAITH IN THE FUTURE AS GROUNDS FOR A RADICAL, LIBERATIVE PRAXIS

The prophetic vision of economic, political, and social justice combined with a conception of the American dream of liberty, equality, and justice to provide concreteness and specificity to King's eschatological perspective. Situated as it was at the intersection of the "is" and the "ought," the horizon of King's "dream" was inclusive of both present needs and future hopes. The vision represented both divine gift and human task.[93] As a human task, the agenda of the future exerted a compelling "pull" on the present, calling it to proactive involvement in the present. King (though affirming humanity's "amazing potential for goodness") was cognizant of the prevalence and potent virulence of sin. Consequently, he conceded that the future vision of a beloved community would be established only through tireless, difficult redemptive work. There would be no guaranteed assurance of the inevitability of the kingdom's coming on the earth apart from radical human participation.

Repeatedly, King asserted that such belief was based on a faulty notion of time itself. Time, in fact, was a neutral commodity. It was the use of time that mattered most. Therefore, effective and efficient management of time as a resource must be encouraged so that liberative work might be done. In light of the extensiveness and intransigence of sin, persistent struggle against the powers of injustice must be undertaken on behalf of the future vision.[94] An unmistakable praxiological emphasis is resident in King's eschatology. The power of this prophetic vision to inspire hope and radical participation in God's future acted to prevent his eschatology from becoming captive to an other worldly focus. Conceived and articulated in concrete social, political, and economic terms, the radical future vision of King was decidedly this worldly in focus. The future was both now and later. God had always incarnated the demands of freedom within the full scope of human history. The Exodus and the nation's history offered demonstrable proof of that fact. God's radical future, then, was not a distant, ahistorical reality. Rather, it was eminent in its presence, compelling in its demand, and historical in its expression. Therefore, humans should expect that progress toward the just human community could at least be partially achieved within history.[95] These emphases enabled King to avoid apathy, complacency, and argue instead for

103

active, radical involvement in the struggle to bring a sane future to realization in the present life.

As divine gift, King's faith in the future was based upon the belief that God was on the side of truth and justice. God was that force working in the universe to pull the present toward its future. The God King knew was already at work in the moral structure of the cosmos and in human history working to transform the "isness" of the present into the "oughtness" of the future. Divine cosmic companionship in the struggle for justice gave him hope that the future agenda would one day be historically realized. At the same time, King held that faith in God's power to ultimately accomplish the aims of the radical future kept those who were actively involved in the freedom struggle from shrinking in the face of suffering and death. Such faith in the future masters fear. It prevents despair from paralyzing freedom fighters into inactivity, and it reenergizes hope when disappointments are mounting. Faith in God's future makes it possible to continuously suffer and endure hardships for the noble cause of justice.[96] In this way, King's deep faith in God's radical future provided the impetus for radical, emancipatory praxis in the present. It is this faith, King claimed, that called for a radical involvement in the freedom struggle. This faith was the basis of hope and the source of strength that undergirded King's continuing battles against injustice in the South after he had left the March on Washington in 1963. This faith, he said, provided grounds for working, praying, struggling against injustice, and going to jail together with others. This faith gave a certain knowledge that one day, freedom and justice would be achieved.[97]

King's faith in the future was, in actuality, faith in a loving God, sovereign over past, present, and future, fully able to achieve divine purpose in history.[98] Faith in God became the basis for public acts of creative dissent, civil resistance, and nonviolent direct action. Based upon agape love in action, this radical future of a beloved human community required actions in accordance with the demands of such love. For King, this meant that one must be willing to go to any lengths to restore broken community. Of course, acts of civil resistance must be held in strict accordance with the philosophic-moral principle of means-ends coherence. Therefore, radical, liberative social action must recognize that the ends one seeks are already preexistent in the means one uses to achieve those ends. At any rate, King's engagement in radical emancipatory acts was not due to a desire to achieve fame or personal privilege at the expense of black and poor people. Neither was he motivated by self-righteous arrogance or a martyr complex. Rather, he was compelled to do so by the ethical demands of love working toward the realization of a radical eschatological vision. A radical future vision required a radical involvement in the present, believing that unearned suffering on behalf of justice was ultimately redemptive in nature. In this way, King's faith in a radical future promoted and inspired radical, liberative action that discouraged and anathematized apathy in the present.

# CHAPTER 4

# KING AS THEOLOGIAN OF RADICAL INVOLVEMENT

laims that King lacked theological grounding for his speech and action are, in the final analysis, both unsubstantiated and unwarranted. Evidence marshaled in the previous chapters clearly demonstrates that a distinctive theological perspective and program did, in fact, undergird and inform King's public witness. Further, the emphatically radical character of that theological perspective was exposed. As he struggled to resolve the crisis of vocational identity, King's nurture in the black faith tradition, formal academic training, existential bent, and experiences of black American life gradually coalesced.[1] By the time of the Montgomery bus boycott, his search for clarity in matters of identity, faith, and intellectual focus had become inseparably interwoven with both his search to know God and his desire to imitate the life of Jesus Christ. There had emerged in King's life a coherence of thought, intention, and action. As a result, King-as-theologian became critically linked to King-as-minister-and-preacher-of-the-gospel and King-as-social-activist.[2] Indeed, from the crisis of Montgomery in 1955 until his death in Memphis in 1968, these three aspects of King's vocational self-understanding operated in such a way as to become virtually indistinguishable.

When King asserted, "I am first a minister of the gospel," he was, at the same time, making a statement about his role as theologian and ethicist.[3] A minister of the gospel also meant commitment to the pastoral and prophetic task of preaching the Word and doing the will of God. For King, the actual doing of theology and ethics would occur through a demonstrated consistency in preaching (voice), teaching (vision), and lifestyle (vocation). Theologian, ethicist, and minister of the gospel represent three legs of the same stool in King's thinking.[4]

107

This is due, in part, to the fact that King's worldview would not allow for a compartmentalization of reality into neat, autonomous, unrelated spheres of activity. Therefore, faith and action, theology and ethics, church and world were linked into the one cosmic reality, over which God exercised providential sovereignty. A belief in the interrelated structure of reality remained foundational for King throughout his life.[5] At the precise moment of engagement through preaching, teaching, marching, picketing, and protesting, King understood himself to be involved in the *doing* of theology.

Every aspect of King's public ministry of proactive social and political engagement on behalf of justice and community was undergirded by a cluster of core theological beliefs, values, and principles that provided the basis for both King's personal self-presentation and his radical social action. King's theological perspective emerged from the context of liberative praxis in a racially oppressive, economically exploitative, and politically unjust human community. It is contextually situated, and utilizes an anthropocentric point of departure.[6]

However, the ultimate goal of King's program was unarguably theocentric or God-centered.[7] Beginning with the human predicament (racism, poverty, war, suffering, black disfranchisement, segregation, and such), he was at the same time involved in a serious quest to discover God. The three areas of tension that drove his vocational crisis—self-identification, faith, and competing intellectual traditions—received their final resolution as King came to terms with the power and reality of God.[8] The God he had discovered was not found solely in—but nevertheless, could not be fully understood apart from—the human predicament of suffering and hope.[9] Consequently, the hub of King's theology is located in an understanding of God as "radically involved agape love in action"—the Divine One who structures the cosmos and works proactively and immanently in and through history to effect the purposes of freedom, justice, and community.[10] King's God-centered perspective led to the conceptualization of a *visio dei* from which he subsequently derived other seminal doctrinal themes.[11]

As a developing theologian, King was never provided the opportunity to weave these thematic and doctrinal cords into a structured, systematic framework.[12] While a student at Crozer and Boston, King was able to make significant progress in forging and refining ideas into a rudimentary theological-philosophical perspective. However, King had not yet tested these conceptual threads in the fires of protest.

Montgomery had provided him with the experience, but not the opportunity to think systematically through his basic conceptual format. The situation of crisis and response out of which King's theology emerged in Montgomery simply would not allow him the time or luxury to hone and systematize his thinking into a fully coherent doctrinal matrix. Because of the pressures and demands on his life from 1955 to 1968, it is to be expected that his theological perspective would be more emphatically systemic and contextual than developmentally systematic in both form and content.[13]

Moreover, as a product of the black religious tradition, King's response to the crisis of vocational identity took on the character of a theologizing faith.[14] Situated in the oral tradition of black religion, his theology was expressed, in large measure, through the medium of sermonic proclamation and jeremiadic exhortation.[15] King's was a "preached theology" in which theological perspectives about the nature and reality of God, the meaning of human existence, the role of the church in the functioning of society, the meaning and relevance of Jesus Christ, and the redemptive power of Christian vision and hope were explicated through powerful rhetoric. Moving beyond the boundaries of the institutional church, King was able to assist these ideas to gain a hearing in the arena of public discourse. King accomplished this by using a language that effectively appropriated the symbols and ideals of American civil religion in order to make prophetic public appeals for justice. At the same time, King's was a "lived theology" that concerned itself more with emancipatory social action than with matters of strict doctrinal orthodoxy.[16]

And yet, King was a formally trained systematic theologian and philosopher of religion. As such, he was familiar with and able to maneuver comfortably in the thought categories of traditional or classical theology.[17] His writings, speeches, and sermons reflect this training. As a Christian theologian, King held theological positions that can be explicated in the theological categories and loci of the classical Protestant tradition as demonstrated in the previous chapters. By presenting King's thinking in this way, one may see more clearly the structured theological formulation that he engaged. Further, one may appreciate more fully King's intellectual integrity and legacy of thought.[18]

The implicit query is now raised. What kind of theologian was King? How are we to understand the content and focus of his theological perspective? In other words, what are we to make of the evidence presented in the previous chapter? The answers to these questions will lead to a greater clarity with regard to the crisis of King's ambiguous identity in popular culture today. The data show the essence of King's theological perspective to be best delineated by the conceptual rubric of *radical involvement.* Radical involvement is the primary theme and touchstone to King's thought, and establishes the essential core and distinctive angle of his theology. The content and meaning of this term as it relates to King's theology will be explored in fuller detail later in this chapter. For now, it is important to state that King's theology of radical involvement promotes a twofold concern. First, it is concerned with the strange ways and actions of a mysterious God who works decisively and continuously throughout history toward the realization of a "justice" community (analysis). Second, it concerns itself with the moral necessity of making a responsible human response to God's ways in and with the world (praxis).

Attentiveness to this twofold concern of King's perspective is crucial for gaining a clear understanding of the essence of his theology. As previously stated, King conceived the theological task as a movement in two parts. The first step of situational analysis, King believed, was dialectically linked to the second step of practical action. It is of paramount importance to remember that King's conceptualization of the task of "doing theology" involved more than simply the rational explication of doctrinal categories and foci. For King, theological statements became "live options" only as they were informed by situational analysis and tested in the crucible of social action.

The thematics of chapters 2 and 3 validate the fact that whatever King discovered by way of situational analysis (first step) would require responsible human initiative. The "problem" must be addressed through some type of divinely mandated radical action as a corrective response (second step). In this way, the concepts of "involvement" and "radicality" are expected to be pivotal in the second step of King's theological movement. And yet, because King's two steps are so dialectically and inseparably linked, these concepts are equally integral to the first step of King's theological method. Therefore, an investigation of the two seminal concepts of "involvement" and "radicality" relative to King's analysis is also indicated.

# INVOLVEMENT AS THE CONNECTIVE THREAD IN KINGIAN THOUGHT AND ACTION

Regarding identity, symbolic role, and function in American culture, King was without question a creative theological thinker of depth and imagination. As an "organic intellectual," King eclectically appropriated insights from a variety of sources: philosophy, theology, ethics, sociology, psychology, economics, and history.[19] As a black Christian thinker, King synthetically arranged diverse intellectual strands into a coherent configuration of thought and belief. He then utilized that intellectual matrix to interpret, critique, and prescribe remedial action for the complex realities of (initially) black and (later) national and global life. Complemented by other factors (optimism and hope in the future, black religious faith, black experience, and such), King's intellectual focus led to a specific methodological approach with regard to the achievement of the democratic ideal and the realization of justice in concrete social, economic, and political terms. In this way, King's approach represents the essence of organic intellectuality in that his engaged activism was effectively linked to and informed by critical intellectual analysis.

And yet, it must be clearly understood that King was also more than an "organic intellectual." King not only linked the active life of the mind in service to the transformation of social structures and institutions. King also linked the active life of mind, soul, and body in sacrificial service not only to the critique and transformation of society, but ultimately in committed service to God. The radical spirituality and activist faith of King exercised decisive influence on his thinking. The central focus of his thought had to do with his relationship with God. This God-centeredness cannot be overlooked or overstated. Indeed, it is the primary reason for an emergent understanding of King as an innovative theologian. It is what sets him apart from exemplary organic intellectuals of the past such as W. E. B. DuBois or Frederick Douglass. Organic intellectuality remains an important orientational commitment and integral component, rather than the definitive core, of King's vocational identity.

Holding the dialectical tension between a human-centered point of departure and a God-centered vision, King imaginatively linked spirituality to the ethical demands of the faith. Human responsibility and divine sovereignty, religion, and life became inseparably connected. Consequently, King advocated a socially active Christianity that stressed a unique type of involvement. It advocated a distinctive participation that combined revolutionary consciousness with a radical pragmatism attentive to the ethical demands for moral-philosophical coherence between means and ends. From the crucible of ideological and sociopolitical conflict, King's theological perspective emerged as reflection upon action in particular situations of struggle against "superpersonal forces of evil" operating in the multiform structural arrangements of society.[20]

The core of King's theological perspective may be located at the intersection of two convergent motifs: first, the motif of *involvement* that emphasized aggressive participation in human affairs aimed at the historical realization of a just social order;[21] second, the notion of *radicality* that emphasized a quest for fundamental, comprehensive transformation in economic, political, and social spheres of human living. Both motifs converge in King's life, work, and thought, and subsequently crystallize into the thematic rubric of radical involvement. Radical involvement becomes the foundational conceptual rubric by which to understand King's theological perspective.

## THE NOTION OF RADICALITY
## IN KINGIAN THOUGHT

Of the myriad images of King available for public perusal and consumption, King's association with radical thought and activism has, unquestionably, been deemphasized. Unfortunately, the persistent public image of King appears to be that of "an all-too-safe dreamer of lofty dreams."[22] Focus remains disproportionately weighted toward the loyalist tendencies in his thinking, and a sterilized interpretation of his advocacy of love, suffering, and nonviolence. Due credence has never been conceded in either the academy, mass media, or ecclesial institutions to King's militant appropriation of principled nonviolence, or his critical linkage of agape love with the demands of justice and the acquisition and use of power. The reductionistic culling of the more radical elements from King's message has resulted in a deradicalization, and hence depotentiation of his legacy.[23] The King of popular consciousness stands as an American loyalist who promotes an essentially liberal-reformist sociopolitical agenda. Skillfully maneuvered into accepting this sanitized image of King, the public has become predisposed to believing that King sanctioned and legitimated precisely those values, judgments, policies, and practices that he so urgently and consistently challenged during his life.[24]

Despite King's enshrinement as a heroic figure of legendary proportions on the national scene, it is difficult to access much of what he said and did beyond 1963. In the same manner that the pre-1963 King has been deradicalized and reimaged for public consumption, the post-1963 King has been domesticated and valorized as an icon of the postmodern liberal establishment.[25] His devastating critiques— of political inertia and corruption; the ethos of ingrained racism, militarism, and imperialism; poverty and economic exploitation fueled by the philosophy of monopoly capitalism—have been muted from public discourse. Hence, his radical social vision, analysis, and action remain effectively blunted from national consciousness.[26]

However, to read King in light of those generative tensions that are permanent features of his theology is also to liberate him from his domestic captivity and expose the radical elements in his thought and action. What, then, does it mean to claim that King's theological perspective is fundamentally radical in its presentation? Unfortunately, the term radical suffers from much misuse and misunderstanding in American culture.[27] In a political sense, a radical is "one who advocates radical and sweeping changes in laws and methods of government with the least delay."[28] Etymologically, the meaning of the word is clear. It is a derivative of the Latin word *radicalis*, which translates "having roots," and the French words *radicix* and *radicis*, which translate "root."[29] Radical means to "proceed from the root," "fundamental," "basal," "reaching to the center of ultimate source." It is associated with efforts to get at the rudiments or fundamentals of a particular reality. To be radical is to be concerned with etiological or causative agency. The true radical is interested not merely in a description or treatment of the symptoms. Rather, the true radical is interested in an analysis and treatment of the root causes or foundational factors that act to perpetuate symptoms. To be a radical, then, involves much more than engaging in militant rhetoric or operating as an angry voice of anarchistic dissent. To be a radical, in the true sense of the term, is to engage in penetrating etiological analyses of the present situation for purposes of identifying and describing the root or causative factors of societal dysfunctionality. It further involves the construction of a programmatic philosophy and methodology that aim at the comprehensive transformation of society in accordance with a progressive vision that is fundamentally and substantively different from the configuration presently in operation.

King's theological-ethical perspective certainly sought a massive and fundamental change. Its aim was to effect comprehensive structural-institutional transformation in the total fabric of American life. In scope, King challenged that which for so long had been considered basic and axiomatic in American culture—its system of values, its notions and use of power, its understanding of and commitment to justice. Speaking to the issue of racial justice in 1968, King argued that judicial decisions or clever rhetoric would not guarantee justice for black folk. Neither would a few strategically placed token changes dissolve the mass discontent of disadvantaged blacks and the poor. The key to justice, he argued, lay in whites' capacity to recognize that nothing short of radical changes in the basic structures of American society would be necessary. Restitution would exact a heavy cost.[30]

We have already identified the radical analysis of King with regard to apathy, moral sickness, and basic injustice. King's theology served as the basis not only for that analysis, but also for his advocacy of a radical vision as well as a radical methodology for change. King's advocacy of sweeping social change at the most basic level went beyond the contours of racial politics. He also spoke of the need for a revolution of values.[31] He argued for a total restructuring of American educational and economic systems.[32] By 1965, in the midst of the Selma Campaign for Voting Rights, King had become thoroughly convinced that "the whole structure of American life must be changed."[33] King's strategic emphasis also reflected this radical thrust. He argued for a socially conscious democracy,[34] as well as for massive civil resistance and disruptive dissent.[35]

King made his jeremiadic appeal for radical social change, in part, by communicating a sense of urgency that steadily intensified during the course of his public ministry. "We want our freedom, and we want it now! We're not willing to wait another hundred or so years for it," he said.[36] Indeed, when viewed from the context of the entirety of his life, King emerges as a thinker and activist who is more radical and antiestablishment (in the truest sense) than has been generally recognized.

It is clear that the emergence of King's radical focus is the result of a developmental process. King always harbored the seeds of this radicality through his nurture in the tradition of radical black religious dissent.[37] Additional seeds were planted through his encounter with intellectual traditions of black critical thought, pacifism, nonviolent resistance, civil disobedience, social gospel, and Christian realism. The soil that provided the medium for King's evolving radicalism to flourish was, of course, the lived experience of liberative praxis in the struggle for justice. Just as his ethic of nonviolent resistance developed and matured over time, so did the elements of his theological program.

It is true, then, that King's radicality had not always advocated or taken the forms that one sees in his last three years of public witness. Montgomery, Alabama, in 1955 serves as a case in point. Coretta Scott King has correctly stated that in the initial stages of the Montgomery bus boycott, "really what we were seeking was a more human form of segregation."[38] Martin King confirmed as much in his account of the movement.[39] After the rejection of extremely moderate demands of blacks in Montgomery, King began to experience a significant (though by no means total) loss of sociopolitical naïveté. The events in Montgomery mark another prominent stage in King's maturational development as an activist theologian. One is able to witness the deepening of his situational analysis and the intensification of radical emphases in his theological and ethical perspective.[40] King became less sanguine about the possibilities for political reform to see that equality would require no less than a comprehensive change in the edifice of segregation.

A meeting of the black representatives of the Montgomery Improvement Association with the white city fathers on December 7, 1955, tested and exposed the limits of a reformist agenda. When the city fathers proved unyielding to their demands, King stated that he had been a victim of unwarranted pessimism because he had approached the meeting with a great illusion. This had caused him, he said, to be a victim of an unwarranted optimism. King learned an important lesson—groups in power do not voluntarily relinquish the privileges of power without strong, radical resistance.[41] Contrary to much scholarly and popular misconception, King's approach to social change had already contained radical elements as early as 1955. The shift in focus of King and his followers from a mere fine-tuning of the American apartheid system to more fundamental and pervasive structural change marks the precise point at which the sharpening of King's radicality occurs. The important "lesson" King learned in Montgomery was that symptomatic analysis and remedial action were inadequate in the struggle for justice. From that point forward, the central objective was to develop those critical tools of analysis and interpretation in order to get at the "root" cause of racial segregation.[42]

To be sure, this radical focus would develop and deepen throughout King's life.[43] The exposure to new intellectual currents and social analyses as well as the experiences of new "campaigns" led to the evolution of King's thought and action.[44] By 1964, King was acutely aware of the interstructuring of oppression and the weblike, systemic connection between racism, poverty, and militarism.[45] By 1965, in the wake of the Selma and Chicago Campaigns, King realized more clearly the complex and insidious nature of racism and poverty. He gained an increased understanding of the devastating impact of laissez-faire, monopoly capitalism on the masses of black, poor, and elderly Americans. Subsequently, he began to see the strong connection between domestic and foreign policy.[46] By 1967, King had come to recognize fully and concede the futility of liberal-reformist approaches to social change in America. King took note of the deep and ingrained nature of racism, the intransigence of power, the unequal distribution of goods and services, the morally bankrupt values of capitalistic consumerism and profit-maximization, and the jingoistic and nationalistic reliance on destructive, militaristic violence. Viewed together, these signposts led King to believe that nothing short of a complete and radical revolution was needed to effect the redemption of America's soul and the restoration of the national community.[47]

King conceded that piecemeal reform of existing societal institutions represented a dead-end street on the path to equality. The radical reconstruction of the total society, including its fundamental value system, was required. This necessitated a "radical redistribution of economic and political power."[48] A respecter of just legislative process and certainly no political anarchist, King nevertheless believed that capitalism simply had to go.[49]

Clearly, one need not ascribe the status of "radical" to the post-1965 King alone. The 1955–56 King of Montgomery had both continuity and discontinuity with the 1967–68 King of New York, Chicago, and

Memphis with regard to radicality in vision, analysis, and social change methodology. On one hand, the "early" King's focus had been, at times, inclined too heavily toward idealism, and ideological and political naïveté. This tendency is more discontinuous with the "late" King of 1965–68 who is, unarguably, more sophisticated in his sociopolitical analysis, self-presentation, and strategic-tactical thrust.[50] Moreover, the more radical and extremist measures that King advocated after 1965—massive civil disobedience,[51] stress upon the acquisition of political and economic power,[52] comprehensive restructuring of America's capitalist economy,[53] searing systemic critique of American foreign policy in Vietnam,[54] the need to eliminate poverty in America[55]—all pointed to a gradual deepening and increasing consolidation of the radical elements in King's perspective.

On the other hand, the post-1965 radical emphases, while distinct from the pre-1965 emphases, show continuity with their analyses and methods.[56] Economic boycotts, marches, pickets, sit-ins, jail-ins, a focus on legislative change, and a belief in the necessity for comprehensive change remain prominent "radical" features of both "early" and "late" Kings. Both Kings see the global interstructuring of oppression.[57] Both Kings recognize the bankruptcy of reformism, and both are willing to suffer and risk their lives courageously for the cause of justice.[58] Both reject violence as an unacceptable response to collective evil, and hold out a nonviolent option as the only viable ethic for social change. Both view community as the ultimate goal of liberative struggle.[59]

In keeping with the strict definition of "radical" presented earlier, both Kings may be legitimately described as radical in thought and action. That is to say, they are both concerned to engage in penetrating analysis of the present situation for purposes of identifying and describing the root causes of problems, and to move subsequently toward the construction of a program that aims at total reconstruction of society in accordance with a radical social vision that is fundamentally and substantively different from that configuration presently in operation. The radical character of King's theology and ethic is to be located in a comprehensive vision of freedom as concrete social, political, and economic empowerment achieved through massive civil disobedience aimed at basic structural change. In both perspective and method, the "early" pre-1965 King is to the "late" post-1965 King as lavender is to purple.[60]

## RADICAL INVOLVEMENT: DISTINCTIVE FOCUS AND ORGANIZING CONCEPTUAL RUBRIC IN KING'S THEOLOGICAL PERSPECTIVE

*Apathy in a Revolutionary Situation:*
*Sign of Spiritual Impoverishment and Moral Irresponsibility*

King's incessant search for the radically involved God of history became coterminous with a deep and personal commitment to "worrying about the things that God worries about." Subsequently, he was driven toward the pursuit of a direction and methodology that would fastidiously avoid indifference, escapism, complacency, and withdrawal in the face of the pressing exigencies of the times. The notion of divine-human coresponsibility in the creation of the beloved community in history led King to reject any lifestyle or pattern of action that exonerated passivity in the struggle against evil. The most glaring example of the disintegrative personality, for King, was the apathetic personality.[61] A personality, lifestyle, or societal ethos infected by apathy was indicative, in the final analysis, of spiritual impoverishment and moral irresponsibility.[62]

Why was apathy so problematic for King? On one hand, the answer was in King's strong faith in a God and the gospel that placed a clear moral demand for engagement in extremist activity in order to effect the restoration of community. There was simply no room in his theology for static nonparticipation in light of the very real presence of structural evil. For King, there was a lethal linkage between apathy and the persistence of injustice in human community. On the other hand the answer was in his assessment of the human predicament. King's contextual analysis of the times heightened his sense of urgency that the society was caught in the grips of a revolutionary crisis.[63] In a revolution, King asserted, apathy was the response of ultimate irrationality and immorality.

King's theological perspective embraced an unshakable belief that all reality hinged ultimately on moral foundations.[64] That belief proved pivotal for King's appropriation of moral integrity as a barometer for measuring the internal, psychosocial health of individuals, groups, and nations.[65] America's social, political, and economic problems, in King's view, were but symptomatic of a more profound and "pervasive moral sickness."[66] The presence of radical and extensive injustice in a society was empirical verification of that community's asymmetrical relationship relative to God's governing universal moral framework. In this way, racism, poverty, and militarism became, for King, theological issues, and their persistent presence indicated a dilemma that was, at bottom, moral in nature.[67] As such, moral as well as political power were required to definitively resolve the crisis at hand. The aim was to redeem the "moral and spiritual lag" and "re-establish the moral ends of our lives in personal character and social justice."[68] Therefore, apathy, for King, was problematic not simply because it unwittingly conspired to validate the perpetuation of a dehumanizing social order. Rather, in the final analysis, apathy represented a form of human recalcitrance against the superpersonal forces of justice and redemption at work in a universe created and governed by moral law, and ultimately redeemed by a loving God. Apathy was not merely a sociopolitical liability. At bottom, it constituted a terminal, moral-spiritual illness.

The moral sickness of America, for King, signaled a problem of ominous proportions. It pointed undeniably to the fact that the nation was caught in the quagmires of a revolutionary situation.[69] Revolutions, of course, are urgent times deserving of the most immediate and focused attention. Assessing the racial, political, and economic crises in America as symptoms of a moral dilemma, King spoke to the urgency of the times.[70]

King argued that a revolutionary climate characterized by abnormally high levels of crisis, tension, and urgency required the development of a revolutionary attitude or consciousness.[71] This "revolutionary spirit" would operate in both the spiritual-moral and sociopolitical spheres to awaken the moral conscience, redeem the soul, and transform societal structures at the most radical or fundamental level.[72]

Apathy represented, for King, the very antithesis of the revolutionary spirit.[73] Circumstances of revolutionary urgency necessitated a lifestyle marked by a particular orientation of personality as well as specific behavioral modalities. Apathy epitomized collective spiritual-moral and psychological deterioration. Appropriating the notion of alienation, King described the cultural conditions under which apathy was induced: lack of moral centeredness or purpose, sense of participation is lost, democratic principle of decision making is abandoned, sense of public responsibility is diminished, vulgarity is ele-

119

vated, social life is imperiled, and safety is elusive. King referred to this as modern culture's most pervasive and insidious development. This type of social alienation, he argued, was like a corrosive acid that slowly ate away at the glue of society.[74]

King had warned of the dangers of apathetic response or "crippling do-nothingism" in the face of revolutionary possibilities.[75] His life had been a constant exposure to the demands of a radical, prophetic, socially active Christianity. With his grandfather, father, Benjamin E. Mays, and others (cut in the grain of the black religious tradition) serving as models, King was given the rudiments of a blueprint for avoiding the apathetic personality.[76] In addition to the dissenting emphasis of the black religious tradition, King was also a product of the broader "American dissenting tradition."[77] Both traditions employ an activistic approach that sponsors public indictments of injustice and stinging criticisms of individual and communal complacency.

King stood squarely within these two traditions of dissent, resistance, and activism. In fact, King admitted that his return to the South was aimed at his intent to become not a mere onlooker or "detached spectator," but a participant in the struggle for justice and freedom.[78] As the newly installed pastor of Dexter Avenue Baptist Church in Montgomery, King wanted to increase the sociopolitical awareness and involvement of the church in the issues of the local community. Therefore, one of his very first acts was the establishment of a social action committee.[79] The advocacy of "creative dissent" in 1955–56 (while not as politically sophisticated or broadly conceived as in 1966–68) was already part of King's guiding theological-ethical framework. Without question, from beginning to end, King was contra-apathy and pro-radical involvement.

Acutely aware of the requirements of a socially active religious faith, King identified the apathy of Montgomery's black church leadership prior to the bus boycott as a "special problem."[80] Expanding the boundaries of his critique, King exposed the depth and breadth of clerical apathy. He expected Christian ministers to stand at the vanguard of the freedom struggle as exemplars of a gospel-based, radical emancipatory social action. Instead, King discovered that the clergy were major contributors to the problem. The "greatest tragedy" of the period, he stated, was not the work of misguided folk, but rather the deafening silence of good people, the "tragic apathy" of the "children of light." King felt deeply that apathy was so prevalent and costly that the entire generation would have to repent in an effort to atone for this serious sin.[81]

King also analyzed the prevailing level of participatory readiness among black citizens of Montgomery. Assessing the future of the city, King identified apathetic indifference among the black electorate as a major obstacle in the quest to achieve equality. Attempting to motivate black leadership to aggressively tackle the problem, King argued that apathy was not simply a moral failure. Apathy was a "form of moral and political suicide."[82] Likewise, speaking to the role of the southern white moderate in the period of transition in 1957, King again stressed the need for deliverance from the sin of apathy.[83] Finally, King warned the nation in 1957 to heed the signs of the times. In a revolutionary situation, apathy and complacency were contraindicated. The nature of the times demanded aggressive, positive action.[84]

King continued, after Montgomery, to issue a prophetic and moral critique against the apathetic, antirevolutionary spirit. In a commencement address at Lincoln University in 1961, King challenged the graduands to be vigilant lest they fall victim to the seductive power of apathy. Nothing could be more conducive to the enhancement of the apathetic personality than to embrace a faulty notion of time in a revolutionary situation. Echoing a theme he had presented in 1957, King urged the listeners to becoming proactively involved in the freedom struggle. Affirming the necessity of engaging in creative protest, King railed against the "myth of time." He contended that patiently waiting on progress worked to encourage social stagnation and induce apathy. History had validated the truth that social progress was never inevitable. Rather, the difficult, tireless, persistent work of committed freedom fighters was necessary for the creation of a new social order.[85]

In the Birmingham Campaign in 1963, King publicly stated that he "stood in the middle of two opposing forces in the Negro community." King identified the first as ". . . one of bitterness and hatred" that came ". . . perilously close to advocating violence." He labeled the second ". . . a force of complacency."[86] Further, King did not limit his critique of apathy to blacks alone, but, as usual, focused on whites as well. In 1967, King was still arguing that apathy and collective self-deception remained white America's chief problems.[87] And yet, the virulence, intransigence, and depth of racism meant that American citizenship was fundamentally incompatible with apathetic passivity in the face of racial injustice.[88]

Until the very end of his life, King sounded the clarion call for a proactive spirituality that took seriously the moral obligation to engage in revolutionary social action against any value, attitude, ideology, policy, practice, or institutional structure that denied freedom and degraded human personality.[89] Nothing could be more indicative of moral hypocrisy and spiritual impoverishment than apathetic withdrawal and passivity in the face of injustice.[90] For King, apathy was the equivalent of "sleeping through a revolution."[91] To stand courageously, in a revolutionary time, against "crippling do-nothingism," the "paralysis of analysis," "silence," the "tranquilizing drug of gradualism," and the "myth of time" was, at the same time, to counter apathy.[92] However, as King looked back on the history of the movement in 1967, he concluded that apathy and complacency had remained perpetual problems.[93]

King's verdict was clear and final. Apathy in the face of injustice symbolized the disintegrative personality in operation. In his belief that the universe was morally structured, and that its arc bent toward justice, King came to view apathy as disharmonious with the very heart of the universe. Further, it was contra-God since it was God (as radically involved agape love in action) who had structured the cosmos through moral law. King's personal and biblical God of love, power, and justice became known through Jesus of the Gospels as the very antithesis of apathetic spirit. Indeed, the gospel of Christianity was thoroughly infused with a revolutionary consciousness. To embrace the Christian faith was to witness a spiritual empowerment in both individual believer and the community of faith. As one experienced spiritual empowerment, one became restlessly dissatisfied with the plight of the victims of social injustice. In the context of revolutionary ferment (times of heightened confrontation between the forces of justice and injustice), apathy amounted to moral irresponsibility. Radical involvement represented the only viable, morally responsible human response to the call of God in the revolutionary situation and the most effective counter to the sin of apathy.

# A THEOLOGY OF RADICAL INVOLVEMENT

The interaction of King's situational analysis with those doctrinal thematics of chapters 2 and 3 crystallized into a theology of radical involvement. "Radical involvement," as an orientational thrust, provided the conceptual blueprint for a distinctive theological vision—historically redemptive activity coinitiated by God and humanity, leading to a revolutionary transformation of relationships at all levels of human existence. That vision was of pivotal importance as King moved into the second step of his theological method, namely applied, liberative action. The essence of that vision promoted a theology of radical involvement that emerged as King's unique and significant theological contribution.

King innovatively revisioned and redefined the nature and task of theology as more than simply a rational explication of the content of the Christian faith. The distinctive and creative element in King's theology lay in his ability to link sustained formulation of the content of the Christian faith to critical social analysis, providing a theological basis for radical, transformative social action. Moreover, King effectively placed race and racism on the table as legitimate moral issues, deserving of serious attention in theological discourse. Indeed, part of King's uniqueness and creativity lay in his ability to critically appropriate and imaginatively connect the particularities of black existence, thought, faith, and struggle with insights and methods from a variety of universalist notions found in liberal theology, American civil religion, Gandhian nonviolent resistance, and theories of social philosophy. The point of theology, for King, was to serve God in the concrete human situation. This meant that theology's usefulness lay in its capacity to serve the interests and objectives of truth, justice, freedom, and righteousness. This approach represents the essence of King's theology of radical involvement.

In this sense, King is not only to be understood as a creative theological thinker. Rather, he is also to be credited with innovatively linking the worship of God to active participation in the concrete exigencies of emancipatory struggle. King forged a unique theological-ethical paradigm that held in balanced tension moral-spiritual development and disciplined, liberative social action. Aimed at the realization of justice in human community, King creatively recovered and elevated social activism to prominence as an indispensable component of both religious faith and the theological-ethical enterprise. In so doing, King modeled a radically new and different understanding of the vocation of the theologian as one who places mind, soul, voice, and body in radical, obedient service to God's will for human community—namely, the beloved community. King's theology promoted a new emphasis on radical, justice-oriented social action as central to Christian discipleship.

King's distinctive contribution, then, was to reconnect theology to the pressing existential realities of his day. In this sense, King modeled a paradigm shift for doing theology, and did more than virtually any other theologian of his time to reestablish the relevance of the Christian faith for the modern era.

## CONTOURS AND CONTENT OF RADICAL INVOLVEMENT THEOLOGY

What, then, were the contours and content of this theology of radical involvement? Paul Garber has perceptively observed that Martin King was

> a pioneer in this theology of involvement, in the effort "to keep going the difficult but not impossible running conversation between the full biblical and theological tradition and the contemporary human situation."[94]

The weight of evidence confirms Garber's point. And yet, Garber does not go far enough in his assertion. Not only was King a pioneer in this regard, but he creatively fashioned a unique type of involvement—*a radical involvement*—as a distinctive theological focus. Holding together inner, contemplative, revolutionary spiritual consciousness with outer, prophetic, social action, King's theology moved beyond the contours of ordinary public involvement. Informed by a dissenting tradition of radical activism, King's theological focus took on a radical edge that qualified the type of involvement his program sponsored. This, in fact, represented the creative aspect of King's theological thought.

King's theology was informed by an urgent prophetic pathos that attempted to respond to the exigencies of a revolutionary ethos. This prophetic element spoke to the moral-spiritual dimension of living as well as to the social, economic, and political realities of society. Simultaneously addressing both spiritual and material realms with equal vitality, King hoped to probe the roots of sin and alienation, effecting a definitive and radical change in the values, relationships, and institutions of the culture. Affirming the inseparability of love of

124

God and love for the neighbor, King's theology directed its energies at both personal and public piety and transformation.

First, King's theology of radical involvement stressed radical obedience to God's will and purpose for the universe and history.[95] For King, the supreme experience for the human is to take a stand for God's truth. The chief end of life was not to seek happiness, maximize pleasure, or minimize pain. Rather the chief end of life was to exhaust all human effort in the attempt to do God's will.[96] As he declared in his final speech in Memphis in 1968, King wanted to be like Jesus—radically obedient to the will of God.[97] This represented the "height" dimension of living that King advocated as a vital part of the integrative personality. To love God was, at the same time, to be committed to God's will for justice in human community. Methodologically, King approached the theological enterprise as a two-step process.[98] For King, "doing theology" (to engage the God question critically in light of human existence) meant, as a first act, analyzing the human situation to ascertain where the mysterious God of radical agape love in action was at work in the universe engaging the superpersonal forces of evil.

This first step also involved a compelling, intelligible articulation of that analysis within the framework of faith. It was aimed at persuading the apathetic personality of the moral obligation to respond to God's radical call to action in the revolutionary situation. The second step of King's theology of radical involvement sought to join God as "coworker" in the struggle to achieve justice in history. King's theology never allowed radical emancipatory struggle to assume a secondary position relative to rational discourse.[99] The proclamation component of King's theology was informed by and dialectically related to the applied practice component.

Christian faith brought with it a moral obligation for aggressive personal and communal involvement against the cosmic forces of sin and evil. It meant protest, resistance, and confrontation against injustice.[100] It promoted a dual emphasis on spiritual-moral empowerment and social action aimed at the radical reconstruction of society at every level of human existence. A "political" reading of the biblical text combined with a study of history and life experience had thoroughly convinced King that ". . . freedom is not given, it is won by struggle." If the "gospel of freedom" was to be relevant and decisively illuminative for the black-led freedom struggle in America, it had to offer a faith that took seriously the sociopolitical realities of the day.[101]

For King, proper attentiveness to spiritual formation was legitimate. Indeed, maturing toward the complete and integrative life required the development of a personal relationship with God. Prayer, for instance, as a faith resource for spiritual-moral growth was vital and necessary. However, prayer without corresponding action represented an inadequate response to the radical demands of a gospel of freedom. Prayer could never be a substitute for radical liberative action. The struggle for justice will not be won by prayer alone. Rather, as Moses and the children of Israel were reminded en route to the Promised Land, God does not do for human beings what human beings can do for themselves through intelligence and work.[102]

Radical involvement sought a balance between the meditative and the prophetic, the personal and the social, the private and the public, the reflective and the active. Both active prayer and prayerful act must be held in dialectical tension. For King's theological perspective, faith without corresponding social action was fraudulent and morally hypocritical. Conversely, social action uninformed by the resources of faith was hollow, and ultimately devoid of sustaining metanoic power.[103]

As early as Montgomery, the correlation between persuasive jeremiadic rhetoric and prophetic action had already been established. King advocated the need for a sacrificial involvement in the struggle for justice and equality. He challenged the federal government, northern white liberals, moderate white southerners, labor unions, the church, and the black community to give "life service" (as opposed to "lip service") to the goal of integration.[104] He appealed to the disruptive tactics of creative protest and militant nonviolence. He argued for a visible and continuous belligerence. "Never let them rest," he said.[105] Realizing that oppositional activity entailed serious hazards to personal safety and survival, King linked such risk taking to a notion of redemptive suffering. He argued that this type of radical involvement expressed the best of Christian discipleship.[106]

While it is true that his strategic and tactical forms of radical involvement did evolve and mature over time, the substance and primary focus were present from Montgomery to Memphis. King never wavered in his passionate appeal for a radical oppositional praxis, based upon the Christian gospel, and aimed at the realization of the shalomic community. Revolutionary times dictated revolutionary responses.[107] The goal and task of radical societal transformation demanded a distinctive type of involvement. Radical involvement required moving beyond the boundaries of moderation and gradualism. It meant pushing beyond the normal limits of giving to a mode of sacrificial self-giving. There could be no advancement made on the path to justice without sacrifice, struggle, and suffering. It was an "anatomical theology" in the sense that it was characterized by an insistence upon the sacrificial placing of body and life on the line in the cause of justice. Such sacrificial giving constituted an adequate response to the radical demands of the Christian faith.[108]

For the citizen, radical involvement entailed more than dispassionate philanthropic giving and attentiveness to civic responsibility. Similarly, it was concerned with more than the pragmatic considerations of political democratization and social and economic justice, namely with the possibilities for a spiritual-moral redemption of the public order. The salvation of society lay not in laws, policies, and programmatic structures, but ultimately in its moral and spiritual power.[109]

And yet radical involvement was a costly endeavor. It would exact a price that most were not willing to pay. As a call to a servanthood ethic of radical obedience,[110] this social-action-driven spirituality ultimately involved "bearing the cross" for the redemption of the nation.[111] King was acutely aware that the individualistic ethos of middle-class America tended to discourage the notion of a service ethic. He was especially concerned with middle-class blacks who, having fallen prey to a culture of conspicuous consumerism and materialistic values, were prone to apathy and inclined to "forget the masses."[112]

King also realized his own personal vulnerability in this regard. His greatest desire was to be remembered as a person who tried to model in word and deed the lifestyle of a radically involved coworker with God and servant to humanity in the cause of justice, love, and peace. In contemplating his legacy, King wanted to be remembered for giving his life to loving and serving humanity; taking a stand for truth; and addressing the needs of the hungry, naked, imprisoned, and homeless. Calling himself a "drum major" for justice, peace, and righteousness, King stressed the core of radical involvement the-

127

ology—the desire to live a life of radical commitment in service to God and humanity.[113]

# SUMMARY

Unquestionably, King's theology was contextually engaged. It emerged out of the crises of the historical moment—first, the peculiar absurdities and issues of black existence, and second, the problematics of general human existence. In turn, his theology spoke relevantly to those crises of the human spirit and communal existence that had given it birth. Further, as a spiritual actualist, King's theological formulation was also firmly and deeply rooted in his vocational identity. A mark of the spiritual innovator is the ability to correlate personal conflicts of identity and vocation with similar crises in others. The resolution of the individual's crisis is joined to that of a larger group in the attempt to establish a new vocational identity not only for him/herself, but for his/her entire generation. In other words, the calling upon that person's life with regard to identity and vocational needs is related to the identity and vocational needs of the historical time in which he/she lives.

The resolution of his crisis of vocational identity related to his analysis of the situational context led to an emergent radical, alternative consciousness in King that mandated radical participation in solidarity with God's revolutionary action in history. King understood this call to radical participation as central to his faith commitment. This faith, in turn, led to acts of selflessness and personal sacrifice aimed at the restoration of human community. It is a type of "radical faith" that promotes a "radical relinquishing" of the self whereby one engages in acts of "redemptive subversiveness" in order to effect societal transformation.[114] The archenemy of this faith is apathy.

In a very profound sense, King's theology of radical involvement may be understood as a lifelong treatise against apathy.[115] King argued, however, that action in and of itself did not constitute virtue. Rather, the objective of that action and the form it took ultimately determined its genuine value.[116] It is precisely the aim and methodological focus—the fundamental reconstruction of society through specific types of human initiative that extend beyond the contours of "normal" social responsibility—that make King's brand of involvement "radical" in the truest sense of the term.

King's theological perspective legitimated a form of contextual involvement in the prevailing social, political, and economic crises that aimed at radical, comprehensive institutional-structural change. At the same time, it left individual Christians and the church free from a too-easy identification with, or conformity to, either the prevailing status quo or the new social order. And yet, the theology of radical involvement did aim at the historical actualization of a just and beloved human community. This had important implications for the central emphasis in King's developing ethic.

# THE PRACTICAL APPLICATION OF RADICAL INVOLVEMENT THEOLOGY: TRANSFORMATIVE PRESCRIPTIONS FOR THE SITUATIONAL CONTEXT

# CHAPTER 5

# THE KINGIAN ETHIC:

## Radical Involvement and the Vision of the Beloved Community

Behind King's public witness lay a theological focus on radical involvement that stressed coresponsible agency—the notion that human beings, in response to the divine agenda for freedom, must become radically active, liberative agents in God's historical project of moral improvement and social redemption. King mounted an effective and sustained (though by no means entirely successful) effort to implement, with programmatic concreteness, the theological program he had formulated and embraced.[1] Because his worldview intimately connected religion and life, body and soul, thought and action, it is not surprising that King's theological perspective is virtually inseparable from his ethical orientation. In fact, his ethic is derivative of his theology.

Clearly, a great deal of similarity and kinship exists between King and the basic orientation of contemporary theologies of liberation. As with King, the liberation theme in these theologies emerges from the context of sociopolitical and economic oppression and psychic dislocation. Therefore, theological reflection is integrally related to prevailing sociohistorical and political realities. Affirming the contextual situatedness of all theology, theologies of liberation press the Christian faith in general, and Christian theology in particular, to take the social context seriously. Therefore, they seek to address themselves proactively to current existential crises and tensions. Specifically, theologies of liberation turn their attention to the plight of the poor and marginalized in society, and concern themselves with working for the transformation of dehumanizing structural arrangements and oppressive social relationships. Starting as they do with analysis of the concrete situation, liberation theologies are intent to maintain an inseparable link between the theological and ethical tasks.[2]

In Kingian thought, Christian faith and sociopolitical praxis became inextricably linked in such a way that theological formulation severed from its derivative ethical implications remained unimaginable. Discursive theological activity without corresponding moral-ethical activity was not only existentially impossible, but also morally hypocritical and spiritually bankrupt. Therefore, any discussion of King's theological program would be incomplete without paying some attention to his ethical orientation. A detailed explication of King's ethical perspective is clearly beyond the aim and scope of this project. This chapter merely intends to briefly present some of the prominent and salient themes found in King's ethics.

Ethics asks the question, "What ought we to be or do in light of the situational options available to us at any given moment in history?" As a minister of the Christian faith, theologian, and social activist, King asked, "What is God calling me to be and to do in this particular situation?" Further, King acknowledged a critical link between the three vectors of moral action, situational analysis, and metaphysical belief. King's conceptualization of the ethical task (moral action) was derivative of his theological platform (metaphysical belief). Both, in turn, were dialectically informed by his situational analysis.[3]

The twofold concern of King's theology (discover where God was at work in the cosmos and to join God there), led to his appropriation of a two-step movement in the doing of theology. The first step of situational analysis was followed by a second step of practical social action. Again, both steps were informed by King's underlying theological perspective. In this way, theology and ethics became inextricably linked in King's program. King's response to the ethical question of "What is God calling me to be and to do in this situation?" was determined, in part, by his understanding of the dynamics of the social context. He relied heavily upon the tools of social, political, psychological, biblical, and economic analysis to uncover the fundamental situational problematics. When combined with a vision of the beloved community (belief) and the activistic thrust of radical involvement (action), situational analysis helped to orient King's ethic toward a communitarian focus. This communal emphasis, in turn, was carried out with a high degree of concreteness and specificity. To better understand the nature of this communitarian ethic, and to appreciate the way in which it emerged from his radical involvement theology, we must turn again to a consideration of King's situational analysis.

## SITUATIONAL ANALYSIS: THE SICK SOCIETY

King's theological perspective emphasized the moral basis of reality. Crucial to this emphasis were King's anthropological belief in the dignity and worth of all human personality, the interrelatedness of all reality, and the sociality of all human life. With a high degree of specificity, King creatively linked concrete social, political, and economic forms of associative human behavior to the demands of a universal, theocentric morality.[4] King established a tight correlation between collective moral health and the degree to which the nation could effectively create and maintain a public ethos that encouraged and sustained interpersonal, intergroup, and institutional relationships based upon the principles of justice, democracy, and egalitarianism. The structured relationships and modes of power distribution and utilization operating within the legal, sociopolitical, and economic systems were to be ultimately judged on the basis of their capacity to enhance the development of human potential. For King, the level of social, political, and economic justice and integratedness was directly proportionate to the degree and depth of moral centeredness operating in the societal context.[5]

King felt that racial estrangement, social alienation, gross disparities in political power, and inequitable, exploitative economic practices and policies were symptomatic of a morally diseased culture. The empirically verifiable "triple evils" of racism, poverty, and war were indicative of massive and chronic moral hemorrhaging.[6] In a sermon entitled "A Knock at Midnight" in 1958, King used the motif of "midnight" to describe the social and psychological crises facing the nation. America, he argued, was in a state of moral fragmentation, social disintegration, racial estrangement, and psychic alienation. This was symptomatic of a deeper "midnight in the moral order." "How we deal with this crucial situation will determine . . . our moral [and] . . . political health as a nation."[7]

By 1963, King had reached the conclusion that America was guilty of serious moral apostasy and in a state of moral declension. Conse-

135

quently, he used his publicly acknowledged moral authority to appeal to the nation to fulfill her destiny of democracy, freedom, and justice in the social, political, and economic arenas.[8] In 1965, the contours and focus of King's situational analysis broadened and deepened as he became increasingly conscious of the interlocking natures of race and class.[9] Analyzing the problems of the nation led King to a more frequent and public description of America as a "sick society."[10] America had managed to skillfully evade the moral responsibility to use her vast resources and power to guarantee equality of opportunity, the privileges of citizenship, and the pursuit of happiness for all her people.

Calling attention to the pervasiveness of racism in the national body politic, King repeatedly used the phrases "schizophrenic personality," "tragic duality," "vacillations," "tragic ambivalence," "compromising duality," "congenital deformity," and "moral dilemma" to describe the diseased moral state of the nation.[11] Addressing the dismal economic reality of massive poverty in America, King asserted that the moral values of the nation had been tragically misplaced. America was badly in need of a cultural values revolution. The items on the nation's moral agenda required immediate reprioritization.[12] The important issue was whether or not America possessed the necessary "soul" or "moral will" to undertake this radical task.[13] With respect to the country's militaristic jingoism and geopolitical imperialism, King's critique of American involvement in the Vietnam War amounted to a public exposure of the nation's moral hypocrisy.[14] For King, "the War in Vietnam [was] but a symptom of a far deeper malady within the American spirit."[15] Maintaining a cautious optimism, King nevertheless became increasingly disillusioned about the nation's capacity to initiate and sustain redemptive agendas for social, political, and economic change. King raised serious doubts about the national moral will and commitment to civil rights. Pointing to a ten-year trend of gradual statistical decline in socioeconomic health for blacks and the poor, King publicly confessed that America was much sicker than he had realized when the movement began in 1955.[16]

## COMMUNITY AS IDEAL AND NORM FOR KING'S ETHICAL EMPHASIS

The remedy for the nation's moral sickness was found in King's theology and ethic. The emphasis on radical involvement was symbiotically related to his progressive social vision of the just and beloved human community.[17] It was this ethical perspective, driven by a radical vision of the future, that motivated him to work for a radically new society.[18] In this sense, King's was a partially realizable future vision that functioned as a catalyst that spurred his commitment to radically involved, responsible human action in the world.[19] The paradoxical hope and cautious optimism that characterized King's eschatological horizon became decisive for the accents of King's ethic. The content of King's radical social vision was the dream of a beloved community in which relationships were characterized by love, justice, and peace mediated through democratic and egalitarian institutions. The resolution of the nation's moral-ethical dilemma lay in its capacity to recommit itself in practice to those ideals of equality, freedom, and justice that were echoed in the foundational documents of the nation's history.[20]

Community, for King, was conceived as a just society in which ethnic pluralism and cultural diversity were embraced as gifts from God. Agapeistic love was the moral foundation upon which community was to be developed, and it was linked to public notions of equality, fairness, democracy, and egalitarianism. Thus, King was led to intelligibly engage in public discourse concerning good citizenship; the ownership, allocation, and distribution of social goods and services; and the construction of structural-institutional networks that empowered the human spirit and enhanced the development of human potential. King often referred to this communal conception as "the good and just society."[21]

King's "dream" of the beloved community was also pragmatically linked to the notion of an integrated society. In a 1962 speech, "The Ethical Demands for Integration," King identified integration as the primary objective of a communitarian ethic. Prerequisite to integration, he stated, must be a recognition of the sacredness of human personality, the solidarity of the human family, and necessity of freedom for human life. He argued that desegregation was a first step on the journey to the beloved society because it merely removed legal and social blocks and barriers to community. It was a short-term goal. He then identified the basic content of integration. Integration, for King, was the needed second step on the road to the good and just society. Integration creatively advocated positive acceptance of blacks into the total fabric of national life. King described integration as "genuine intergroup, interpersonal living." Integration was the long-term goal because it ultimately sought the creation of a genuine national community.[22]

Expressing fundamental disagreement with John Killens's thesis that integration comes only after liberation, King argued that liberation and integration were inseparably linked. Neither could be achieved without the other. King further defined integration in political and ethical terms as "the mutual sharing of power." The only means to liberate black and poor folk from inferior education, legal oppression, substandard housing, and poverty was to integrate them fully into all levels of American life. This, he argued, would require power. King asserted that in struggles for national independence, liberation and integration could be theoretically and sociologically separated. However, when the racially oppressed struggle for justice in a society where the oppressor is of a different race, liberation and integration could not be divorced. Liberation was achievable only through integration.[23]

The beloved or integrated community became, for King, the all-embracing sociopolitical ideal and moral-ethical goal. King never wavered from this idealistic progressive social vision.[24] The notion of community also functioned as a normative prescription for purposive human action, which King applied to the movement for justice in America. Believing that the end of all life ultimately moved toward the actualization of community, King asserted that the aim of the justice struggle must never be to defeat or humiliate whites. Rather, the aim was to win friendships and gain mutual understanding. This was the only way to create a society of justice and peaceful coexistence.[25]

King believed that the struggle to actualize the beloved community in history was, at bottom, a struggle between the forces of justice and injustice, chaos and community, rather than between black and white humanity. Therefore, from the time of Montgomery in 1956, he advocated action that would harmonize the interests of blacks and whites. Since mutual respect must be the basis of integration, at the bus boycott's end, King called for a move "from protest to reconciliation."[26] Again, the normative guide and objective for all revolutionary action was community. Hence, King stated that to work against community is to work against creation itself, the entire cosmic moral foundation. This is why one must not respond reciprocally to hate or

violence. These types of actions intensified the brokenness and fragmentation of community. However, radical agape love acts to heal the
brokenness and restore the unity of community. Appealing to the
sociality of human life and the interrelatedness of reality, King argued
that human personality could only be fulfilled in community. Inflicting harm of any type on another, regardless of that individual's
actions against you, ultimately meant inflicting harm on oneself.
Human life could be adequately sustained only through community.
This communitarian perspective would have important implications
for King's strong advocacy of nonviolent resistance and massive civil
disobedience in the struggle for justice.

## GOD AND THE COMMUNITARIAN ETHIC

The organizing principle for King's communitarian impulse was,
of course, his faith in the radically involved, loving, and redeeming
God of history. King not only believed that God was able to effect
divine purposes in history but he was also convinced that he had
discovered God's ultimate will for humanity. King asserted that as
radical agape love in action, God's primary concern with human
history was the restoration of the beloved human community.[27] King
understood God as radical agape love in action seeking to create,
redeem, sustain, and restore community. Even when purposive human action tries to destroy it, God insists on community, and demonstrated (through the cross of Christ), that no sacrifice was too great
to effect its restoration. Jesus became source and norm for this
communitarian ethic, embodying the communitarian virtues of love,
forgiveness, sacrificial suffering, and risk taking on behalf of justice.[28]
Likewise, the Holy Spirit was the community-creating Spirit that
moved continuously throughout history seeking the restoration of the
human family.[29] Unquestionably, community was the defining eschatological motif in King's theology of radical involvement.

The belief that God's will for humanity was the historical realization of a beloved community remained a consistent and prominent
theme in King's public utterances throughout his twelve years of
public service. King's statement in 1956 that "the end is the creation
of the beloved community" is entirely consistent with his bold claim
in 1967 that humankind was faced with the urgent choice "between

139

chaos and community."[30] God, as radically involved agape love in action, seeking the freedom and justice of humanity was, in the final analysis, working toward universal wholeness and the restoration of the beloved community.[31]

## ETHICS AND ANTHROPOLOGY: *BEING* AND *DOING* AS RECONCILING AGENTS

King's theological perspective was inseparably connected to his ethic. This fact remains crucial to King's ethical perspective for two reasons. First, it both forms and informs his anthropology or how he understood human *being*. Second, the theological-ethical linkage in King's thought provided both form and content for his doctrine of the Christian life. In both cases, the human being is morally obligated to choose a lifestyle of radical involvement in light of the demands of ethical coresponsibility. King held firmly to the belief that each person bore the "indelible stamp of the Creator." Individuals were to be "respected" as members of the one family of God living in the "world house." Every person was deserving of "human freedom"—the capacity to "deliberate, decide, respond."[32] King argued that every act of injustice defaced the image of God in the individual. The consequences of such acts increased the degree of self-alienation as well as separation among and between human beings. Since King also held to the sociality of human life, he identified alienation as a countervailing force that acted to thwart and frustrate efforts at the creation of community.

King held a belief in the interrelated structure of reality in tension with both the morality of the universe and the sacredness, worth, and dignity of human personality.[33] Consequently, he was able to see the connection between oppressed black people and other groups of marginalized poor people in American society. Further, King grasped the connection between oppression in the United States and oppression in other countries around the globe.[34] As King's communitarian ethic matured, he was able to see more clearly the interstructuring of oppression. Subsequently, he was able to make deeper connections between domestic and foreign policy, race and class, war and poverty. By the end of his life, King's communitarian ethic was truly nonsectarian and ecumenical in scope.[35] God, he argued, was interested primarily in the freedom of all persons, not one particular group or race. God desired the creation of a society, a community where all people can live with dignity. Indeed, community was at the very heart of history—mutual cooperation and concern for the other. The universe is so structured, King asserted, that without this impulse of mutual responsibility for others, no individual can fulfill his/her potential. We can become full persons only as we interact with other persons.[36]

Community implied individual freedom to deliberate, decide, and respond.[37] However, freedom, for King, was dialectically linked to responsibility. King embraced an *individual-within-community* model that linked personal liberty to communal consciousness. Genuine community meant the opportunity for each person to develop, mature, realize his or her full potential as children of God, and to be respected as a person of inherent value and worth. Each individual and every institutional structure in society must act responsibly to ensure, as a minimum, that the basic subsistence necessities of all persons were met. For King, concern for the needs of the least advantaged members of society was tantamount to a moral responsibility from which no person, group, or institution could hope to escape. Mutual social concern represented a vital indicator of community.

## COMMUNITARIAN ETHIC AND
## THE CHRISTIAN LIFE

If the chief end of life was "to do the will of God, come what may," the Christian life was to be characterized by purposive response in concert with God's will. Since King understood God's ultimate concern to be coterminous with the restoration of love and justice in human community, his conception of the Christian life was informed by a theological emphasis on radical involvement aimed at the actualization of the good, just, and beloved community. King's emergent communitarian ethic for Christian living placed emphasis on the struggle for justice; the protest against all forms of injustice; the revolutionary consciousness that focused spiritual-moral resources to promote radical action aimed at comprehensive restructuring of social institutions, political ideologies and values, economic struc-

141

tures, and power relationships; the willingness to risk personal safety and to endure suffering in the pursuit of justice; and a lifestyle dedicated to the creation of an integrated, just, and loving human community.

As a first act, King's communitarian ethic insisted upon a moral obligation to engage in personal acts of empathy, compassion, non-possessive warmth, genuineness, and sacrificial self-giving aimed at the concrete actualization of "freedom and justice through love."[38] As a second act, King's communitarian ethic promoted the ideal of community as normatively prescriptive. Radical involvement in both individual lifestyle and corporate action was restrained and guided by the content and focus of community. Every thought, word, and deed was to be judged by its capacity either to enhance or to impede the restoration of alienated and broken human community. King's ethic of community merged both descriptive and normative realities. Descriptively, this ethic functioned as the future goal or theological-philosophical ideal toward which all human life was striving. At the same time, this ethic represented a prescriptive ethical norm that guided and critiqued both individual and corporate behavior.[39] In this sense, community as moral "ought" represented both divine gift and human task.

## LOVE, POWER, AND JUSTICE IN SERVICE TO THE BELOVED COMMUNITY

King acknowledged the presence of sin and evil in interpersonal relationships and corporate structures. There were, in fact, personal and social barriers to the historical actualization of community. King identified those barriers as racism, poverty, and war.[40] King consistently leveled radical, prophetic criticism against racially based, de jure and de facto segregation, poverty, militarism, and materialism. These realities (along with the values, policies, and institutional structures that perpetuated their continued existence) were not only anti-God and anti-Christian, but unequivocally anti-community. King's communitarian ethic emphasized courageous action designed to remedy the impact of alienating, oppressive policies and practices that worked to diminish freedom and deface the image of God in human personhood.[41] Therefore, nothing less than a revolution of values and a radical restructuring of American society was required.

King also affirmed the presence of sin and evil in personal living. He held to the dual nature of human personality—the capacity for both good and evil. While he acknowledged the positive side of humanity, his reading of Reinhold Niebuhr and his experience in the struggle for justice never allowed him to underestimate the radicality and pervasiveness of sin.[42] On the personal level, King specifically stressed moral-spiritual and scientific education as a response to sin and evil.[43] On the corporate level, the social manifestations of sin and evil required the presence of agape love. In the final analysis, King relied upon both a radical analysis of power and a doctrine of loving grace in order to overcome these personal and social barriers to community.[44]

For King, the social power of love operating in society was both morally and sociopolitically redemptive. Having found a unity of love and power seeking justice in his conception of God, King established theological and existential grounds for correlating the redemptive power of love with the just use of power. In this way, King was able to link a conception of "loving power" with that of "just love," to engender a commitment to the actualization of community.[45] Only radical agape love could overcome the forces of social alienation and cultural disintegration. Love was the empowering reality that motivated individuals and groups to pursue reconciliation. Agape love operated on both the personal and social levels to overcome barriers to community.

King believed that the route to the beloved community lay in a right use of power aimed at the establishment of justice.[46] Love was the foundational aspect of justice, but justice was achieved only through the concrete utilization of power. In holding to the close correlation between the three realities of love, power, and justice, King was able to wrest power from its negative connotations.[47] Pointing to a distinction between conscienceless or immoral power and powerless morality, King asserted that the realization of justice would require more than moral suasion alone. It would require the organization, development, and morally sensitive use of power.[48]

King affirmed that God's grace alone was ultimately sufficient to bring about genuine justice. Love was certainly a gift from God. And yet, as freely deliberating, purposive beings, humans, at birth, as-

143

sumed the task to respond to God's historical initiatives to restore community. The human task was to join God in the liberative praxis of radical involvement as coresponsible moral agents of justice and reconciliation, working together to actualize the beloved community in history. Unquestionably, this included the right use of power to achieve justice in a loving community.[49]

## MEANS-ENDS COHERENCE IN KING'S COMMUNITARIAN ETHIC

The ideal vision and pragmatic norm of the beloved community were decisive in shaping King's ethical response to the situation of oppression. In seeking community, King was constrained to demonstrate consistency and moral coherence between the end sought and the method utilized to achieve that end.[50] With respect to the Montgomery bus boycott in 1955, King admitted doubts as to the moral soundness of the method of boycotting. Was it in keeping with Christian values and principles? Even if it were effective in achieving their ends, was it morally defensible as a method? Since community was the goal of the struggle, the question of means and ends was not unimportant. Critically appropriating the nonviolent resistance ethic of Gandhi,[51] King argued that the key to peace and justice in community lay in the capacity to see that means and ends must be coherent in the struggle for freedom. Justice and peace were not distant goals, but means to achieve the goal. The universe was morally coherent. That meant that the end was preexistent in the means. The goal sought must cohere with the method used to achieve that goal. Therefore, one cannot achieve moral ends by using immoral means. Constructive ends cannot be brought about by destructive means. [52]

King also applied the means-ends focus at the level of societal critique to expose the nation's "poverty of the spirit." Pointing to the gulf between the nation's scientific and technological progress on one hand, and its moral regress on the other, King exposed the moral decay in collective American life. As it achieved increased material abundance, it became proportionately impoverished morally and spiritually.[53] King identified the problem of the nation as allowing the technological means by which it lived to outdistance the spiritual ends toward which it had expressed commitment.

The philosophical assent to means-ends coherence found practical expression in King's vigorous and unyielding embrace of nonviolent resistance. Throughout his life of public service, King consistently argued that nonviolence was the only viable method for the oppressed in the struggle for justice, the "only road to freedom."[54] King embraced nonviolence because of its efficacy in achieving the beloved community. For King, violence was both immoral and impractical as a method or means for achieving justice. Its impracticality lies in its predisposition to destroy the very peaceful community it seeks to create. Violence thrives on brutality in its action. Its immorality is in its aims—to humiliate and annihilate the other. Violence sees the other as enemy and is vulnerable to forces of hatred and bitterness. Ultimately, violence destroys community.[55]

For King, a choice of the nonviolent option was clear and unequivocal. The nonviolent option was preferable because it was morally consistent with the goal of the peaceable community.[56] The imperatives of community-building necessitated the use of a nonviolent methodology.[57] The goal was to achieve redemption and reconciliation in human community. Violence was thought unsuitable as a means to this end because it produced only bitterness and alienation.[58] The movement's ultimate goal was integration, which he defined as genuine living on both intergroup and interpersonal levels. King aggressively asserted that this goal was attainable only through the revolutionary public witness of nonviolent direct action.[59]

King applied this principled nonviolence at both the personal and corporate levels of human existence. Internal violence of the spirit and physical violence in the public order were equally self-defeating in their effect on interpersonal, intergroup, national, and international relations. Because King was concerned with the "moral uprightness" and "health of the [nation's] soul," he categorically rejected any attitudinal perspective, value system, or liberation methodology that sanctioned the use of violence or hatred.[60] King held that if the aim was to "make the world and our nation better places to live," the world was in desperate need of "the nonviolent man."[61] The nonviolent personality exhibited the *tridimensional integrativeness* of length, breadth, and height (relationship to God, concern for other, rational self-interest). This individual possessed the capacity to combine the forces of militancy and moderation, love and power, into a new kind of nonviolent power—a "power infused with love and justice."[62] The communitarian ethic, by its very nature, promoted the nonviolent ethic as an integral component in overall content.

In this way Kingian nonviolence must be understood as more than a tactical or strategic method for radically restructuring the social order. Ultimately, for King, nonviolence became a way of life.[63] Until the very end of his life, King was still arguing that the fundamental choice for the nation and the world was "nonviolent coexistence or violent coannihilation . . . chaos or community."[64]

# SUMMARY

King moved fluidly between the boundaries of theology and ethics in his worldview. His theology of radical involvement remained inseparably linked to his communitarian ethic. In fact, his ethic is derivative of his theology. King's ethical orientation emphasized radical social action aimed at the establishment of a beloved community. This community was to be marked by the normative operations of love, justice, and peace. King's ethical method related situational analysis with both his commitment to a radical vision and his stress on radical social action. This communitarian ethic operated on both individual and corporate levels.

On the individual, interpersonal level, the ethic stressed the development of the integrative personality—tridimensional balance between spiritual-moral growth, rational self-interest, and concern for the other. Further, the ethic promoted a lifestyle that stressed personal commitment to nonviolence and solidarity with those who are engaged in the liberative struggle for love, justice, and peace in human community. On the corporate level, King's communitarian ethic legitimated the use of disruptive acts of nonviolent resistance and massive civil disobedience. The intent was to generate a type of creative tension that would compel a decisive confrontation with those forces that would fragment human existence and perpetuate exclusionary practices with regard to blacks, the poor, and other marginalized groups. The ultimate aim of King's communitarian ethic was to effect a radical transformation of American culture in concrete social, political, and economic terms. In this way, the ethic employed both prophetic consciousness and radical involvement in service to the beloved community.

# CHAPTER 6

# THE RELEVANCE OF KING:

## Radical Involvement, Generative Tensions, and Radical Transformation

The relevance and enduring legacy of King can be established only through a clear understanding of his vocational identity. King's resolution of a personal crisis of vocational identity led to an emergent vocational self-understanding as a theologian. King's theological perspective may be best described as a theology of radical involvement. Emerging from a revolutionary context of ideological and existential conflict, King's theological perspective was concerned primarily with moral-spiritual revitalization and sociopolitical-economic reconstruction. On the individual level, it aimed at the resuscitation of the apathetic personality. On the social-communal level, it sought radical, comprehensive institutional-structural transformation.

This resurrectionist thrust emphasized the necessity of moral, social, and political engagement through restorative acts of creative dissent, nonviolent militancy, and sacrificial suffering. King's theology was undergirded by a strong and unwavering commitment to an activist religious faith and provocative moral-spiritual values. As a religionist, he viewed the content and meaning of the Christian faith as essentially a vocational call to radical, emancipatory action aimed at the establishment of freedom and justice in programmatically concrete psychic, sociopolitical, and economic terms. Consequently, his theological program emphasized an extremist, radical brand of involvement in the cosmic struggle against evil and injustice in human community.

Since King's theology was informed by a cosmological wholism that affirmed the interrelatedness of all reality, it is not surprising that his ethical approach emerged naturally from his theology. Radical involvement theology provided the fundamental orientation for King's central ethical concern—the realization of the beloved community of love, justice, and peace. King's ethic, then, might best be understood as a communitarian ethic. Its primary concern was the restructuring of society into relational configurations that would nullify asymmetrical patterns of power sharing, decision making, and resource distribution, production, and consumption. By structuring human relations in accordance with a communitarian moral-ethical vision, King sought to ensure equal access to the community's social, political, and economic goods for all its members—hence, a beloved community. In solidarity with God's active love and power working within history to restore fragmented community, King's communitarian ethic stressed radical, purposive human activity aimed at societal redemption.

What can we learn from this theological and ethical perspective? Having established the vocational identity of King and the content of his thinking, how may we assess the contemporary relevance of King? What did Martin Luther King think, say, and do, and why is it still important for us today? What one sees in King's worldview is a pattern of thought and action that leads to certain generative tensions that emerge as permanent features of his theological-ethical program. Contemporary society will neither grasp the radical character of his intellectual formulation and social activism nor come to fully appreciate his legacy, until King is reread through the lens of the generative tensions present in his thought. This more political reading of King offers a clearer and more profound comprehension of the critical issues he addressed, the scope and magnitude of his radical analysis, the urgency of his prophetic challenge, and the depth, breadth, and boldness of his radical moral vision for America and the world.

King's theology, embodied in a lived commitment to the Christian narrative, makes rather intense moral claims upon the lives of both Christians and non-Christians alike. In the life perspective and public witness of King, one discovers a paradigmatic model for confronting the generative tensions that inevitably surface in all cultures, and that every generation must unavoidably face. It is at those historical moments, where we are able to collectively discern and critically engage these generative tensions, seeking their resolution for our own time, that the relevance of King's perspective is immediately established.[1]

Tension may be understood as a condition of existential strain resulting from the pressure generated in the encounter between oppositional forces. Symptomatically, tension is empirically verified in heightened states of anxiety and stress.[2] Generativity is linked to notions of procreation and productivity. To speak of a reality as "generative" is to acknowledge its power to function as a reproductive agent.[3] Consequently, a "generative tension" is a tension, the presence of which continually re-creates or reproduces a heightened need for resolution. It represents those issues or concerns that arise inevitably at precise points in human history, assertively presenting themselves, seeking resolution to the unsettling psychic stress, moral turbulence, and social conflict that accompany its arrival.

Generative tensions illumine those areas of personal and social human existence where the necessity and challenge for change induce the highest levels of discomfort. As such, they represent those undesirable areas of growth that we least like to face, and are prone, most often, to fastidiously avoid. In the crucible of struggle, situations of crisis and revolutionary possibilities, generative tensions present the urgent demand for searching inventory and difficult choices. Generative tensions scream for definitive resolution regarding which moral values, ethical principles, social and economic policies, political judgments will inform our personal as well as our public actions. Generative tensions call us to either justify or judge the current arrangement of our individual and corporate priorities.

Generative tensions unleash great conscientizing power, arousing a heightened sense of contextual awareness, and inducing moral urgency about pressing personal and social concerns. In this way, generative tensions are necessary for the continued maturation of individuals and communities because they assist in unmasking and demythologizing the illusions, untruths, and false choices that exist in every society. They help us identify and move beyond blind spots, defensive mechanisms, denials, rationalizations, mental gymnastics, and uncritical justifications of our behavior.

A generative tension represents the kairotic moment in the life of a person or community—a time of crisis and demanding choice, where decisions for or against specific options are unavoidable, and where not to choose, is to choose. In this sense, generative tensions represent occasions where opportunity presents itself in the form of choices for either problem or promise, pain or progress.

The creative tensions in King's perspective generated then, as they do now, moments of unavoidable choice between opposing options:

149

spiritual uplift or moral degeneracy, progressivism or traditionalism, redemptive conversion or perpetual decay. This is why King focused so intensely on disciplined moral deliberation and ethical decision making. The generative tensions in his perspective had helped him to clearly discern those conflicting moral, sociopolitical, and economic options emerging in the historical moment. Indeed, King had acutely felt the reality of those tensions in several areas that he subsequently articulated in the public square—nonviolence, integration, the Vietnam War, democratic socialism, the focus on poverty. In fact, King sought to induce creative tension in an effort to force individuals, the church, and the nation to face difficult areas of collective decision making that had materialized as matters of both moral necessity and existential survival.

## GENERATIVE TENSIONS IN THREE
## POSTMODERN PUBLICS

What, then, were these generative tensions that King's theology and ethic raised so acutely for his generation? King's perspective acknowledged the necessity for critical intellectual exchange and collaborative emancipatory action between church and culture. In this sense, it generated significant creative tension between the radical demands of the Christian faith and the hard-core existential realities of modern society. Drawing upon insights from David Tracy, Richard Mouw has perceptively argued that the relevance of the Christian faith is dependent upon its capacity for attentiveness to the real needs and vital human concerns of three publics—the church, the academy, and the society.[4] Stressing the unity of human life, the need for radical liberative participation, and the public moral vision and social dream of the beloved community, King's thought and action raise generative tensions in the three publics of contemporary postmodern culture.

### Crises of Contemporary Postmodern Culture

There is no universal agreement about what constitutes "postmodern culture." As Cornel West observes, the term is used promiscuously to describe a variety of crucial features of contemporary life at differing levels of interpretation—popular, academic, and existential.[5] Following West, I shall use the existential interpretive view of the current crises of our culture as offering the best grasp of the major determinants of postmodern culture. Postmodernity is a complex, multifaceted phenomenon. An exhaustive exploration of postmodernity is beyond the scope of this work. However, I want to lift up two prominent features of postmodern culture, identifying several elements of each feature, for purposes of this discussion. In so doing, I aim to better delineate and understand the fundamental crises of postmodern culture. In turn, I hope to illumine the way in which generative tensions raised by King's perspective and program establish the relevance of his thought and action for the three publics of postmodern culture.

The first prominent feature of postmodern culture relevant to this discussion is the unprecedented impact of market and commercial forces on every facet of American life, especially the everyday lives of ordinary people: careers, professions, values, knowledge, religion, technology, language, music, ideology, politics, and sexuality. The upshot is that a unique capitalist culture has been created in which powerful market forces reduce human beings to a mass of consumption-oriented, pleasure-seeking, addictive personalities.

The powers of decision making, resource distribution, and image production, however, are concentrated in the hands of a small minority of wealthy business corporations, institutional complexes, and managerial elites. These forces are driven fundamentally by a motive of profit maximization. As the corporate mentality meets with the pleasure-seeking consumers through powerful telecommunications networks, individuals' lives become centered around the buying and selling of goods (commodity exchange). This mass commodity consumption is required to satiate the need for pleasure that is stimulated by subtle and insidious marketing strategies used by the purveyors of market values. Fashionability and satiability emerge as new cultural standards. Ideas, clothes, narratives, curricula, food, music, and technological gadgets are judged by their ability to fashionably satisfy the consumer who craves for pleasurable escape from the depersonalizing effects of contemporary postmodern life.

Already wealthy corporations, in turn, benefit from large profits while the consumers pay exorbitant fees to get "fixed," stimulated, and titillated. Consequently, a few corporate elites reap large monetary benefits while the masses are stripped of both financial resources and personal dignity. An increasingly widening gap emerges between

151

haves and have-nots as power, wealth, and profits become concentrated in the hands of a minority at the top of a hierarchically structured culture. One witnesses the breakup of the middle class, the increasing impoverishment of the working poor, and the emergence of a permanent underclass, perpetually marginalized and effectively denied access to the social and political goods of society.

All this points to the second feature of postmodernism, which constitutes a major paradox. As the cultural masses become susceptible and vulnerable to market forces seeking pleasurable release and stimulation, they spend increased amounts of time, energy, and resources trying to achieve what ultimately proves to be elusive. Market forces refuse to be saturated, and the more folk taste and acquire, the more they need and desire. Hence, a perpetual and insatiable fixation on conspicuous consumption aimed at the maximization of pleasure, comfort, and technological convenience. This is testament to the power of raw, market values to seize, subdue, and subtly regulate the thought processes, and decisively shape the values and priorities of consumers. As the messages of the market culture are transmitted continuously, on a daily basis, the culture is able to engender intense loyalty, even from those who suffer most and benefit least from these arrangements of power and wealth. Even the poor and marginalized in the culture often tenaciously defend the "system" as the best of what is possible. While the masses are distracted with matters of survival, market culture stimuli simultaneously provide technological and consumer anodynes that deaden revolutionary sensibilities. As persons become increasingly energized by market forces, the more they become desensitized to ways the culture anesthetizes the analytical impulse.

The second feature of postmodern culture relevant to this discussion, then, highlights the paradox of unprecedented consumer technology existing alongside heightened societal anomie. It speaks to the pervasive and deep levels of moral decay and fragmentation, social-cultural disintegration, and psychic dislocation operating in the culture. Postmodern culture sustains a lack of moral centeredness; the collapse of a commonly held, public vocabulary; and the segmentation of society into distinct, alienated, and xenophobic associative human groupings.

Further, market forces have had a devastating impact on the ability of ordinary working and poor folk to meet basic subsistence necessities. At the same time, we witness the withdrawing of public provisions designed to mitigate the effect of corporate downsizing, increased unemployment, and rising levels of impoverishment. While the culture sustains significant increases in the number of poor, the government plays a decreasing role in public assistance for the needy. Moreover, the master narratives that once guided people's interpretation of reality and provided a way to make sense and meaning of life have been replaced by the seductive, fashionable narratives of the marketplace. And yet, these market-driven narratives lack the power to either provide meaning or to sustain hope in the cultural wasteland. Under different cultural conditions, certainly prior to 1945, the culture was able to produce a common vocabulary, and to maintain certain social-cultural buffers that helped to sustain life, provide love and care, and help folk interpret life in meaningful ways. In the deindustrialized, highly technocratic, postmodern society, the social-cultural buffers—family, church, community, school—that once operated in the culture have sustained serious attack by adversarial commercial forces. Hence, they appear to be crumbling, in serious disarray, and in some cases have virtually collapsed.

We are witnessing the serious erosion of life-sustaining, meaning-making, hope-giving virtues, values, principles, ideas, and ideals. As the market ethos saturates every facet of private and public life, human beings are forced into lives of quiet desperation, constantly underneath a hovering, psychic Damoclean sword. The values of the marketplace become the central guiding force in individuals' lives. Preoccupied with immediate gratification, individuals find it increasingly difficult to embrace and hold on to nonmarket values such as love, commitment, sacrificial self-giving, risk taking, caregiving, honesty, trust, concern, and support for others in their liberation struggle.

Sustaining excruciatingly high levels of misery, people become increasingly desensitized to pain and violence while, at the same time, expressing deep fears about it. One of the ironies of postmodern culture is the contradictory embrace and rejection of violence. Violence is pervasive in postmodern society. On one hand, violence is marketed and sold to American consumers who have developed voracious appetites for its imagery. On the other hand, American consumers fear violence as a prominent feature of life—rape, homicide, robbery, assault, spousal and child abuse, suicide, racial antagonism, crimes of passion, not to mention structural violence inflicted upon the marginalized poor, elderly, and children. Violence is also personal and felt in an immediate sense. Living under the constant threat of violence makes everybody victims, in a sense. Hence, the market culture preys upon its citizens in yet another way by playing to the fear and threat of violence while providing the necessary "hardware" (guns) by which a feeling of psychic safety is induced. The convergence of these varied cultural forces wreaks havoc on the capacity of ordinary folk to survive daily with dignity. They become apathetic persons, politically lethargic, socially withdrawn, victimized by a culture that promotes meaninglessness, hopelessness, and love-lessness.[6]

The insidious and tragic forces of contemporary culture become especially heightened and problematical when pondering the African American postmodern predicament. Along with the normal elements of postmodern culture, blacks face additional and unique pressures and threats to their physical and psychic well-being. Cornel West appropriates the marxist term "nihilism" to describe a sense of detachment and a posture of self-destructiveness many blacks assume toward life. It is the result of trying to cope with a culture devoid of meaning, hope, and love. Again, market forces shatter the social-cultural buffers that once provided meaning, love, care, a feeling of self-worth and dignity, and a sense of future possibilities. However, among a people already devalued, dehumanized, degraded, and marginalized, the impact of capitalistic consumer market forces becomes even more devastating, and black cultural and existential disempowerment occurs to an even greater degree.

Resultantly, the masses of oppressed black folk who are among the poorest of the poor in America, experience escalated levels of destruction and self-destruction, self-devaluation, and contempt. This appears to be especially true among the growing black underclass. In black life in general, deindustrialized market forces drive increasing class divisions between middle-class and working-class blacks. Suicide has increased among blacks at an alarming rate, unprecedented in the history of blacks in America. Homicide, drug addiction, alcoholism, divorce, abuse, rape, assault, robbery, high anxiety rates, the explosion of psychotherapeutic counseling as a resource for psychic survival, and the proliferation of gangs are all symptomatic of black nihilistic despair in postmodern America.

In addition, while the same market values of immediate gratification, stimulation, pleasure, consumption, and the institutionalization of wealth and prosperity are pumped into the black psyche, the normal avenues to achievement remain effectively blocked. The younger generation of blacks becomes especially vulnerable to the market forces of commodification, and more susceptible to what West refers to as a "gangster mentality." Like the corporate successes they see and imitate, the aim is to get by and get over, by any means necessary. Among many young black entrepreneurs, the moral critique tends to drop out of black agency in several ways—the exploitative use of black women's bodies by some rap artists, or the seemingly indiscriminate ease with which some blacks kill other blacks over drug turf, for example. In both cases, the devaluation and commodification of black life is market-driven in the black postmodern context.[7]

The convergence of these multiple forces produces a cultural context within which King's perspective proves to be highly relevant. As it raises generative tensions in the three postmodern publics, King's worldview also offers significant clues for responding to contemporary societal crises.

## Generative Tensions in the Ecclesial Public

In the ecclesial public, King's theological-ethical perspective challenged religion and the church to an involvement in efforts at shaping public ethos and public policy. As the moral guardian of society and the social factor of salvation, the church became the custodian of moral values and virtues that were seminal in the formation of Christian character. As a radically involved community of faith, the church must seek to shape the outlook and direction of the social order. For King, the axis of tension revolved around the role of the church in both character formation and the actualization of justice in human community.

In today's postmodern culture, King's theology challenges the church and individual Christians to take seriously the radical nature of the faith and its accompanying call to costly involvement in overcoming barriers to the restoration of human community. Will their loyalties be adjudicated in allegiance to the forces of sin, evil, and injustice or the forces of justice and morality? In King's own phraseology, the issue is whether or not and to what extent the ecclesial public chooses either "chaos or community."[8] Understanding the

155

essence of God, the gospel, and human life as freedom, King challenged the church to deal with how its words and actions either enhance or impede the realization of freedom, justice, love, and peace.

The creative tension that King raised focuses on the ethical commitment of the church. In a time of great debate on the pressing issues of the day, is the church a guardian of the status quo or does it possess the revolutionary spirit of Christ that challenges the status quo in a way that makes it tremble? If commitment to the Christian faith and the gospel of Christ means anything, it cannot evade those important and difficult practical human choices. Relative to the ordering of human community, that means concrete and specific choices for or against communism and capitalism, egalitarianism and hierarchialism, narrow sectarianism or public engagement. All attempts at ecclesial neutrality in situations of social crisis will only sanction preexistent states of moral-spiritual and theological impoverishment. King clearly understood the essence of the gospel as a radical, prophetic call to the church to get its hands soiled (and upon occasion, bloodied if necessary) in the justice struggle. He believed that the church could not keep its hands clean in the revolutionary situation of emancipatory struggle and remain true to its mission. If the church would be the church, it must avoid apathy, abandon all attempts at situational neutrality, and face the problem of dirty hands. The church simply had to decide whether its real identity and conscience lay in its pocketbook or in the prophetic, Christian narrative. For King, the church had to confront and resolve its own identity crisis.

The past presidential candidacies of Jesse Jackson and Pat Robertson (along with the rise of the Religious Right and the Moral Majority of Jerry Falwell and others) press the issue of ecclesial engagement to a level of urgency that it enjoyed during King's day. Leaving aside the ideological and theological content of these movements, they have at least publicly answered King's concern about the role of the church in the reconstruction of society. Like King, they have reminded us that the church does *not* enjoy the luxury of deciding whether it will be involved in societal matters. The church's involvement in the important issues of its day has never been optional. Rather, the only remaining issue is a collective decision about the form of public witness the church thinks most socially and politically pragmatic and morally resonant with Christian values and principles.[9] While some see ecclesial political involvement as perhaps extreme, King reminds us that the question is not whether we are either for or against extremist behavior. In a revolutionary situation, such pro or con arguments become vain and fruitless. The questions King will not allow us to avoid are these: "What kind of extremists will we be? Will we be extremists for love or hate, justice or injustice?"[10]

Like Calvin in Geneva in the 1500s, King in the 1950s and 1960s did not sanction ministers' becoming professional politicians. However, he both understood and approved of the unique role that many black ministers (and some white ministers) had assumed throughout the black experience of struggle in America. And yet, he saw the necessity of the church to become a major participant, radically involved in the reconstruction of society. Consequently, King was openly willing to qualify notions concerning the separation of church and state.[11] It is worth remembering that King's deepest publicly stated disappointment concerned the church's failure to radically involve itself in the freedom struggle. At issue was how the church might avoid becoming a major disappointment to God. In a word, King challenged the church to deal with its "loss of prophetic consciousness."[12]

Part of the creative tension generated by King is how the church can recapture its prophetic spirit. In postmodern times, the church must offer more than rhetoric and individual security. It has to decide if it is interested in becoming the truly revolutionary community it is called to be at this time. Such a decision involves a change in its vision and method. It has to be concerned about addressing institutional-structural realities as well as personal salvation. It has to offer a relevant word about power, wealth, and culture utilizing the tools of systems analysis. It has to be willing to promote and to engage in serious intellectual as well as moral-spiritual warfare. In addition to providing moral vision and values, the church simply cannot avoid an inescapable responsibility to be the organizational basis for social-political and educational activity. While the church provides anchoring amid social disintegration and loss of hope, it must also provide concrete, programmatic strategy and action designed to achieve the reconstruction of culture.

Like Karl Barth, King understood that a primary task of theology was to provide a critical self-test for the church.[13] Since the mark of maturity is the capacity to undergo self-criticism, King's perspective

157

challenges the church to come of age and demonstrate signs of theological and ethical maturity. Indeed, the very nature of radical involvement theology generated a tension that demanded the church's continuing critique of the nature of its public witness. This kind of ecclesial interrogation remains equally relevant for the contemporary church as well. We must ask whether or not the church is capable of honest self-assessment. Can it acknowledge its duplicity in the perpetuation of alienating, chaotic, and fragmenting ideologies and institutional practices? Can the church divest itself of ideological collusion with the state? Does the church possess the spiritual-moral resources necessary to resist the dangerous seductiveness of the postmodern market culture? Does the church have the moral courage required to assume the lead in societal transformation? Does the church really want to tap into the tradition of prophetic, subversive memory that fosters radical dissent? Or is it content to rest comfortably in the fog of historical amnesia, disengaged and disinterested in matters of cultural survival and social change?

King's challenge to the church was to recommit itself to that to which God and the very structure of the universe are committed—the restoration of the just and beloved human community. In light of that challenge, we are constrained to investigate the extent to which the church fully participates in the continuing struggle for all people's opportunity to live free from the tyrannies of poverty and want, fear and discrimination, and free to develop their vast, God-given potentialities of mind, body, and spirit. Beset by internal conflicts and often ignored by culture, we must now honestly face some serious questions about the relevance of the church in today's world.

As a beginning, the church is challenged to recover the visual acuity to discern and the moral courage to affirm and pursue justice and peace as that goal and mission to which it is called by the God of the Christian Gospels. The publicly activistic nature of true religion demands that the spiritual-moral content of the faith is infused with a complementary sense of the necessity of social-political engagement. The challenge is to balance the important, powerful message of hope and meaning with the challenging message of the need for radical involvement. This challenge speaks to the heart of the generative tension in King's program: a recognition that sin is rooted in systems and corporate structures (a powerful truth in light of the racism scandals at Texaco and Avis Rent A Car as well as the sexual harassment scandals in the army and navy) as well as in the individual personality.

Consequently, the tension for us has to do with how we are able to address the balance between moral vision and moral outrage, the connection between spiritual awareness and social action. The church certainly has to concern itself with consciousness-raising and training in the moral virtues of love, faith, hope, justice, prudence or temperance, courage, and wisdom. And yet, King's description of the church as a "colony of dissenters" moved beyond merely an emphasis on the formation of Christian character. It also had to do with an emphasis on participation in the historical, public drama of the freedom struggle. This emphasis carries important implications for an insistence on courageous moral action as an unimpeachable component of Christian discipleship. The church simply cannot justify glaring inconsistencies between speech and action, rhetoric and practice.

Here, generative tensions challenge the ecclesial public's capacity to continually examine its motives and its practices. If revolutionary efforts to overthrow oppressive and exploitative political and economic systems are to be viewed as a Christian duty and a moral responsibility, then the tension between ecclesial involvement and ecclesial apathy is sharply emergent.

In this sense, the postmodern church (and especially the black postmodern church) is left contemplating the importance of discerning relevant aspects of the Christian faith and human living that are too often ignored in traditional religion. In light of the church's three fold task of kerygma (proclamation of the good news of the gospel), koinonia (nurturance of fellowship and community), and diakonia (service to humankind), King's perspective of radical involvement acutely raises the issue of how "radical" or "revolutionary" the church is prepared to be. Carrying out important ecclesial tasks must be done in light of the radical, revolutionary nature of a religion that has always had the tradition of principled prophetism woven tightly throughout its intellectual fabric. As a socially active force for moral and political good, the Christian faith requires the pronouncement of a radical critique upon the culture of its day. The real mood of the Christian gospel, King reminds us, has turned "upside down" customs and practices that run contrary to its true spirit of justice, love, and peace.

159

The church is challenged to come to terms with just how true to the gospel it will be. Does the church possess the necessary "soul" to embrace the corporate ethos and lifestyle demanded of a radically involved community of faith? King's perspective will not allow the ecclesial community to escape the responsibility of making hard choices about the content, goals, and methods of its present-day agenda. Either the church will choose an agenda that is explicitly concerned about personal and social empowerment or it will be irrelevant as a force for sustenance, hope, and meaning in the twenty-first century. Ultimately, the church has to decide whether it will be an *instrument* or merely a *symbol* of the liberative struggle for freedom and justice in human community.

## Generative Tensions in the Academic Public

In the academic public, King's perspective generates tension around some of the prominent issues facing ministerial training today. Specifically, what some scholars have identified as "the crisis in theological education" must be addressed.[14] Simply put, the crisis speaks to the more fundamental issue of ascertaining "what it means to be a Christian minister in our time."[15] In this regard, David Kelsey correctly points out that the issues of "living the faith" relative to the seminary involve a resolution of the debate about "theological education vs. education for ministry."[16]

At stake is the resolution of a new form of the resurgent theoria-praxis debate. However, we are also faced with the issue of whether or not the academic preparation of future Christian ministers (in light of the crises of American religion in general and theological education in particular) can give serious intellectual attention to a more holistic concept of ministry.[17] Does the conception of vocation and existential orientation of faculties, along with institutional curricula, address those critical ministerial competencies that are most required in the crisis-laden postmodern context? How relevant is the program of academic preparation to the vicissitudes of everyday living? What kinds of minds are being produced in academia? What is the correlation between the intellectual agendas these minds absorb in the aseptic schoolhouse and the existential agendas they will confront in the battle-scarred neighborhood?

As a treatise against apathy and an oppositional force against the stagnancy of theological, political, social, and economic conservatism,

King's theology of radical involvement placed heavy stress on the nature and role of the prophetic in the doing of theology. Theological education today, in response to the Kingian approach, must reconsider its relationship to the demands of social ministry. As a perspective that advocates radical involvement for the purposes of social change, King's theology places squarely before us the issues of focus and method in the education of ministers.

Ministerial focus concerns that which receives the highest level of attention. Simply put, it is a matter of priorities. To affirm religion as an integral feature of all aspects of life is to admit the need for an educational experience that will equip prospective ministers for a "socially responsible ministry." As King reminds us, ministry involves "lived Christian practice . . . rooted in spirituality and love, guided by the vision of shalom," "social analysis and consciousness of the ethos in which we live," a "radical critique of society," "personal, institutional, and ecclesial self-critique," "praxis or struggle for liberation of the oppressed," "doing justice, making peace, and caring for creation," and "critical analysis and institutional reform."[18]

Ministry that purports to heighten consciousness with regard to social activism must also deal with the issue of theological method. To be a relevant force in society, theology must clearly define the nature and task of its existence. King's theology emerged from commitment to a radical faith that was concerned not only with humanity's moral-spiritual, but also its sociopolitical existence as well. Since traditional splits of secular-sacred, spiritual-material, public-private, personal-social represented false dichotomies, King affirmed the moral necessity of religion to be attentive to mundane affairs. In so doing, his perspective creates tension about the starting point of the theological enterprise.

As a matter of method, one's point of departure for doing theology is extremely important. To a great extent, it is determinative of the focus of one's theology, the issues and questions one's theology raises, and the answers it proposes. King's theology and ethic took their points of departure from the undeniable, concrete predicament of massive human suffering and social dislocation. Racism, poverty, and war—King's triple evils—provided the points of departure for King's emergent perspective. It was through these "windows of particularity" that King attempted to offer a public word about God. In this sense, King used the view from these narrow windows to help illumine a

161

broader picture of the mysterious ways of God at work in a fallen and fragmented world.

Thus, King spoke directly to the particular versus universal tension present in all theology.[19] He reminds us that theological speech that references the universalist redemptive claims of God and the gospel is always asserted against the backdrop of human frailty and sin. Moreover, the human condition is discernible only in and through particular situations of human living. Theology cannot be heard by everyone (universal) until and unless it can speak a word to and for someone (particular). King's thought celebrates the universal-particular tension, and resolves it by affirming the particular as the only valid starting point for doing theology.

Likewise, King's ethic emerged from the crucible of broken community and the tragic character of human existence. Like Tillich, King held to the dialectical tension between the Cross and the Resurrection.[20] If Easter and the resurrected possibilities for communal restoration held any vibrancy or vitality, it would be through (not around) the sociopolitical alienation represented by Good Friday's pseudotriumphalism. The beloved community as moral-ethical mandate would be heard only to the extent that it spoke clearly and forcefully to issues of estrangement and disintegration. King's method was to allow the suffering of broken humanity to speak for itself, on its own terms, in its own way. His perspective attempted to give voice to the unspoken, silent suffering of the marginalized masses as he sought to move issues of pain and fragmentation from the periphery to the center of theological discourse and ethical deliberation. Further, King's reading of the biblical text moved from experience-to-text-to-experience predating the action-reflection model of liberation theology. To speak the truth about what God was doing in the revolutionary situation meant delivering a word of hope in the midst of a dynamic confrontation between forces of life and death, sanity and insanity.

In this way, King ascribed theological status to the problems of the day, raising issues of racism, poverty, and war as fundamental theological-moral problems to be solved not only at the level of politics but also at the level of faith and spirituality. His ethical proscriptions took the form of a universalist, internationalist moral vision, which, at the same time, was remarkably specific to the national context. In concrete programmatic terms, community also meant a particular societal arrangement of shared social goods.[21] In this sense, King was pragmatic, and challenged the postmodern intellectual (especially the black postmodern intellectual) to connect critical thinking to engaged, oppositional praxis in particular situations of dehumanization and exploitative manipulation.

The tensions regarding methodology, point of departure, and particularity versus universality in King's theology are also raised for the postmodern sojourner. How are we to speak of God in a broken, suffering world? From whence does our God-talk take its point of departure? For whom is theology done? To whom and for whom does it speak? For what purpose? At whose cost? For whose benefit? At a minimum, King forces us to deal with the fact of the contextual situatedness of all theology. The subjective nature of theology means that one has to be both deliberate and honest about where one begins one's theology.

Of equal importance is the question of focus. What are the seminal issues that drive one's theology? Undeniably, the dominant, popular theology continues to remain captive to the interests of those in power (academic, corporate, political, and financial elites). How will our theology speak to the needs of those least able to fend for and defend themselves against the power brokers of society? The tension King raises centers around the issue of whether or not our theology, and subsequently our ethic, speaks *to* or *for* power. Certainly, we must be suspicious of theology that is written for those who enjoy unlimited access to bombs, guns, planes, and money. Is our theology handicapped by an insensitivity to the existential dilemmas of daily living? Does our theology have the capacity to "speak the truth to power with humility"? Our theology has to face and respond to these generative tensions.

King's conception of a socially active Christianity affects the academic public of the seminary at a deep, existential level because it insists upon a method of correlation as the most viable methodology available for doing theology. If theology really is the *logos* about the *theos* (a pregnant word about God) King reminds us, it is also a word about radically involved agape love seeking the fulfillment of human potential in a particular, historical community. God is to be esteemed above and beyond the limits and vagaries of the created order (though not deistically detached from it). At the same time, God is to be linked to the created order (though not pantheistically coterminous with it). Theology is not merely a word *about* God. Theology is also a word *from* God *to* a fallen world. Like the church, the academy must decide what kind of theology it will do. The academic public has to decide whether its intellectual agenda will promote relevant critical analysis and pragmatic engagement with the felt existential crises of postmodernity. At issue is whether or not the academy can move beyond the more self-serving needs of what Cornel West has referred to as "Alexandrian cynicism," "flaccid careerism," "flagrant denominationalism," and "mediocre professionalism."[22]

### Generative Tensions in the Cultural Public

In the broader cultural public, generative tension arises in King with regard to what H. Richard Niebuhr has already identified as the "enduring problem of Christ and culture."[23] Niebuhr defined culture as

> that total process of human activity and that total result of such activity. . . . Culture is the "artificial secondary environment" which man superimposes on the natural. It comprises language, habits, ideas, beliefs, customs, social organization, inherited artifacts, technical processes, and values . . . to which Christians like other men [sic] are inevitably subject.[24]

If Christians are to culture as fish are to water, how one adjudicates between the competing claims and loyalties of Christ on the one hand and culture on the other hand represents an issue of great importance. How does one resolve conflicts between the proximate loyalties of culture (family, job, nation), and ultimate loyalty to the gospel of Jesus Christ?

# CULTURAL PARTICULARITIES: THREE GENERATIVE TENSION AREAS IN KING'S THOUGHT

To the cultural public, King's theology and ethic raise creative tension in several areas. I shall present and briefly describe three such areas: values, personal lifestyle, and societal ordering. By no means are these meant to be exhaustive. I merely want to suggest these areas as indicative of how King's perspective, in fact, appears to generate tensions for the postmodern era.

*Values*

King repeatedly warned America and the world about the need for a revolution of values. The caveat was indicative of King's concern with moral harmonization between the universal principles of justice, love, peace, nonviolence, and democracy and those values that operated to guide human action. The generative tension in this area has to do with the nature of choice with regard to those fundamental norms or moral principles that orient, motivate, and guide the construction of human community.

The tension in this area has implications for both the individual citizen and the broader society. Personal and social values determine, to a large extent, the agenda, priorities, and ends for which persons, institutions, groups, and societies live. King was not "against" culture. He recognized the marvelous accomplishments that human beings had made throughout history. However, he was highly critical of many of the prevailing values and practices of his day. His perspective advocated the critical affirmation and reappropriation of the best of culture (e.g., democracy, rights, representative government, and so forth). Conversely, King sought to emphasize the role of the Christian faith in the shaping of moral values and norms in the public domain. In this way, he had hoped to affect the direction in which the communal ethos and public policy were subsequently oriented. Likewise, he was intent on having a direct impact upon the manner in which corporate institutions operated in the social sphere. Arguing that the gospel had social and political relevance, King mounted a sustained, prophetic critique against the cultural values of hedonistic materialism, conspicuous consumerism, political and economic individualism, and jingoistic militarism.

King's focus on corporate values and virtues (public piety) elevated tension around which basic, communal beliefs and norms can be agreed upon to serve as moral coordinates or ethical blueprints for how we conceptualize our common life together as a Judeo-Christian nation dealing with the realities of cultural, religious, and ideological pluralism. What moral-ethical code will guide our modalities of thinking about the way we understand and structure our interpersonal and communal relationships? What anthropological assumptions do we sanction? Is human life sacred? Are all persons deserving of worth and dignity regardless of rank, station, education, or income? Are people to be commodified and "thingified" in a market culture that reduces persons to disposable units? On what grounds is the treatment of people as means to commercial ends ever justifiable? What about competing notions of the communal ideal? What values mark our vision for community? Inclusivity? Diversity? Egalitarianism? How do we view the plight of the poor, unemployed, underutilized, and disadvantaged? Do we bear any collective responsibility for their welfare? Do we value human life enough to seek remedies to human misery? What are our guiding values? Are they justice, love, utility, personal security and self-aggrandizement, power, money, maximization of profit?

A brief look at the prevalence of violence in American culture highlights the relevance of King's focus on values. In today's accepted "culture of violence," King raises very sharply the tension between principled pacifism or absolutist nonviolent philosophy and self-defense on the personal, societal, and national levels.[25] H. Rap Brown's requiem on American culture amounted to the undisputable claim that "America is as violent as cherry pie."[26] Stokely Carmichael further asserted that due to the systemic, institutional nature of violence in America, the debate between violence versus nonviolence had become irrelevant.[27] Floyd McKissick argued in 1967 that nonviolence had become a thing of the past totally unsuited to the demands of future liberation struggle in America.[28]

In light of these analyses, how do we assess the cogency of King's assertion that the ultimate choice we face is nonviolence or nonexistence? In a world where persons are victimized and assaulted daily through structural violence endemic to the culture (e.g., police brutality, or under- and unemployment that breed massive, cyclical poverty, and hence the inability to access basic subsistence necessities or participate in making decisions that affect one's destiny); in a culture where violence in mass media representation is valorized and virtually enshrined as a way of life; in a society marked by proliferating gang violence and a gunslinging, gangster mentality that encourages citizens to arm themselves at alarming levels; in a world of geopolitical unrest, ethnic civil wars, clashes and conflicts between national self-interests (e.g., the Gulf War of the early 1990s), crucial questions must be raised and answered. In a world such as this, what does it mean to speak of nonviolence? Is it possible to live nonviolently in such a violent society? What values should we teach our children about the right to self-defense, the justice of war, or the nonviolent ethic? Can the possession and use of weapons of mass destruction be morally justified, even for purposes of national defense? What does a categorical rejection of violence and war mean in a world where not only violence, but also the threat of violence and conflict remain all too real and commonplace?[29]

The challenge of King's advocacy of nonviolence is apparently quite radical in this regard. A categorical rejection of claims that advocate the moral justification of violence (in a world whose cosmic fingerprint traces the cruelest expressions of inhumane and barbarous treatment) is to cut against the very grain of reality as we know it.[30] King argues that we are obligated to apply responsible moral critiques against acts of personal and systemic violence in any form. Further, King does not allow us to escape a collective responsibility to explore philosophical and strategic alternatives to violence.

Kingian thought pushes us to raise hard questions about those seminal societal values we embrace and perpetuate. In a market culture driven by notions of excessive narcissism and egoistic acquisitivism, what does it mean to speak of a "revolution of values"? How can we critique and transform fundamental values so that they enhance our collective capacity to achieve love, justice, and peace in community? King's reliance upon the traditions of cultural criticism (black tradition of radical critique and protest, instrumental Marxism, democratic socialism, and the social gospel, among others) points to a way out of the maze of our own moral crisis. As a public moralist, attempting to deal with communal norms and values, King challenged us to come to terms with the correlation between our professed moral values and our operative sociopolitical-economic practices. The creative tension in King raises serious doubts about whether or not we can legitimately expect lasting political, social, or economic transformation apart from a prerequisite revolution of bedrock cultural values. In this way, King highlights the inescapable tension between the moral and political dimensions of culture.

### Personal Lifestyle

The focus on values revolution is related to another area of generative tension in Kingian thought—personal lifestyle. In view of King's anthropological assertions and conception of the Christian

167

life, the creative tension present in the choice between apathy and radical involvement is illumined. His faith commitment to the tradition of prophetic Christianity and his analysis of the demands of the contemporary situation led King to a particular discernment about the moral requirements for radical involvement in human affairs. King wanted citizens (both Christians and non-Christians) to take seriously the dialectical tension between personal moral renewal and collective moral conversion, private metanoia and public transformation. In King's radical faith, the locus of tension is found at the intersection between the vectors of inner, contemplative spirituality and outer, prophetic social action.

In this sense, King's perspective and program raise uncomfortable questions about the dangerous inclination of individuals to sacrifice redemptive potential at the altars of excessive individualism, exaggerated egoism, and narcissistic self-aggrandizement. To what extent does the culture predispose persons to cooperate with their own enslavement to the mythology of self-reliance? When King raises the issue of moral choice between egoism and altruism or self-preservation and neighbor-love, he is essentially raising the issue of lifestyle orientation. We have to consider the multifarious, subtle ways we are each seduced and manipulated daily to embrace styles of living in pursuit of hollow, superficial, and morally bankrupt ends.

Together, King's emphasis on values and lifestyle reminds us that whether rich or poor, members of the middle class or the permanent underclass, we are each of us fallen creatures who live in a fallen world. We live our lives in contradiction, often compromising right for wrong and truth for expediency. Each of us is prone too often to choose lesser goods when greater goods present themselves. Even when we have known what was right, true, and good, we have too often failed, as individuals and groups, to do it. King affirmed what James Baldwin once reminded his nephew—that although folks "know better . . . people find it difficult to act on what they know."[31]

King advocates that we take the extent, intransigence, and virulence of sin seriously, but that we also take responsibility for the decisions and actions over which we can exercise control. In our self-negotiations about how we will live complete, integrative lifestyles, King never allows us the luxury of forgetting that we must be equally attentive to the tridimensional concerns for God, self, and other. In matters of personal living, King challenges us to hold the tension between love of God and love of neighbor. For the Christian especially, King offers the life and ministry of Jesus Christ as the definitive statement about the moral requirement to hold both beams of the cross in dialectical tension—vertical and horizontal, pastoral-priestly and prophetic. A lifestyle that refuses to sever either aspect is required in revolutionary situations of injustice, brokenness, meaninglessness, and despair. The question is explicitly raised: "Will our lifestyle promote the virtues of selfishness or a communal consciousness that pursues a concern for freedom and justice? How closely will our styles of living conform to the moral dictates of the gospel?"

In today's culture, we are challenged to embrace personal lifestyles that embody the principles of compassion and egalitarianism. How, then, ought we to live in light of the "isms of separatedness" so prevalent in our society—sexism, racism, classism, other xenophobic forms of elitism, and hierarchialism? The first aspect of the tension in personal lifestyle concerns how one models certain values, virtues, and principles of love, justice, and peace in relationship with and treatment of others. The second aspect of the tension in personal lifestyle has to do with the extent to which we are committed to live for others. This altruistic emphasis in King is tempered and heightened by the view that "good Samaritan neighbor-love" (not to be equated with acts of pity, condescension, or paternalism) insists upon "cross-bearing" as an indispensable part of integrative living. To live for others in a revolutionary situation, and to combat sin and evil proactively in both interpersonal and social dimensions require the acceptance of a moral challenge and responsibility to live life in what Martin E. Marty calls a "risked mode of living."[32]

To do justice, love mercy, and walk humbly with God will ultimately entail risk taking. Tension is bound to be generated when the personal concerns of job, career, family, personal fulfillment, and security clash with the more publicly focused concerns of justice and love. The challenge for the individual, church and nation is to enable personal objectives to make peace with public ones. Much has been written about the captivity of the human spirit to ideological currents in the contemporary American situation. The upshot has been a capitulation toward apathy and complacent conformity with the way things are.[33] This is especially true of middle-class consciousness.[34] And yet, King reminded us that a lifestyle marked by radical involvement and commitment to the actualization of a just and beloved community may not, in essence, be a happy one. The "risked mode" of prophetic living requires standing in the marketplace of deception and speaking truth about the human condition. This public presentation has historically exacted heavy tolls on psychic, emotional, and physical well-being. Guarantees of personal safety will always remain tenuous in these circumstances. The fundamental question is whether or not we are prepared to pay the cost in orienting our personal lifestyles that is required of a coparticipating agent in God's restoration of the human community.

King admitted that this lifestyle requires moving beyond token gestures and individual acts of moralistic philanthropy based on notions of pity. Personal, sacrificial suffering through the dogged emancipatory praxis of nonviolent civil resistance becomes both a moral and a political necessity. This meant that some might suffer the loss of home, family, property, power, prestige, security, and possibly life itself. King's perspective continues to ask whether or not any of us are ready, willing, and able to pay the price to achieve the justice we claim we desire.

*Societal Ordering*

Finally, King's theological-ethical focus generates tension in the area of societal ordering. In light of the compelling values (freedom, justice, egalitarianism, democracy) and lifestyle (radically involved, risked modality of thought and action) that King advocated, postmodern society must face the responsibility of deciding for or against the beloved community. In the vision of King, we are presented with the unavoidable tension between present and future, is and ought, real and ideal, already and not yet.

Several related issues emerge. First, the issue of membership. American society has to finally decide the matter of who's in and who's out. In view of increasing cultural pluralism and diversity (that cuts across religious, racial-ethnic, gender, ideological, and class lines) we now must collectively grapple with how to structure a society that will ensure justice and maximization of democratic participation. We have to provide citizens wider access to the channels of power and decision making. Moreover, we have to make room for the poor, marginalized, and disfranchised to have a voice in the decisions that affect their lives.

King asserted that the measure of a nation's greatness lies in its capacity to be sensitive to the needs of the "least of these." In this assertion lies a moral challenge for America to assess her treatment of the voiceless, powerless masses who are least able to defend their dignity or to lay claim to their rights as citizens. The level of tension is elevated significantly when King insists that salvation in the public realm cannot take place apart from the renewal of hope. Society has to be concerned about those who are still deprived of the opportunity and resources with which to achieve a livable dignity. In this regard, the nation has to come to terms with the problematical issues of racism, sexism, and other "isms" of separatedness. The rising trends in racial tensions and conflict—confirmed by the Rodney King beating and the Yusef Hawkins murder; among schools and college campuses like Michigan, Alabama, and Stanford; in communities like South Central Los Angeles, Howard Beach (New York), Liberty City and St. Petersburg (Florida), and Virginia Beach; and in boardrooms like Texaco and Avis—have empirically verified America's continuing racial crisis. These incidents validate what C. Eric Lincoln said over a decade earlier about the nation's deep-rooted and pervasive racial xenophobia.[35]

Recent published analyses by ad hoc commissions and cultural critics continue to serve notice that racism is flourishing in the national body politic.[36] Moreover, the matter of gender bias and discrimination (to which King was less sensitive than issues of race and class) remains a cancerous malignancy on the society's historical ledger.[37] King challenged individuals, churches, and the nation to confront and deal with racist philosophies, social policies, and institutional practices. It is a well-documented and undeniable fact that we are currently facing the very same "impasse" in race relations that King addressed in his day. Vital indicators in the areas of housing, education, employment, infant mortality, and health care reveal that blacks have statistically regressed since King's assassination in 1968.[38] If the nation is to be redeemed, King reminds us, it must accept a moral and political responsibility to address the issues of membership and inclusion. Given the intransigence of racism and sexism in America, the creative tension between chaos and community continues to assert itself and to seek definitive resolution.

Second, tension in the area of societal ordering involves the issue of agenda prioritization. How will the nation address the thornier

171

issues attendant to the production, ownership, and distribution of societal resources and goods? Probing questions about the content and quality of society's public moral vision must be explicitly raised. At this point, King's critique of capitalism and its concomitant ideological framework of values and ends is instructive. The nation's challenge is to decide whether it will be guided by a concern for the maximization of profit and the acquisition of material comfort at the expense of developing its human potential and pursuing the quest for relative social justice.

This involves questions about spending priorities as well. King's criticism of foreign policy in Vietnam, for instance, carried the perceptive insight that foreign and domestic policy were inseparably linked. Defense spending in the hegemonic military-industrial complex had ominous consequences for the quality of life of millions of poor- and working-class Americans. An honest look at America's last decade reveals the undeniable truth that America has placed most of its economic eggs in the basket of foreign policy, and embraced "peace through strength" military initiatives. Bulging defense budgets have shunted badly needed fiscal resources away from critical areas of domestic need. Undeniably, this has had a devastating impact on masses of elderly, poor, illiterate, semiskilled, untrained, jobless, and homeless Americans.[39] King's focus on the issues of housing, education, guaranteed annual income, employment, and poverty are highly germane to a discussion about where America will channel the greatest proportion of its massive resources. The tension remains for us to decide where our spending priorities will be, at whose cost, and for whose benefit.

Further, hard choices must be made about the form of political and economic structuring that would more justly distribute wealth and opportunity, thereby effectively eliminating incongruous poverty in the land of plenty. It is not accidental that King described himself as a "democratic socialist."[40] King's analysis of capitalism had led to the conclusion that it was incapable of providing the necessary structure for the actualization of economic justice or the alleviation of poverty. Linking racial justice to comprehensive economic restructuring, King was able to move beyond the boundaries of race to a consideration of poverty and class. King's efforts to organize a "Poor People's Campaign" amounted to a symbolic public presentation of radical involvement's efforts to call attention to shameful economic deprivation in affluent America.[41]

At this point, King's understanding of the systemic nature of the theological and ethical task becomes evident.[42] If religion would be relevant to the vital concerns and issues of the day, it must address the totality of human needs, including economic and sociopolitical ones. With regard to the multiplicity of pressing social problems, King was able to see what others both before and after him had also argued— that as important as race and gender issues were and are, these will never be addressed in any significant manner without simultaneously addressing the issue of class.[43] So long as economic justice proved to be elusive, so too would the quest for racial justice and gender equality.

Postmodern America cannot casually dismiss King's bold assertion that the entire economic edifice of America required radical restructuring. It now seems unarguably clear that apart from the elimination of poverty, racism and sexism will never be fully resolved. Can the case be made convincingly that poverty will never be eliminated in America without the radical restructuring of monopoly capitalism? These are issues that require serious consideration at the levels of national forum and public debate. In the wake of the disintegration of the Soviet Union, the death knell for socialism has been pronounced by proponents of democratic capitalism.[44] And yet, Americans appear to have a penchant for confusing socialism with communism. The two are hardly synonymous, although some historical connectionality is certainly evidenced.[45] It may well be the case that some combined form of capitalism-socialism will be needed to address the massive problems of poverty, national debt, inflation, recession, deindustrialization and joblessness in America. In any case, Kingian perspective calls the nation (and especially the church) to understand the tradition King was relating to when he (in assessing the role of religion in sociopolitical-economic conflict) affirmed democratic socialism as the most viable approach for achieving economic and social justice.[46]

The currently adjourned debate on national health care insurance promoted by the Clinton administration is a prime case in point. The current health care system has failed to guarantee all citizens equal access to adequate health care. Is a health delivery system in the form of socialized medicine now required at this point in the nation's life? Will the current system require comprehensive restructuring? Can we ensure all Americans adequate health care under the present system of "democratic capitalism"? King had already begun to raise these questions during the final years of his public ministry, and his continuing legacy presses us to give them due consideration at this time in the nation's history. In fact, King's concern with societal ordering reveals the public nature of his theological-ethical program, and raises sharply the creative tension between private faith and public responsibility.[47]

## Summary

Heinz Dietrich Wendland has argued that relative to the social crises of contemporary society, the theologian is required to offer, "not a new language, but a new involvement in those places in the world where God is most dynamically at work. . . ."[48] Unquestionably, King's approach sanctioned intensive intellectual and existential participation in the effort to respond prudently to the radical demands of the Christian faith. Probing the radical elements in King's theological and ethical framework reveals a decided emphasis upon a new type of radical involvement in the world. Tenacious commitment to a belief in the inseparability of faith and action pulled King into the vortex of creative tension between what theologian James Cone has identified as the orthodoxy-orthopraxy debate.[49]

For King, the central question emerged, "How can the church of Jesus Christ speak a relevant word about God in the revolutionary situation of ideological crisis, massive human suffering, and existential despair without, at the same time, employing radically involved, emancipatory praxis?" King had issued numerous warnings to the church about the glaring contradictions between ecclesial rhetoric and action. In fact, King's theology was particularly concerned with the match between the church's public utterance and its communal practice. The theology of radical involvement was not content to merely sanction discourse about sacrificial suffering and nonviolent resistance on behalf of freedom. It required modeling these approaches in one's personal lifestyle. Consequently, King raised the implicit query (for the ecclesial community as well as the individual Christian) about the extent to which our programs of discipleship are preparing us to follow the way of the Cross.

King's legacy, however, moves far beyond the boundaries of the ecclesial community. King bequeathed the nation and the global village both a hard challenge and a subversive hope. When reread through more intellectually honest and critical eyes, King presses the hard challenge of balancing the moral requisites of radical analysis, responsible decision making, and courageous social action. Here King's "prophetic realism" demands the continual rethinking of every judgment, action, policy, or institution we create.[50] The challenge is to be vigilant in our efforts to ensure that differences are celebrated as gifts of God, and that principled egalitarianism and democratic participation in the decision-making process become normative.

The element of subversive hope is clearly discernible when one considers King's radical, eschatological vision for human community. This metaphysical, moral vision of a beloved community had international implications for the ordering of planetary living. It promoted a revolutionary attitude that inspired radical action on behalf of the just and loving human community. King's vision, with its dimensions of sociopolitical and economic specificity, was based upon an unshakable faith in the justice of God and the power of God to defeat evil and injustice. This radical faith claim enabled King to maintain both subversive hope and paradoxical joy amid pernicious social negligence, political unresponsiveness, and economic privation.

The power and cogency of King's personal and public witness amount to a forceful invitation to deal with the content of our own faith and the kind of vision that faith inspires. The spiritual component in Kingian thought invites us to ask whether or not we can extricate ourselves from a broadening moral and sociopolitical morass. In today's postmodern world, it may well be a choice between spirituality and self-destruction; sane, insurgent, radical involvement and apathetic madness. The visionary component in Kingian thought invites a continuous interrogation into personal and communal aspirations, motives, and priorities. Hence, we cannot avoid the haunting question of the future, "What on earth are we hoping for?" The answer will, in large measure, determine our most compelling personal and collective loyalties and priorities.

Relative to King's theological and ethical perspective, we have discovered a creative thinker whose vision, voice, and vocation as theologian, Christian minister, and social activist speak relevantly to the culture of our day. When allowed to speak, we are enabled to hear the more radical elements in King's thinking. When heard, we are enabled to experience the piercing critique and relentless challenge of his message and ministry. A consideration of the popular images of King as a national icon is quite revealing. King remains a victim of the politics of image making in the context of a market culture that commodifies its heroes into innocuous and banal insularity. Consequently, King must be viewed as a casualty of the more narrowly circumscribed, licentious business interests inherent in America's market establishment.[51]

Unfortunately, the public is unsuspectingly maneuvered into naively accepting these powerfully seductive but false images. No sane observer can deny the high levels of psychic and existential angst operating in today's culture. Because of the capacity of images to placate the phobias and anxieties that accompany high levels of cultural chaos, the public remains vulnerable to the skillful marketing of images of King. Further, there exists hidden but undeniable ideological content and political force in public images. In view of this, King (despite the radicality of his message) is still in danger of becoming the culture's most celebrated saint and symbol of postmodern market ideology. Given King's explicit critique of capitalist values and objectives, there can be no greater paradox in American history.[52]

The corrective, of course, is to seek ways to transform many of the current, popular images of King operating in the culture. To be of real assistance in the justice struggle, King must be liberated from his captivity to hollow, superficial, publicly championed versions of the "American Dream." To accomplish this requires that we begin to think more critically about how images of King have been and are being constructed. If American culture and the world court could access and "hear" the things King said and did, our nation's professed love affair with him might be exposed for the hypocrisy it is rapidly becoming. As an organic intellectual, prophetic realist, radical visionary, cultural critic, and nonviolent activist, King pronounced a devastating critique against the culture of his day. Although he was an American loyalist to a degree, he did not uncritically embrace the misguided values and practices prevalent in the social, psychological, moral, political, and economic dimensions of modern culture. Indeed, King tried to apply radical, transformative action in these five circles of death.[53]

And yet, King did offer a qualified optimism about the capacity of justice-oriented, oppositional praxis to finally triumph over encroaching fatalism. In today's postmodern culture of violence, poverty, and emptiness, hope often lies prostrate in the subterranean recesses of individual and collective consciousness. There are many folk in America and the world languishing in captivity to forces of bland apathy, escapist romanticism, and paralyzing nihilism. Many persons have simply given up or have dropped out of the political and educational processes, believing that, ultimately, no significant moral or social improvement can be achieved.

Yet, ironically, a prominent feature of postmodern culture is the bold flaunting of technological supremacy. Incredible advances subtly promote a false security in mass consciousness that somehow every problem will be eventually brought under the control of superior technology. This posturing tends to mask states of rising meaninglessness, hopelessness, and lovelessness that operate in the culture at alarming levels.[54] For many peoples, the structures of meaning have snapped, crumbled, and altogether disappeared. The ability of folk to interpret and make sense of frightening, complex realities—rising criminality, drug addiction, AIDS, absence of a cohesive and coherent public agenda, inability to establish a commonly held moral center, public skepticism and loss of faith in the political system, the devastating impact of joblessness, lack of adequate educational and skills retraining opportunities, growing numbers of those falling below the poverty line, the devaluation of the dollar's buying power, hyperinflation—has been dangerously undercut. Traditional, sociocultural buffers that once offered some measure of protection against the perils and uncertainties of the future—church, school, family, and community—have suffered serious erosion, and in some cases have simply been lost. Too many people see no possibility for any appreciable improvement in the fundamental quality of their lives in the foreseeable future. They have lost hope, and languishing in the politics of deprivation, "lead lives of quiet desperation."[55]

At the same time, never before in the history of the nation have we witnessed the kind of anomic morbidity and nihilistic despair that seem to grip sizable segments of the African American community. The crises indicative of the black postmodern predicament are witnessed to an excessive degree among the truly disadvantaged who find residence in the ethos and exigencies of the urban, inner city, and pockets of the rural enclaves of the nation.[56] Moreover, centrist, mainstream, middle-class America (both African American and European American) finds itself preoccupied with a struggle to find meaning and hope amid the sociopolitical and economic nightmares that have risen ominously on the cultural landscape.

177

King invites our generation to accept the moral, intellectual, and political challenge of hammering out a vision, a voice, and a vocation of radical involvement in an engaged struggle for love, justice, and peace. Our children must not become the first generation to fail to advance the agenda of justice one step more. In today's postmodern culture, the church has to insist that questions about the meaning of the Christian faith and the requirements of Christian discipleship continue to be raised. We are a generation in desperate need of "a word from the Lord." The voice of prophetic empathy must, once again, speak with power and clarity in the public arena. And yet, King reminds us that if the beloved community is to be realized at all, it will be on divine rather than human terms. The issue is whether or not church, nation, and world have ears to hear and eyes to see the path that leads to a recovery of prophetic vision, service, and hope.

The final months of King's life were marked by elevated levels of resignation prevalent among the cadre of dedicated freedom fighters who were witnessing the nation's abandonment and betrayal of the civil rights agenda. In fact, King himself suffered from periodic bouts of depression. And yet, he never lost the paradoxical hope that justice would be ultimately achieved.[57] Facing the crises of faith, meaning, and hope in postmodernity, the task before us is to enable persons to begin to embrace life (despite its tragic dimensions) as a gift to be celebrated, rather than an obstacle to be overcome. This is precisely what King helped empower me to do with my own life at age fifteen, some twenty-eight years ago.

If individuals, the church, and the nation intend to move with integrity into the twenty-first century, it will be through, not around, the perennial issues of identity, ethics, and the future that ask the questions, "Who am I?"; "What ought I to be and to do?"; and "What am I to hope for?" Of paramount importance is the culture's coming to terms with those generative tensions in vocational identity that offer themselves continually for resolution. What are we being collectively called to do and to be at this time in history to assist God in the process of humanizing the social, political, and economic order?

King does have something to offer in this regard that might be critically reappropriated in the postmodern situation. Serious national problems are not going to disappear simply because we ignore them or engage in the politics of denial. The generative tensions raised by King's perspective help to restore many vital social issues to

178

a more prominent place on the public agenda. A theology of radical involvement and a communitarian ethic simply will not allow public debate on important social problems to be permanently adjourned.

King's enduring legacy lies in keeping before us the challenge continually to probe, locate, and articulate with power, passion, and persuasion the relevance of the gospel as a solution to the ongoing crises of the human situation. In this regard, King invites us to revision the essence of the Christian faith as a vocational call to address the perennial economic, social, and political problems of culture with a view toward seeking the radical transformation of society into a community where love, justice, and peace are normative. King's perspective, lifestyle, and public witness illuminate the human vocation to live a life of radical commitment to the goal of humanizing the human community. If we are serious about accepting the forceful invitation to join God in the struggle to restore cosmic community, King's intellectual and activist legacy will prove to be highly relevant to our efforts in undertaking this human calling.

# NOTES

## PREFACE

1. See Joseph Washington's *Black Sects and Cults* (Garden City, N.Y.: Doubleday/Anchor, 1973) for a discussion of the religious perspective of these various groups. Other helpful sources include E. Franklin Frazier, *The Negro Church in America* (New York: Schocken, 1964); and Nans A. Baer, *The Black Spiritual Movement: A Religious Response to Racism* (Knoxville: Univ. of Tennessee Press, 1984).

Significant pockets of this more religiously and politically conservative attitude were also to be found in some of the larger denominations. For example, King was challenged and opposed by Joseph Jackson of the powerful National Baptist Convention. Jackson did not agree with King's more progressively activist approach to social change and was able to influence a large slice of that body to reject King's leadership. Consequently, King and others withdrew from that body in order to form the Progressive Baptist Convention in the 1960s. See *Frustrated Fellowships* by James Melvin Washington and *Fire in My Bones* by Charles King.

2. See King's chapter "The World House" in his book *Where Do We Go from Here: Chaos or Community?* (Boston: Beacon, 1967).

## INTRODUCTION

1. See Lewis V. Baldwin, *There Is a Balm in Gilead: The Cultural Roots of Martin Luther King Jr.* (Minneapolis: Fortress, 1991), pp. 11-14 and *To Make the Wounded Whole: The Cultural Legacy of Martin Luther King Jr.* (Minneapolis: Fortress, 1992), p. 5.

## CHAPTER 1

1. See Joseph Washington, *Black Religion: The Negro and Christianity in the United States* (Boston: Beacon, 1964); Albert Cleage, *The Black Messiah* (New York: Sheed and Ward, 1969); and *Black Christian Nationalism: New Directions for the Black Church* (New York: William Morrow, 1972).

2. Cleage, *Black Christian Nationalism*, pp. 139-41, 150-51, and 224-25.

3. Washington, *Black Religion,* p. 5.

4. See Gayraud S. Wilmore and James Cone, eds., *Black Theology: A Documentary History, 1966–1979* (New York: Orbis Books, 1979); and Lewis V. Baldwin, *To Make the Wounded Whole: The Cultural Legacy of Dr. Martin Luther King Jr.* (Minneapolis: Fortress), pp. 57-162.

5. For a general discussion of the many images of King, see Carol Carr, "Public Images of Martin Luther King, Jr." (Ph.D. diss., Ohio State Univ., 1977); see also James P. Hanigan, "Martin Luther King, Jr.: Images of a Man," *Journal of Religious Thought,* 31 (Spring-Summer 1974), pp. 68-95; James Washington, ed., *A Testament of Hope: The Essential Writings of Martin Luther King, Jr.* (San Francisco: Harper & Row, 1986), pp. xvi-xvii, xxii-xxiii.

6. James H. Cone is perhaps the leading proponent of this view. See Cone's *Speaking the Truth* (Grand Rapids: Eerdmans, 1986), p. 23. Also see Cone, *A Black Theology of Liberation* (Philadelphia: J. B. Lippincott, 1970), p. 77.

7. Among these are Paul Garber, "Martin Luther King, Jr.: Theologian and Precursor of Black Theology" (Ph.D. diss., Florida State Univ., 1973); Also Garber, "King Was a Black Theologian," *Journal of Religious Thought,* 31 (Fall-Winter, 1974–75), pp. 16-32; Herbert Richardson, "Martin Luther King, Jr.: Unsung Theologian," *New Theology No. 6,* Martin E. Marty and Dean Peerman, eds. (New York: Macmillan, 1969); John Rathbun, "Martin Luther King: The Theology of Social Action," *American Quarterly,* 20 (Spring 1968), pp. 38-53; John Harris, "The Theology of Martin Luther King, Jr." (Ph.D. diss., Duke Univ., 1974); Katie Cannon, *Black Womanist Ethics* (Atlanta: Scholars Press, 1988), pp. 9, 160-74; L. Harold DeWolf, "Martin Luther King, Jr. as Theologian," *Journal of the Interdenominational Center* 4 (Spring 1977), pp. 1-11; Ralph Abernathy, "Our Lives Were Filled with the Action," in C. Eric Lincoln, ed., *Martin Luther King, Jr.: A Profile* (New York: Hill & Wang, 1970), pp. 219-27; Larry Miller, "King's Liberating Theology," *Quaker Religious Thought,* vol. 23, no. 1 ( January 1988), pp. 5-24. I support those who argue that King is best seen as a theologian.

8. See especially Washington, *Black Religion.*

9. Adam Fairclough, *To Redeem the Soul of America* (Athens: Univ. of Georgia Press, 1987), esp. Introduction and Chapter 1.

10. Lawrence Reddick, *Crusader Without Violence: A Biography of Martin Luther King, Jr.* (New York: Harper & Brothers, 1959); James P. Hanigan, *Martin Luther King, Jr., and the Foundations of Nonviolence* (Latham, Md.: University Press of America, 1984).

11. Lionel L. Lokos, *A House Divided: The Life and Legacy of Martin Luther King* (New Rochelle, N.Y.: Arlington House, 1968); Alan Stang, *It's Very Simple—The True Story of Civil Rights* (Belmont, Calif.: Western Islands, 1965).

12. William R. Jones, "Martin Luther King, Jr.: Black Messiah or White Guardian?" audiotape of unpublished lecture presented at Florida A&M Univ., Tallahassee, Florida, February 20, 1973.

13. Robert Bellah, *Habits of the Heart* (New York: Harper & Row, 1985), pp. 249, 286; Coleman B. Brown, "Grounds for American Loyalty in a Prophetic Christian Social Ethic—With Special Attention to Martin Luther King, Jr." (Ph.D. diss., Union Theological Seminary, 1979).

14. On King as a militant, see Robert Brisbane, *The Black Vanguard* (Valley Forge: Judson, 1970), pp. 220, 248-50; on King as conservative militant, see August Meier, "On the Role of Martin Luther King," *New Politics* 4 (Winter 1965).

15. James Smylie, "On Jesus, Pharaohs, and the Chosen People: Martin Luther King as Biblical Interpreter and Humanist," *Interpretation* 24 (1/70), pp. 74-90; John C. Harris also claims that humanist thought in the mid-twentieth century significantly influenced King's thinking. See his Ph.D. diss., "The Theology of Martin Luther King, Jr.," Duke Univ., 1974.

16. Ralph David Abernathy, *And the Walls Came Tumbling Down: Ralph David Abernathy—An Autobiography* (New York: Harper & Row, 1989).

17. Taylor Branch, *Parting the Waters: America in the King Years 1954–63* (New York: Simon & Schuster, 1988); Herbert Richardson, "Martin Luther King, Jr.: Unsung Theologian," *New Theology* 6, Martin E. Marty and Dean Peerman, eds. (New York: Macmillan, 1969).

18. *David Garrow, Bearing the Cross: Martin Luther King, Jr. and the Southern Christian Leadership Conference* (New York: William Morrow, 1986).

19. Reddick, *Crusader Without Violence.*

20. See Frederick L. Downing, *To See the Promised Land: The Faith Pilgrimage of Martin Luther King, Jr.* (Macon, Ga.: Mercer University Press, 1986), p. 279.

21. James Cone has reintroduced the image of King as a prophetic dreamer in his latest book, *Martin and Malcolm and America: A Dream or a Nightmare* (Maryknoll, N.Y.: Orbis Books, 1991). Cone has also described King as a creative theologian who, in the tradition of black religious faith, engages in oral theologizing or a type of proclamation theology.

22. Among the few who take King's experience of personal identity crisis seriously is Frederick Downing, *To See the Promised Land;* Lerone Bennett, *What Manner of Man* (Chicago: Johnson Publishing, 1976); and James Cone, *Martin and Malcolm.*

23. Gayraud Wilmore describes an "identity crisis" as ". . . a critical event in the development of a person or group when a decision is made either to affirm or to deny a historical individuality. By historical individuality we mean that distinctiveness, that uniqueness, which belongs to someone in a particular place, at a particular time, under a particular set of circumstances that all go into making that person who she or he is." Gayraud Wilmore, *Black and Presbyterian: The Heritage and the Hope* (Philadelphia: Geneva Press, 1983), p. 83.

One may also note that such a crisis of identity appears to be emblematic of both the black church and black culture in the context of white American culture. W.E.B. DuBois, for instance, has spoken of the crisis of double-consciousness or dual identity of blacks in America who are faced with the problem of the "two irreconcilable strivings" as one attempts to be both African and American. Cecil Cone has pointed out the crisis of identity as it relates to the theology of the black church. Black theology, he argues, suffers from an identity crisis with regard to its point of departure. It seeks to be identified with both the academic structure of predominantly white seminaries and with the black power motif of black radicals. In this way, says Cone, it loses a connection with its only appropriate point of departure—black religion.

King, as product of both a black culture in general, and the black church in particular (who is also educated in the finest of white institutions of higher learning) does not escape this identity crisis as articulated by both DuBois and Cone. See W. E. B. DuBois, *The Souls of Black Folk* (Chicago: A. C. McClurg, 1903), pp. 3-5; Cecil Cone, *Identity Crisis in Black Theology* (Nashville: AMEC, 1975), pp. 15-25.

24. Bennett, *What Manner of Man*, p. 80. Clayborne Carson, ed., *Papers of Martin Luther King, Jr., vol. 1: Called to Serve, January 1929–June 1951*, p. 57.

25. In speaking of *kairotic* moments, I am referring to a moment of urgency regarding pressing decisions for or against a perspective, understanding, or action. A kairotic moment presents a choice of such urgency that immediate decisions for or against it emerge at the moment of presentation. Not to decide is also to decide. This kairotic urgency accompanies King at several points in both his private and public life.

26. Bennett, *What Manner of Man*, p. 24; several of King's comments about nonconformity, extremism, maladjustedness regarding the posture one assumed toward structures and realities that sought to stifle one's personality and narrowly circumscribe one's horizons of development can be found in *Strength to Love* (Philadelphia: Fortress, 1963), pp. 23f., 31, 139; and in Washington, *Testament of Hope*, pp. 14, 33-34, 89, 163, 216, 218, 251, 291, 297, 349, 356, 482.

27. Bennett, *What Manner of Man*, pp. 17-21.

28. Ibid., pp. 19-20.

29. Bennett lists some of these incidents to include the white neighborhood grocer who refused to allow King to play with her boys; the bus incident while traveling to the oratorical contest in Valdosta, Georgia; the trip to Hartford, Connecticut, and other cities in the North in the summer of 1944; his membership in an integrated intercollegiate council; see Bennett, pp. 19-25.

30. As George W. Forell asserts in *Christian Social Teachings* (Minneapolis: Augsburg Publishing House, 1966), p. 214, puritanism is a complex term that refers to a religious orientation that is neither unambiguously conservative nor progressive in its emphasis. Historically, puritanism has held both a conservative pietism and a more liberal reformist emphasis that stresses democracy and freedom. As such, it is marked by a diversity in thought and action. In its broader sense, puritanism refers to an effort at moral reformation in all areas of life, and as such it promoted four main emphases: *godliness* (simply obey God's will in decisions and affairs of daily living); *righteousness* (moral rectitude in matters of personal piety and behavior such as honesty, truth telling, dependability, and such); *sobriety* (moderate and responsible use of life's enjoyments and pursuits so that worldliness is avoided); and *vocation* (each person had a particular role to fulfill in political, social, and economic life, and was called to a *vocational task* that acknowledges responsibility for the public order).

King, as a black Baptist minister, is certainly influenced by this puritanist strain with its dual (and at times conflictual) emphases on public and private piety on one hand, and conservative and progressive ethics on the other. For King, the puritanist focus on *vocation* will become crucial. The resolution of his crisis of identity, faith, and tradition will take the form of a vocational response.

For a more detailed discussion of puritanism, see "Ethics of Puritanism and Quakerism" in *Christian Ethics,* 2nd ed. (London: Alfred A. Knopf, 1973), pp. 298-326, Waldo Beach and H. Richard Niebuhr, eds. For a detailed discussion of the influence of puritanist thinking on black religious thought, see Henry Mitchell, *Black Belief* (New York: Harper & Row, 1975); and Monroe Fordham, *Major Themes in Northern Black Religious Thought, 1800–1860* (Hicksville, N.Y.: Exposition Press, 1975).

31. Bennett, pp. 34-35; see Stephen Oates, *Let the Trumpet Sound* (New York: Signet, 1982), p. 23

32. Bennett, p. 35.

33. Downing, *To See the Promised Land,* pp. 53-71, 115.

34. Interestingly enough, King initially chose against the ministry as a vocation. His choice had much to do with his critique of black religion as intellectually unrespectable and socially irrelevant. However, it also had to do with King's standing over against his father and asserting his own right of agency to participate in choosing his own destiny. See Oates, *Trumpet Sound,* pp. 12-13.

35. See Coretta Scott King, *My Life with Martin Luther King, Jr.* (New York: Holt, Rinehart & Winston, 1969); Stephen Oates, *Trumpet Sound,* pp. 44, 48, 89; and Garrow, *Bearing the Cross,* pp. 44, 47-49.

36. King's struggle with his father's authoritarianism was also accompanied by a profound sense of admiration and respect. In a Crozer paper written in 1950, King admitted that despite marked differences in theology and life, his father had remained his personal hero. See Carson, *Papers,* 359-63.

37. DuBois, *Souls of Black Folk,* p. 4.

38. James W. McClendon Jr., *Biography as Theology* (Nashville: Abingdon Press, 1974), pp. 47-48.

39. Bennett, p. 25; Garrow, pp. 34-37.

40. See King, *Stride Toward Freedom* (San Francisco: Harper & Brothers, 1958), pp. 132-50.

41. Ibid., pp. 58-70, 132-70.

42. King, *Why We Can't Wait* (New York: Signet, 1964), pp. 73, 122-25; Garrow, *Cross,* pp. 283-86; McClendon, pp. 57-58.

43. King, "A Testament of Hope" in Washington, *Testament of Hope,* pp. 313-30; also "Death of Evil Upon the Seashore" in his book of sermons, *Strength to Love,* (Philadelphia: Fortress, 1963), pp. 76-85.

44. King, *Strength,* pp. 65, 133, 134; McClendon, pp. 64-65.

45. Several scholars have attempted to trace both the intellectual and nonintellectual factors that shaped King's thought. Among the best are John Ansbro, *Martin Luther King, Jr.: The Making of a Mind* (Maryknoll, N.Y.: Orbis Books, 1982); Kenneth Smith and Ira Zepp, *Search for the Beloved Community: The Thinking of Martin Luther King, Jr.* (Valley Forge: Judson, 1974); James Cone, *Martin and Malcolm and America* (Maryknoll, N.Y.: Orbis Books, 1991); William D. Watley, *Roots of Resistance: The Nonviolent Ethic of Martin Luther King, Jr.* (Valley Forge: Judson, 1985).

46. King, *Stride,* p. 20.

47. Ibid., pp. 90-91.

48. Bennett, pp. 26-29. King maintains enough critical distance from the black church and the black religious tradition to be able to critique it from time to time, as he does in the sermon, "A Knock at Midnight" in *Strength*, pp. 56-66. King also critiqued other traditions to which he was exposed. See King, *Stride*, pp. 90-101.

49. King, *Stride*, pp. 90-107; also see Bennett's chapter "Seed," in *What Manner of Man*, pp. 30-51.

50. See King, *Stride*, pp. 92-95; and "How a Christian Should View Communism" in *Strength*, pp. 96-105. King admits that he also learns much from Marx and is challenged to a growing concern for social and economic justice, poverty, and the profit motive of capitalism. King reveals this influence in the sermon "Paul's Letter to American Christians," also found in *Strength*, pp. 138-46.

51. King, *Stride*, pp. 95-96.

52. King, *Strength*, p. 147.

53. King, *Stride*, pp. 91-92, 95-107; *Strength*, pp. 147-52.

54. See King's Ph.D. dissertation entitled "A Comparison of the Conceptions of God in the Thinking of Paul Tillich and Henry Nelson Wieman," Boston Univ. Press, 1955.

55. King, *Strength*, pp. 154-55.

56. King, *Stride*, p. 95.

57. Bennett, p. 11; King, *Stride*, pp. 100-101.

58. Washington, *Black Religion*, p. 3.

59. Cornel West, *Prophetic Fragments* (Grand Rapids: Eerdmans, 1988), p. 3.

60. Ibid., pp. 3-4.

61. See William D. Watley, *Roots of Resistance.*

62. Increasingly, more scholars are recognizing the foundational impact of black religious faith upon King's life and thought. Among them are James Cone, *Martin and Malcolm and America;* Cornel West, *Prophetic Fragments;* C. Eric Lincoln, *Race, Religion, and the Continuing American Dilemma* (New York; Hill & Wang, 1984); and William D. Watley, *Roots of Resistance.*

63. Washington, *Testament of Hope*, Introduction, pp. xi-xii; Aldon Morris, *Origins of the Civil Rights Movement* (New York: Free Press, 1984), pp. x-xiii, 291 n. 2; David Howard-Pitney, *The Afro-American Jeremiad: Appeals for Justice in America* (Philadelphia: Temple Univ. Press, 1990), pp. 3-16, 133-83.

64. C. Eric Lincoln in *Race, Religion, and the Continuing American Dilemma* (New York: Hill & Wang, 1984), pp. 131-37, 138 defines Americanity as ". . . the religion of the American culture, the religion of the Republic . . . the national religious self-understanding that embodies and cherishes the ideals, aspirations and hopes that have been traditionally associated with America. . . . Americanity is the semi-secular, unofficial, but characteristic religion to which most Americans appeal when an appeal to religion is indicated. It is the religion most Americans feel when they feel any religion at all."

65. Zepp and Smith, *Search for the Beloved Community*, pp. 19, 24, 29.

66. King, *Strength*, pp. 147-48.

67. King, *Stride*, p. 100.

68. Ibid., pp. 91-95. On King's reference to Gandhi as the "little brown saint," see Washington, *Testament of Hope*, p. 17.

69. Ibid., 96-97. It was Gandhi's philosophy of soul-force love (*satyagraha*) and noninjury (*ahimsa*) demonstrated in his method of nonviolent resistance that enabled King, in part, to overcome the devastating critiques of Christianity by Marx and Nietzsche. Gandhi's life and thought influenced King so profoundly that King would come to describe him as ". . . one of the half-dozen greatest men in world history." King had a picture of Gandhi hung in his home as well as in his office. Bennett, pp. 3-4, 21, 24, 37, 101, 123-24, 207.

70. King, *Stride,* pp. 84-85.

71. Keith D. Miller, *Voice of Deliverance: The Language of Martin Luther King, Jr., and Its Sources* (New York: Free Press, 1992), offers a provocative discussion of King's use of language in public discourse. See also Calvin Morris, "Martin Luther King, Jr., Exemplary Preacher," in *The Journal of the Interdenominational Theological Center* IV (Spring 1976), pp. 61-66.

72. West, *Fragments,* p. 11.

73. See numerous instances where King appeals to the U.S. Constitution, Declaration of Independence, Bill of Rights, and so forth in Washington, *Testament of Hope,* pp. 89-90, 98, 103, 165, 277, 286.

74. King, *Strength,* pp. 151-52.

75. William H. Becker, "Vocation and Black Theology" in *Black Theology II* (London: Associated Univ. Press, 1978), edited by Calvin E. Bruce and William R. Jones, pp. 27-51. Becker makes the point that the concept and symbol of vocation is deeply rooted in the black experience in America. This notion of vocation among blacks, he contends, has four historical roots: two—the call to acknowledge, affirm, and live true to an African heritage and the notion of suffering as somehow redemptive—are distinctively black: two others—philosophy of the natural rights of man, and the biblical concept of Israel as God's chosen people—are shared with whites.

76. By this, King means taking care of the business that befits a person by virtue of being a human creature. This includes a focus on self-development of body and mind, nurturing of proper virtues of love and caring. See King's speech "What Is Man?" in his little volume, *The Measure of a Man* (Philadelphia: Fortress, 1959), pp. 7-32 and King's speech "The Three Dimensions of a Complete Life" from the same volume, pp. 33-56.

77. See *The Words of Martin Luther King, Jr.* (New York: Newmarket Press, 1983, 1987), ed. by Coretta Scott King, pp. 17, 21.

78. King, *Stride,* p. 91; *Strength,* p. 150.

79. King, *Stride,* pp. 15-34; *Strength,* pp. 56-66.

80. Garrow, *Cross,* pp. 558, 560, 561.

81. See King's sermon "The Drum Major Instinct" in Washington, *Testament of Hope,* pp. 259-67; it is also revealing that King throughout various points in his life refers to himself by several other "handles" that point to his evolving sense of vocational identity—extremist, nonconformist, evangelical liberal, soldier, democratic socialist, to name a few.

82. Washington, *Testament of Hope,* pp. 40, 44, 50-51, 80-81, 85-90, 98, 313-14, 338-39, 349-50.

83. King, *Strength,* pp. 86-95, 115-26.

## CHAPTER 2

1. The claim here is *not* that King has done no theology prior to the call to public service in Montgomery. For instance, there are *already* developing formulations of God in several papers written as part of course work at Crozer Seminary and Boston University. One might also make reference to King's Ph.D. dissertation that deals with conceptions of God in Tillich and Wieman. Rather, the claim *is* that everything that King wrote *prior to* Montgomery must be now seen *in light of* his engagement in prophetic, social action on behalf of justice and community. King himself says as much in *Stride Toward Freedom* (San Francisco: Harper & Row, 1958), pp. 101, 134 and *Strength to Love*, (Philadelphia: Fortress, 1963), p. 112.

2. See Abernathy, "Our Lives Were Filled with the Action"; John Rathbun, "King: The Theology of Social Action." For an in-depth discussion and analysis of the concept of praxis in both its theoretical and practical dimensions, see Gustavo Gutierrez, *A Theology of Liberation: History, Salvation, and Politics* (Maryknoll, N. Y.: Orbis Books Books, 1984), pp. 6-19, 66-77.

3. See DeWolf, "King as Theologian"; John Rathbun, "King: Theology of Social Action," Ph.D. diss.; James Cone, "The Theology of Martin Luther King, Jr., *Union Seminary Quarterly Review*, 40, January 1986, pp. 21-39.

4. See, for instance, King's sermon "Love in Action" from his book of sermons, *Strength to Love* (New York: Harper & Row, 1963), pp. 36-46. King uses the Cross as symbol par excellence as an expression of divine love in action. From this view of God as proactive love, King is able to extract doctrines of the Christian life, the church, eschatology, Christology, anthropology as well as offer critiques of war and racial segregation.

5. Ibid., pp. 15-16, 83-84, 106-14, 122-26.

6. See King's Crozer Seminary paper "Examination Answers, Christian Theology for Today," *Papers of Martin Luther King, Jr. vol. I: Called to Serve, January 1929–June 1951*, Clayborne Carson, ed., pp. 289-94. Hereafter written as "Papers."

7. See King, *Strength*, pp. 154-55; *Stride*, p. 100.

8. King, *Strength*, pp. 19, 33-35.

9. King's conceptualization of God and gospel led him to a theological perspective that was highly pragmatic in nature. This focus affirmed the need for a socially active Christian witness and discipleship in both ecclesial community and personal lifestyle. This practical emphasis is found in several places throughout his life. See King's column "Advice for Living," *Ebony*, 1956–1957; "Action for Interracial Understanding," *Franciscan Herald and Forum*, vol. 42, October 1963, p. 289; "Suffering and Faith," *Christian Century*, vol. 77, April 27, 1960; "Is It Alright to Break the Law?" *U.S. News & World Report*, vol. 55, August 12, 1963, p. 6; and *Trumpet of Conscience* (San Francisco: Harper & Row, 1967), pp. 59, 70-78.

10. King, *Strength*, pp. 26-35, 36-46, 47-55.

11. King, *Stride*, pp. 103-4.

12. *Strength*, "Love in Action," pp. 36-46.

13. John Ansbro, *Martin Luther King, Jr.: The Making of a Mind* (Maryknoll, N.Y.: Orbis Books, 1982), pp. 1-36.

14. King, *Strength*, p. 50. This quotation merits commentary about the contextual situatedness of King's language. Without question, King was as much a product of the culture of his day as a shaper of it. As such, his speech reveals an insensitivity to the issue of gender-inclusivity in communication. Like others in the 1960s (prior to the public awareness of the bias inherent in gender-exclusive language), King used the prevailing speech and journalistic patterns of the times. He was just not conscious of the issue of gender bias. His quoted material reflects this lack of critical awareness. Certainly, King's universalist-humanitarian emphases as well as his notions of community and the *imago Dei* provided the intellectual and moral bases upon which to mount an effective appeal for the use of sexually inclusive language. Therefore, despite the fact that he did harbor sexist notions, I believe that King would have been open to a critique of his use of sexist language. In order to hold to a minimum any interruptions in the power and force of his rhetoric, I will avoid the use of "sic" when quoting King's words or the words of others written prior to an awareness of the need for an inclusive language.

15. James Washington, ed., *A Testament of Hope: The Essential Writings of Martin Luther King, Jr.* (San Francisco: Harper & Row, 1986), p. 20.

16. *Strength*, pp. 77-78.

17. Ibid., pp. 36f., 47, 120.

18. Washington, *Testament of Hope*, pp. 20, 88; King, *Strength*, p. 114.

19. King, *Papers*, "Religion's Answer to the Problem of Evil," pp. 416-17.

20. Ibid., pp. 422-32.

21. King, *Strength*, p. 69

22. See Borden Parker Bowne, *The Principle of Ethics and Personalism* (New York: Harper & Brothers, 1892); Edgar S. Brightman, *Moral Laws* (New York: Abingdon Press, 1933); Albert C. Knudson, *The Principles of Christian Ethics* (New York: Abingdon Press, 1943).

23. King, *Strength*, pp.109-10.

24. For a detailed discussion of the laws of Bostonian personalism, see Brian M. Kane, "The Influence of Boston Personalism on the Thought of Dr. Martin Luther King, Jr.," Master's thesis, Boston Univ., 1983, pp. 58-77.

25. See Knudson, *Principles of Christian Ethics*, pp. 118-21; Bowne, *Studies in Christianity*, (Boston and New York: Houghton Mifflin, 1909), pp. 95-98; Brightman, *Moral Laws* (New York: Abingdon Press, 1933), pp. 270-72; DeWolf, *A Theology of the Living Church*, rev. ed. (New York: Holt, Rinehart, and Winston, 1969), pp. 115-16.

26. King, *Stride*, p. 106; Washington, *Testament of Hope*, p. 88

27. King, *Stride*, p. 117; *Why We Can't Wait*, pp. 82-84; *Strength*, p. 128.

28. King, *Strength*, pp. 133, 134; Washington, *Testament of Hope*, pp. 200, 270, 296.

29. King, *Trumpet of Conscience*, pp. 76-78.

30. Washington, *Testament of Hope*, p. 89.

31. It should *not* be forgotten that King (by his own admission) was *first* and *foremost* a product of the black religious tradition. This tradition provided significant and foundational theological insights about God's goodness, justice, and power in the face of evil. King's conception of God as personal, caring, tender, and strong reflects the influence of black religion. See King's *Stride*, p. 100, and his unpublished paper, "My Call to the Ministry" (King Center Archives, Atlanta, Ga.). See also William D. Watley, *Roots of Resistance: The Nonviolent Ethic of Martin Luther King, Jr.*

(Valley Forge: Judson, 1985), pp. 41-45 and Lewis V. Baldwin, *There Is a Balm in Gilead: The Cultural Roots of Martin Luther King, Jr.* (Minneapolis: Fortress, 1991), pp. 159-228.

32. See Thomas Hoyt, Jr., "The Biblical Tradition of the Poor and Martin Luther King, Jr.," *Journal of the Interdenominational Theological Center,* vol. IV, Spring 1977, no. II, pp. 12-32.

33. King, *Why We Can't Wait,* p. 78; *Where Do We Go from Here,* p. 170; Washington, *Testament of Hope,* pp. 37-38, 282.

34. King, *Strength,* pp. 65, 83-84, 90.

35. Ibid., pp. 76-85.

36. Ibid., p. 45; Washington, *Testament of Hope,* pp. 9, 40, 88, 141.

37. Washington, *Testament of Hope,* p. 88.

38. Ibid., pp. 9, 88, 141.

39. Washington, *Testament of Hope,* pp. 88, 219; King, *Strength,* pp. 65, 82, 85, 95, 106, 111-14, 122, 128, 134.

40. John Calvin's *Institutes of the Christian Religion* begins in Book I with the claim that "without knowledge of self there is no knowledge of God. . . . Without knowledge of God there is no knowledge of self" (pp. 35, 36). In this way, Calvin maintains an inseparable connection between the two forms of theological and anthropological knowledge. King's approach follows a similar methodological path.

41. King, *Stride,* p. 100; this did *not* mean that King held optimistically to a belief in the innate or essential goodness of human beings. A strong conception of sin combined with life experiences as a member of an oppressed group made King ultimately reject liberal theology's optimistic anthropology. See King's "How Modern Christians Should Think of Man" (quoted in Watley, *Roots,* p. 43). See also King, *Measure of Man,* pp. 9, 21.

42. King, *Where Do We Go from Here,* pp. 73, 84, 97, 180.

43. Garth Baker-Fletcher, *Somebodiness: Martin Luther King, Jr. and the Theory of Human Dignity* (New York: Fortress, 1993).

44. Washington, *Testament of Hope,* p. 122.

45. King, *Where Do We Go from Here,* pp. 43-44; *Why We Can't Wait,* p. 30.

46. King, *Stride,* p. 75.

47. King, *Strength,* p. 160; Washington, *Testament of Hope,* p. 119.

48. King, *Trumpet of Conscience,* p. 72.

49. King, *Stride,* pp. 101-7 and *Where Do We Go from Here,* pp. 54-66.

50. Washington, *Testament of Hope,* pp. 119-22.

51. King, at times, links this phrase with "the interrelatedness of all reality" to mean that all existence (including human existence) has a social character. That is to say, the development of the individual personality is achievable only within the social dimension of corporate living. See King, *Strength,* pp. 65-66; *Trumpet of Conscience,* p. 68; and *Measure of Man,* pp. 48-49.

52. Washington, *Testament of Hope,* pp. 117-25; King, *Where Do We Go from Here,* pp. 180-81.

53. King, *Where Do We Go from Here,* pp. 97-98.

54. King, *Measure of Man,* pp. 18-31.

55. King was able to overcome a negative view of whites' human nature largely by looking at whites through the lenses of the *imago Dei* concept (see *Stride,* pp. 102-3).

King himself consistently faced the necessity of moral choice as his capacity for violence and hatred was tested in the midst of virulent acts of white violence.

56. King, *Measure of Man*, pp. 12, 18.

57. See King, *Why We Can't Wait*, pp. 89-93.

58. King, *Strength*, pp. 62-63; King has edited out a very significant statement in the written text of this sermon. It is found in the phonodisc version of "A Knock at Midnight." King says, "A doctrine of black supremacy is as evil as a doctrine of white supremacy!"

59. King, *Where Do We Go from Here*, pp. 180-81, 193-202.

60. King, *Measure of Man*, p. 9.

61. Ibid., "Three Dimensions of a Complete Life," pp. 35-37.

62. Ibid.

63. Washington, *Testament of Hope*, pp. 47-48.

64. King, *Where Do We Go from Here*, pp. 132-34, 186-90; "Declaration of Independence from the War in Vietnam," A. J. Muste Memorial Institute Essay Series, no. 1, pp. 35-36, 46.

65. King, *Measure of Man*, pp. 42-49.

66. King, *Strength*, pp. 28, 96-105, 138-46; *Where Do We Go from Here*, pp. 132, 186.

67. King, "The American Dream," Lynchburg, Va., March 12, 1961, audiocassette recording, B & S Recordings, Bladensburg, Md.

68. Washington, *Testament of Hope*, pp. 105, 111.

69. King, "Impasse in Race Relations," in *Trumpet of Conscience*, pp. 1-17; *Where Do We Go from Here*, "Where We Are," pp. 1-22.

70. King, *Strength*, pp. 130-31, 133.

71. Ibid., pp. 20, 80, 202; *Stride*, pp. 218, 222; *Trumpet of Conscience*, p. 46; *Why We Can't Wait*, pp. 43, 89; "The Civil Rights Struggle in the United States Today," 1965, p. 12 (quoted in Ansbro, *Making of a Mind*, p. 227).

72. King, *Trumpet of Conscience*, pp. 76-78.

73. See King, *Strength*, "On Being a Good Neighbor," "Love in Action," and "Loving Your Enemies," pp. 26-55.

74. King, *Trumpet of Conscience*, p. 68.

75. King, *Measure of Man*, p. 49; Washington, *Testament of Hope*, pp. 138, 210, 269-70.

76. King, *Why We Can't Wait*, p. 77.

77. King, *Trumpet of Conscience*, pp. 69-70.

78. King, *Measure of Man*, pp. 48-49.

79. King, *Where Do We Go from Here*, pp. 167-91; *Trumpet of Conscience*, pp. 25, 68, 72.

80. King, *Stride*, pp. 104-5.

81. King, *Strength*, pp. 27, 29, 31, 35.

82. Ibid., p. 27; *Measure of Man*, pp. 41-44.

83. In addition to comments in the "Letter from a Birmingham Jail" in *Can't Wait*, King's Memphis campaign demonstrates his willingness to place the needs of others above personal objectives and safety. In the first foray into Memphis, King acted against the judgments and caveats of his closest advisers who repeatedly argued that Memphis was a dangerous place for him to go. In the famous "Mountaintop" speech

on the eve of his assassination, King said that the question was not what would happen to him if he came to Memphis, but rather, what would become of the sanitation workers if he did not stop to help them. See Washington, *Testament of Hope,* p. 285.

84. King, *Strength,* p. 31.

85. King, *Where Do We Go from Here,* pp. 187-88.

86. King, *Strength,* p. 27.

87. Ibid., pp. 34-35.

88. King, *Where Do We Go from Here,* p. 86.

89. King, *Stride,* p. 103.

90. King, *Why We Can't Wait,* pp. 88-89.

91. See, for instance, King, *Stride,* pp. 84-85, 96-98; *Strength,* pp. 21-25.

92. King, *Stride,* p. 103.

93. Ibid., p. 54.

94. Ibid., pp. 189-224.

95. King, *Strength,* p. 25.

96. Garrow, *Bearing the Cross,* pp. 166, 355, 365, 447, 555, 560, 564.

97. See King, *Strength,* pp. 143-44; see also Washington, *Testament of Hope,* p. 10 and especially p. 143, where King expands the statement beyond a Christian ethic to embrace a broader, more inclusive social ethic. Here King replaces the phrase ". . . nothing could be more *Christian,*" with the phrase ". . . nothing could be more *honorable.*" Or again, note King's rephrasing of the ethic in *Stride,* p. 216, to read ". . . if physical death is the price that a man must pay to free his children or his *white brethren from a permanent death of the spirit,* then nothing could be more *redemptive.*" For King, the mandate for suffering and self-sacrifice in the cause of justice is *not* the sole, exclusive domain of the professing Christian alone.

98. It is significant and instructive that King made this statement from the Reidsville State Prison in Tattnall County, Georgia, October 26, 1960.

99. Washington, *Testament of Hope,* p. 42.

100. Coretta Scott King, *Words of MLK* (New York: New Market, 1987), p. 17.

101. Washington, *Testament of Hope,* pp. 41-42.

102. King, *Stride,* pp. 121, 179; *Where Do We Go from Here,* pp. 55-66; and *Trumpet of Conscience,* pp. 74-75. See also Washington, *Testament of Hope,* pp. 281-82.

103. Washington, *Testament of Hope,* p. 222.

104. King, *Where Do We Go from Here,* p. 20.

105. Dorothy Soelle, *Suffering* (Philadelphia: Fortress, 1975), pp. 1, 4-5, and chapter 1.

106. King used the terms "maladjusted personality" or "creatively maladjusted person" frequently to refer to persons who are non-neutral in situations of injustice. They courageously refuse to endorse circumstances whereby one group enjoys an unfair advantage of power over another. In King's mind, the "maladjusted personality" is that person who remains "disturbed" by the presence of injustice to the point that he or she cannot morally acclimate or accommodate to any prevailing cultural ethos or structure that degrades human personality. See King, *Strength,* pp. 23, 139. Also see Washington, *Testament of Hope,* pp. 14, 89, 163, 216-18, 291, 349, 482.

107. Washington, *Testament of Hope,* pp. 33-34, 68-69, 256.

108. Ibid., pp. 284-86; King, *Why We Can't Wait*, pp. 88-89; *Where Do We Go from Here*, pp. 91, 133-35; *Trumpet of Conscience*, p. 50.

109. King, *Why We Can't Wait*, pp. 88-89.

110. King, *Where Do We Go from Here*, pp. 91, 133-34.

111. King, *Strength*, pp. 17, 22, 23, 24.

112. Washington, *Testament of Hope*, pp. 222, 265-67.

## CHAPTER 3

1. Clayborne Carson, ed., *Papers of Martin Luther King, Jr.* vol. 1, *Called to Serve, January 1929–June 1951,* "The Humanity and Divinity of Jesus," p. 261.

2. Ibid., pp. 245-48.

3. King does attempt to resolve the christological problem of how to maintain both the full divinity and full humanity of Christ. It is clear, though, that King's resolution emphasizes the utility of Jesus for the modern Christian. Jesus' divinity, lay "not in his substantial unity with God, but in his filial consciousness and his unique dependence upon God. . . . The true significance of the divinity of Christ lies in the fact that his achievement is prophetic and promissory for every other true son of man who is willing to submit his will to the will and spirit of God. Christ was to be only the prototype of one among many brothers." The humanity of Jesus focused on his "moral and religious life" and the "constancy of his will." Together, both divinity and humanity opened the possibility for progressive moral improvement in history through individual and collective social effort. See *Papers, vol. I,* pp. 257-62.

4. See Martin Luther King, *Stride Toward Freedom* (San Francisco: Harper & Row, 1958) pp. 61-63.

5. Ibid., pp. 84-85; James Washington, ed., *A Testament of Hope: The Essential Writings of Martin Luther King, Jr.* (San Francisco: Harper & Row, 1986) pp. 16-17.

6. King, *Strength to Love,* (Philadelphia: Fortress, 1963), pp. 21-22; *Stride,* pp. 44, 61-63, 69-70.

7. King, *Stride,* p. 117; *Papers,* vol. 1, pp. 246-48.

8. King, *Stride,* pp. 93-94, 117.

9. Washington, ed., *Testament of Hope,* p. 255.

10. King, *Stride,* pp. 88, 137-38, 157; *Strength,* pp. 26, 28, 36-39, 48.

11. King, *Strength,* p. 33.

12. King, *Stride,* pp. 39-40.

13. Ibid., p. 210; *Papers,* vol. I, pp. 266-67.

14. King, *Papers,* vol. I, pp. 247, 261-62.

15. Ibid., pp. 244, 247-48; *Strength,* pp. 34-35.

16. King, *Strength,* p. 76.

17. Ibid., pp. 18-19.

18. Ibid., pp. 103-5; Washington, *Testament of Hope,* pp. 37, 282.

19. Taylor Branch, *Parting the Waters: America in the King Years 1954–63* (New York: Simon & Schuster, 1988), pp. 114-16; Lerone Bennett, *What Manner of Man* (Chicago: Johnson Publishing, 1976), p. 57; Stephen Oates, *Let the Trumpet Sound* (New York: Signet, 1982), pp. 53-55.

20. Cone, *Martin and Malcolm and America: A Dream or a Nightmare* (Maryknoll, N.Y.: Orbis Books, 1991), p. 230. Cone points out correctly that King's view of

the importance of the color of Jesus underwent marked change in light of the black power movement that forced him to deal seriously with the concept of blackness in the freedom struggle.

21. Washington, *Testament of Hope*, pp. 266, 297, 356, 538.

22. Ibid., p. 298.

23. Ibid., pp. 14-15, 16, 90, 216, 447.

24. Ibid., pp. 89-90.

25. *Papers,* vol. I, pp. 266-67.

26. King, *Strength*, pp. 25, 45-46.

27. Ibid., pp. 93-94.

28. Ibid., pp. 60-63, 88-89.

29. Ibid., pp. 68-69, 100-101, 105.

30. Ibid., p. 63.

31. King, "The Negro Is Your Brother," *Atlantic Monthly*, vol. 207, Aug. 12, 1963, pp. 78-81, 86-88.

32. King, *Where Do We Go from Here*, pp. 97-99.

33. Washington, *Testament of Hope*, pp. 92, 119-20, 142-44.

34. Martin Luther King, *Why We Can't Wait* (New York: Signet, 1964), p. 77.

35. King's critical exegetical-interpretive framework emerged from the black experience of suffering and oppression. Therefore, his perceptual filter and hermeneutical lens predisposed him to be drawn toward the biblical prophetic tradition of critique, challenge, and conversion. His use of the prophetic texts of Amos, Micah, Isaiah, and others confirms this bent. Furthermore, King's understanding and use of the Scripture reveal a decided inclination toward a "political reading" of biblical texts—how the text speaks to the pressing social issues of the day. Indeed, the very questions and assumptions King brought to the narrative all but guarantee the appropriation of a "liberation paradigm" with regard to the black condition of suffering, survival, and resistance in America. For a more thorough discussion of King's approach to the Scripture see Thomas Hoyt, Jr., "The Biblical Tradition of the Poor and Martin Luther King, Jr.," *The Journal of the Interdenominational Theological Center*, vol. IV, Spring 1976, No. II, pp. 12-32.

36. See Gayraud Wilmore, *Black Religion and Black Radicalism* (Maryknoll, N.Y.: Orbis Books, 1984); C. Eric Lincoln, *The Black Experience in Religion* (New York: Doubleday, 1974).

37. King, *Stride*, p. 91.

38. King, *Strength*, pp. 68-69.

39. King, *Stride*, pp. 35-36.

40. Ibid., pp. 116-17.

41. Henry Hampton and Steve Fayer, *Voices of Freedom: An Oral History of the Civil Rights Movement from the 1950s Through the 1980s* (New York: Bantam Books, 1990), p. 465.

42. King, *Strength*, p. 100.

43. King, *Stride*, pp. 75-76.

44. Kenneth Smith and Ira Zepp, *Search for the Beloved Community: The Thinking of Martin Luther King, Jr.* (Valley Forge: Judson, 1974), pp. 33, 37, 42-43.

45. King, *Strength*, pp. 43-44.

46. King, *Stride,* pp. 205-7.
47. King, *Where Do We Go from Here,* pp. 96, 99, 132, 186.
48. King, *Strength,* pp. 142-43.
49. King, *Where Do We Go from Here,* p. 100.
50. King, *Stride,* pp. 207-10.
51. King, *Strength,* pp. 58-64.
52. Ibid., pp. 21, 43-44.
53. Ibid., pp. 103-4; King, *Why We Can't Wait,* p. 91.
54. King, *Why We Can't Wait,* pp. 89-92.
55. King, *Strength,* p. 62.
56. King, *Stride,* p. 207; King, *Strength,* pp. 58-64.
57. King, *Why We Can't Wait,* pp. 84, 89-92.
58. King, *Where Do We Go from Here,* p. 96.
59. King, *Why We Can't Wait,* pp. 91-93; King, *Strength,* pp. 58-64.
60. King, *Strength,* pp. 62-63.
61. King, *Why We Can't Wait,* pp. 34, 87, 90-91; *Where Do We Go from Here,* p. 124.
62. King, *Stride,* p. 89.
63. King, *Strength,* pp. 63-66.
64. It is interesting to note that during his student years at Crozer, King affirmed the efficacy of hope in the concept of the kingdom of God. For King, an important social emphasis was inherent in this reality, focusing on a future reign of God on earth. However and whenever it came, King felt it would be "a society in which all men and women will be controlled by the eternal love of God . . . social relationships controlled by . . . trust, love, mercy, altruism." King found it difficult to specify with exactness what such a society would be like, "for it runs so counter to the practices of our present life. But we can rest assured it will be a society governed by the law of love." See King, "The Christian Pertinence of Eschatological Hope," *Papers,* vol. 1, pp. 272-73. Beyond this, the young King of 1950 can say little more. As King matures, however, this future vision takes on more concreteness and specificity with regard to social, political, economic justice, and the distribution and configuration of power and wealth in society.
65. Ibid., pp. 109-10; Washington, *Testament of Hope,* pp. 13-14, 20, 40, 88.
66. King, *Strength,* pp. 110-11.
67. Ibid., pp. 76-85, 106-14.
68. Ibid., pp. 65, 133, 134.
69. Ibid., pp. 82-83.
70. Ibid., pp. 77-82, 106-11, 114.
71. Washington, *Testament of Hope,* p. 226
72. King, *Strength,* pp. 133-34.
73. Washington, *Testament of Hope,* pp. 9, 52, 313, 375.
74. King, *Strength,* p. 71; Washington, *Testament of Hope,* pp. 339, 371, 381.
75. Washington, *Testament of Hope,* p. 314; King, *Strength,* pp. 82-83.
76. Ibid., pp. 86-95.
77. King, *Stride,* pp. 181-88.
78. King, *Why We Can't Wait,* pp. 92, 126; Washington, *Testament of Hope,* pp. 219-20.

79. Washington, *Testament of Hope,* p. 226.

80. Ibid., pp. 228-30.

81. Ibid., p. 286.

82. King, *Strength,* pp. 59-60, 64-66.

83. King, *Stride,* pp. 36, 91, 117.

84. Ibid. See also Zepp and Smith, *Search for the Beloved Community,* pp. 43-45.

85. Walter Rauschenbusch, *A Theology for the Social Gospel* (New York: Macmillan, 1917), pp. 142, 155; *Christianity and the Social Crisis* (New York: Harper & Brothers, 1907), p. xiii.

86. Rauschenbusch, *Theology for Social Gospel,* esp. chapters 13 and 18; *Christianity and Social Crisis,* p. 420.

87. Washington, *Testament of Hope,* p. 219.

88. See King, "Speech to the United Auto Workers Union," Detroit, Michigan, June 1963, audiocassette; Washington, *Testament of Hope,* pp. 105, 144, 151, 206-7, 208-16.

89. Washington, *Testament of Hope,* p. 151.

90. Ibid., pp. 104, 111, 219. See also Zepp and Smith, *Search for the Beloved Community,* pp. 125-31; James Cone, *Martin and Malcolm,* pp. 58-88.

91. Washington, *Testament of Hope,* p. 111.

92. Ibid., p. 350.

93. Here King is consistent with his anthropological view of humanity as "coworker" with God, each coresponsible for effecting the realization of God's purposes in human history. See this chapter's section dealing with King's anthropology.

94. Ibid., pp. 47-48, 51, 110-11.

95. James P. Hanigan has argued, correctly, I believe, that King was at least semi-Pelagian on this point. While King took sin seriously and denied the perfectibility of humanity, he nevertheless held that some significant moral and social improvement could be made. See Hanigan's Ph.D. diss. (Duke University, 1973), "Martin Luther King, Jr. and the Ethics of Militant Nonviolence," pp. 59-61.

96. King, *Strength,* pp. 85, 95, 122-26.

97. Washington, *Testament of Hope,* p. 219.

98. King, *Strength,* pp. 154-55.

## CHAPTER 4

1. It cannot be overemphasized that King's vocational calling into the ministry must be seen within a developmental framework. In King's own words, his choice for the ministry while at Morehouse College grew out of a desire to serve the church and humanity (see Clayborne Carson, ed., *Papers of Martin Luther King, Jr., vol. 1: Called to Serve, January 1929–June 1951,* pp. 44-45, 363). That desire led him, as a minister, to search simultaneously for a method to eliminate social evil while at Crozer (see King, *Stride Toward Freedom* [San Francisco: Harper & Row, 1958], p. 91); aspire to the highest development as a theological scholar at Boston (Carson, *Papers,* pp. 49, 333, 390); and pursue a pastorate in the South upon completion of course work at Boston (King, *Stride,* pp. 9-24).

2. See King, *Stride,* pp. 208-11; also John W. Rathbun, "Martin Luther King: The Theology of Social Action," *American Quarterly* 20; (Spring 1968): 38-53 and Herbert Richardson, "Martin Luther King—Unsung Theologian," *Commonwealth* 89 (May 3, 1968), pp. 201-2.

3. David Garrow, *Bearing the Cross: Martin Luther King, Jr. and the Southern Christian Leadership Conference* (New York: William Morrow, 1986), p. 561. It is important to note that King made this statement at a press conference in New York in the context of a meeting with anti-Vietnam War activists in 1967. After making this public statement, King flew to Cleveland, Ohio, to announce SCLC's intent to initiate a voter registration drive, tenants' rights organization, and the formation of a Breadbasket program to alleviate hunger and malnourishment in that city. This action is entirely consistent with King's viewpoint in Montgomery in 1958 that the Christian gospel was both personal and social, and that religion must ultimately deal with the entire range of human needs—social, psychological, political, and economic as well as spiritual (King, *Stride,* pp. 36, 37, 91, 117). Undeniably, ministry for King involved giving equal attention to both theory and praxis, theology and ethics, faith and action. The basis of King's disappointment with the white ministers of Montgomery in 1955 was a failure to "serve the cause of Christ in the South." This entailed a moral obligation to "stand up courageously for righteousness" and to be "willing to suffer courageously for righteousness" (King, *Stride,* pp. 208-10).

4. In a student evaluation at Crozer in 1951, one of his professors, Charles E. Batten, indicated that King already demonstrated that "while interested in social action . . . he has a fine theological and philosophical basis on which to promulgate his ideas and activities." King himself admits, in a paper entitled "An Autobiography of Religious Development" at Crozer in 1950, that "my call to the ministry was . . . an inner urge calling me to serve humanity. . . [R]eligion has been real to me and closely knitted to life. In fact the two cannot be separated; religion for me is life." See *Papers,* pp. 406, 363.

Coretta Scott King has corroborated this in her observation that at the bus boycott rallies in Montgomery, King and Ralph Abernathy worked as a duo in this regard. According to Mrs. King, Abernathy would supply the down-home folk humor and inspiration, while King (as leader of the boycott, social activist minister, and resident theologian) would provide the philosophical and theological analyses that undergirded their actions. See audiocassette series *Eyes on the Prize: America's Civil Rights Years—1954 to 1965,* "Awakenings, 1954–1956" and *Eyes on the Prize II: America at the Racial Crossroads—1965 to 1985,* "The Promised Land, 1967–1968" Henry Hampton, exec. producer (Boston: Blackside, Inc., 1985).

5. King, *Stride,* p. 199; *Trumpet of Conscience* (San Francisco: Harper & Row, 1967), pp. 68-70.

6. Paul Russell Garber's doctoral dissertation ("Martin Luther King, Jr.: Theologian and Precursor of Black Theology," Florida State Univ., 1973) has argued that like that of all liberationists, King's is essentially an anthropocentric point of departure. His emergence from the black religious experience, his exposure to the black predicament, and his concern to take social problems seriously make Garber's thesis quite tenable. One might also note another rather obvious but surprisingly disregarded source for King's theology—Paul Tillich. King wrote his doctoral

dissertation on Tillich and Henry Nelson Wieman, and was very much influenced by Tillich's method of correlation (correlating the message of the gospel with the questions of human existence). See Paul Tillich, *Systematic Theology*, vol. 1 (Chicago: University of Chicago Press, 1951), pp. 3, 8, 11-15, 53.

7. As late as King's final public speech (the "Mountaintop" speech in Memphis, 1968), King's theological and ethical focus remained solidly theocentric. Out of all that he had hoped to accomplish, he said, "I just want to do God's will." Although the starting point is human-related, clearly the ultimate aim is God-related.

8. Again, King's efforts to answer questions about the conception of God definitively came to a head with his formal research on the dissertation project. And yet, King admitted that it was not until the Montgomery bus boycott that he "experienced the presence of the Divine as I had never experienced him before." See King, *Stride*, p. 134.

9. See, for instance, King's sermons "Death of Evil on the Seashore" and "Our God Is Able" in King, *Strength*.

10. In virtually all of King's writings, the allusions to God are quite prominent. King's book of sermons alone (*Strength to Love*) is riddled with God language—God as just and forgiving (p. 15); ultimate concern and refuge (p. 73); active in history working to defeat evil (pp. 83, 97); caring parent (p. 90); sovereign, provident, and triumphant in history (p. 95); essence and ground of all reality (p. 97); cosmic law-giver (p. 98); Savior and sustainer of the universe (p. 99); eternal source of courage and hope (p. 124); coresponsible agent in history (p. 136); love (p. 145); personal (p. 154).

11. Eminent John Calvin scholar John Leith's analysis of the basic structure of Calvin's theology has merit for attempts to describe King's theology. Leith has argued rather persuasively that Calvin cannot be understood as a systematic theologian, per se. For Leith, Calvin's theological perspective may best be understood by comparing it ". . . to a wagon wheel without the rim. There is a center which holds it together and from which spokes extend, but there is no outer rim which brings the spokes into a self-contained order . . . [T]he hub of the wheel is the personal relationship between God and humankind. . . . The spokes represent the various attempts to explicate this relationship according to particular themes which are developed . . . but which are never fully related to other particular truths." See John Leith, *John Calvin's Doctrine of the Christian Life* (Louisville: Westminster/John Knox, 1989), pp. 12-21.

This evaluation represents an apt description of the basic structure of King's theology. King's theological hub consists of his conceptualization of God. King used that hub as a focal point from which to articulate other doctrinal thematics (e.g., Christology, anthropology, and such). King never completely tied all the strands together in systematic fashion. Some theological issues, while addressed, were never thought through completely. L. Harold DeWolf, ("Martin Luther King, Jr. as Theologian," *Journal of the Interdenominational Center* 4 [Spring 1977], p. 10) has alluded to King's doctrine of evil as a case in point.

12. Several factors contribute to King's never being able to explicate his theological viewpoint fully in the more orthodox manner—the manner in which King's thought process operated (synthesizing, eclectic borrowing), the situational

context out of which his understanding of God emerged (black suffering, poverty, militarism), the daily pressures and constraints upon his time, his untimely death, and such.

13. King's situational context and view of God acted in concert with his theological method of action-reflection as well as his teleological focus on the concrete realization of justice, freedom, and equality in community to result in a theological perspective that was highly practical in nature. This pragmatic focus in King's thought can be seen in his column "Advice for Living," *Ebony*, 1956–57; and in his remarks in "Action for Interracial Understanding," *Franciscan Herald and Forum* 42 (October 1963), p. 289.

14. James Cone, *Martin and Malcolm and America: A Dream or a Nightmare* (Maryknoll, N.Y.: Orbis Books, 1991), pp. 121-25.

15. See David Howard-Pitney, *The Afro-American Jeremiad: Appeals for Justice in America* (Philadelphia: Temple Univ. Press, 1990), pp. 3-16, 133-83.

16. See for instance, King, *Stride*, pp. 36-39, 91. See also Lewis Baldwin, *Balm in Gilead*, pp. 58, 66, 166-67, 180-81, 227.

17. King's doctoral dissertation represents a formal, written demonstration of his ability to think in and use the categories of traditional theology. Also see Cone, *Martin and Malcolm*, pp. 131-35; Ralph Abernathy, "Our Lives Were Filled with the Action," in C. Eric Lincoln, ed., *Martin Luther King, Jr.: A Profile* (New York: Hill & Wang, 1970), and "Dr. King's Theology in Action," unpublished paper, author's files, n.d.; and L. Harold DeWolf, "Martin Luther King, Jr., as Theologian."

18. It is interesting to note that the very same problematic existed for James Cone in 1969 relative to black theology. In the text *A Black Theology of Liberation* (New York: J. B. Lippincott Company, 1970), Cone faced head-on the necessity of offering a sustained, systematic delineation of black theology through the classical doctrinal categories and foci of the Christian tradition. This work attempts the same relative to Kingian theology. To date, there is still a dearth of research focusing on King's thinking about traditional Christian doctrines. This fact has serious implications for a resolution of King's crisis of ambiguous identity in the public square. I would contend that if King is to be better understood as a distinctively Christian theologian, his thinking, writings, and social activism must be correlated more closely with the doctrinal categories and foci of traditional Christianity—God, ecclesiology, anthropology, Christology, eschatology, doctrine of the Christian life, and so forth.

To my knowledge, only L. Harold DeWolf, "Martin Luther King as Theologian," (*Journal of the Interdenominational Center* 4 [Spring 1977]: 1-11); James P. Hanigan, "Martin Luther King, Jr. and the Ethics of Nonviolence" (Ph. D. diss., Duke Univ., 1973); and Ervin Smith, "The Role of Personalism in the Development of the Social Ethics of Martin Luther King, Jr." (Ph.D. diss., Northwestern Univ., 1976) have attempted to show how King's theology might look in the categories and foci of traditional doctrine. This is not to say, however, that some other scholars have not teased out doctrinal categories found in King's thinking. See, for example, Shin Lee, "Concept of Human Nature, Justice, and Nonviolence in the Political Thinking of Martin Luther King, Jr." (Ph.D. diss., New York Univ., 1979); or John Colin Harris, "The Theology of Martin Luther King Jr." (Ph.D. diss., Duke University, 1974), which focuses on King's doctrine of reconciliation, but fails to show how this doctrine is related to King's other doctrinal emphases.

James Hanigan's dissertation is helpful, but limited in that it focuses primarily on King's ethical philosophy of nonviolence as King's main orientation. Here, I think, Hanigan is mistaken. King's primary focus is love (of which nonviolence is only a part). King's love is understood as an "involved love" derived from his view of God. Hanigan seems to miss this point. In a similar fashion, Ervin Smith organizes King's thinking more systematically in light of King's claim that Bostonian personalism was his primary philosophical commitment. Smith provides helpful clues to King's understanding of God and humanity. However, he fails to give due credence to King's more forceful and most oft-repeated self-description as a committed minister of the Christian gospel. Smith fails to take seriously King's statement that it is the Spirit of Christ that guides the movement he is leading. Hence, Smith pays virtually no attention to King's Christology, ecclesiology, or doctrine of the Christian life.

19. The notion of "organic intellectual" has been popularized by Cornel West in *Prophetic Fragments* (Grand Rapids: Eerdmans, 1988). West appropriates the term from Antonio Gramsci and applies it to King to mean an individual who is "linked to prophetic movements or priestly institutions" in such a way as to "take the life of the mind seriously enough to relate ideas to the everyday life of ordinary folk. . . . Organic intellectuals are activistic and engaged."

20. King had certainly engaged in critical reflection prior to his public ministry. However, from Montgomery to Memphis, all of his theological statements are made either *in* or *after* his involvement in organized efforts aimed at comprehensive social change. In fact, participation in liberative social action acted to clarify and hone King's thinking. In reading the evolving Kingian corpus, one observes an increased level and skill in sophisticated analysis over time. For instance, *Why We Can't Wait*, written during and after the Birmingham Campaign of 1963, contains a much stronger line against gradualist politics. It is also more piercing in its critique of white liberals and the white church as compared to *Stride Toward Freedom* of 1957. Similarly, *Where Do We Go from Here*, written in 1967 after the lessons learned in the Selma Campaign of 1964–65 and the Chicago Campaign of 1965–66, offers a more searing critique of American capitalism, a focus on poverty, and a more detailed and complex analysis of power compared to *Why We Can't Wait*. The same maturation of thought can be seen in King's oral statements. Compare, for instance, "Nonviolence and Racial Justice" (1957) to "Ethical Demands for Integration" (1963) and "Remaining Awake Through a Great Revolution" (1968).

The primary point must not be lost, however, that King's written and oral statements take place within and beyond the fires of struggle and protest. In this sense, King's theological methodology is consistent with that of liberation theology's action-reflection model. In fact, King might be viewed as a precursor, of sorts, to liberation theology, at least in its written form of the 1960s and beyond.

21. On the concept of involvement, I am influenced by Benjamin Reist, *Toward a Theology of Involvement: The Thought of Ernst Troeltsch* (Philadelphia: Westminster Press, 1966).

22. Paul Garber, "Too Much Taming of Martin Luther King?" *Christian Century* XCI (June 5, 1974), p. 616.

23. Andrew Hacker (*Two Nations: Black and White, Separate, Hostile, Unequal* [New York: Charles Scribner's Sons, 1992], pp. 18-19, 63) is correct, I believe, in his contention that King has become a choice of whites in America because he fits their comfort zones. He had been heavily credentialed by the white academy. He spoke the language of mainstream American religion. His nonviolent rhetoric and philosophy and his willingness to engage in biracial coalition politics made him palatable to many whites. The radicality of King's thought, however, is clearly demonstrable. In fact, if the American public were to seriously examine the things King said and did, it might not be so quick to embrace him as a national hero. On the other hand, the disturbing radicalism of King may be a reason why he has been so domesticated and reimaged according to national specifications. For a discussion of King's myriad public images, see chapter 1 of this work. Also see Luther D. Ivory, "Dr. Martin Luther King, Jr.: More Than a Dream," *Union Theological Seminary Focus,* Spring 1992, p. 4.

24. An honest and serious look at how the message of King has been packaged for public consumption reveals how and why he is often portrayed as little more than an idealistic social visionary. It is clearly demonstrable in media presentations of his famous "Dream" speech. Selective sound bites provide innocuous renditions of King's rhythmic refrains, "I have a dream . . . ," "Let freedom ring . . . ," "With this faith . . . ," "Free at last . . . !" Conspicuously absent is the rather lengthy and incisive critique of American historical precedent, social policy, economic reality, legal thrust, and political will relative to the status of blacks. The text has been redacted, and the prophetic analysis has been excised. Hence, apart from King scholars, very few Americans are familiar with the total breadth and depth of King's argument in the speech. The text has come to us too truncated to do justice to the full force of its cutting edge critique. For a discussion of this tendency to sanitize King's speeches, see Haig Bosmajian, "The Inaccuracies of Martin Luther King's 'I Have a Dream' Speech," *Communication Education* 31 (4/82), pp. 107-14; also James Cone, *Martin and Malcolm,* pp. 19-20.

25. I am thoroughly convinced that King has been effectively "commodified" as a marketable "product" in America's market-oriented, profit-driven culture. On one hand, he has been long held in captivity by many loyal admirers (both black and white) who recognize his greatness, but fail to appreciate and take seriously his humanity. For these, King becomes a "commodity" who must be apologetically defined and defended on their own terms. On the other hand, representatives of the liberal white power establishment (through its monopoly control of the media) tend to hold King captive in an even more insidious manner. These are motivated by a desire to shape the image (and hence, legacy) of King according to their own special interests and specifications. They embrace King, in death, in a way they never could or would in life. Consequently, he is reduced to "product" status and is often made to serve the more prurient interests of a market-driven culture and, at the same time, used to legitimate aspects of the status quo, namely liberal notions of success and philanthropic pity, consumeristic values, and the "triumphant" capitalist spirit.

Paradoxically, the national holiday tended to exacerbate this problem. It did for King what the Constantinian paradigm did for Christianity. Christianity lost much of the cutting edge it had developed while marginalized in the broader culture. The

King holiday, while certainly necessary and potentially uplifting, ironically assisted in co-opting King as a hero of the American state. In this sense, it represents both promise and problematic, gift and task.

26. This undeniable fact is a primary factor in James Cone's perceptive insight that our culture has transformed "a genuinely prophetic voice into the 'voice of America.'" Paul Garber has contended that in America there has been "too much taming of Martin Luther King." See Cone, *Speaking the Truth* (Grand Rapids: Eerdmans, 1986), p. 76; Garber, "Too Much Taming of Martin Luther King," *Journal of Interdenominational Theological Center 2* (Spring, 1975):100-113.

27. The term has been used so often by so many that it has lost much of its true content and meaning. The connotative sense of the word is usually associated with vehement rhetoric that emphasizes violent overthrow of the existing social order. The pervasive and stereotypical caricature of guerrilla-style, paramilitary activity tends to inhibit one's capacity to see the usefulness of the word. This imagery has too often been promoted by angry militants and other ideologues who are self-described "radicals." In ascribing radical status to King's theology, my intent is to recover and to critically reappropriate the denotative meaning of the term. For a discussion of the perceptual imaging of radicals in public consciousness see Saul Alinsky, *Rules for Radicals* (New York: Vintage Books, 1971), pp. xix-xxii, 10, 48-62; and Robert Allen, *Black Awakening in Capitalist America* (Trenton, N.J.: Africa World Press, 1990), pp. 246-73.

28. *Webster's New College Dictionary*, p. 697.

29. Ibid.

30. See "The Case Against Tokenism" in James Washington, ed., *A Testament of Hope: The Essential Writings of Martin Luther King, Jr.* (San Francisco: Harper & Row, 1986), pp. 106-11, and "Bold Design for a New South," pp. 112-16 in same; King, *Trumpet of Conscience*, "Impasse in Race Relations," pp. 3-20.

31. King, *Where Do We Go from Here*, pp. 132-34, 186-91; *Trumpet*, pp. 32-33.

32. King, *Where Do We Go from Here*, pp. 193-202.

33. Garrow, *Bearing the Cross*, p. 564.

34. King, *Where Do We Go from Here*, p. 187.

35. Ibid., pp. 133-34; *Trumpet of Conscience*, pp. 49-50.

36. "Martin Luther King, Jr.: From Montgomery to Memphis," 16mm, Bailey Films Associates, Santa Monica, California, 35 minutes, black and white, 1968.

37. The best of the black religious tradition has always taken seriously the inseparability of faith and life. As such, it has held to a strict tension between divine sovereignty and human responsibility. Radicalism in black religious thought has concerned itself not only with the ways and acts of a mysterious God, but also "the thrust of blacks for human liberation expressed in theological terms and religious institutions" (see Wilmore, *Black Religion and Black Radicalism*, [Maryknoll, N.Y.: Orbis Books, 1984], pp. 167-74). As an inheritor of this tradition, King held that religion was linked to life (King, *Stride*, pp. 37, 117). Nurture in the bosom of the black church had caused King (even prior to his intellectual search in seminary) to be concerned with issues of social and economic justice. King's black religious faith not only spurred his radical pragmatism, but also provided theological grounding for his efforts at social change.

38. "Martin Luther King, Jr.: From Montgomery to Memphis," 16mm film, 35 minutes, black and white, Bailey Films Associates, Santa Monica, California, 1968.

39. King, *Stride*, pp. 63, 109-11, 113-14.

40. James Cone has convincingly argued that King's early period in Montgomery was marked by "an optimistic belief that justice could be achieved through love, which he identified with nonviolence. At the beginning of the Montgomery bus boycott, he placed justice at the center of his thinking." This had the net effect of making King "radical" enough in his methodological approach to "insist that black people stand up and demand their rights." However, King was not yet radical enough in his thought to advocate the kind of comprehensive, revolutionary structural change that he would in 1967. This point is very important in establishing that King already harbored radical elements in his thinking, but these would undergo continuous deepening and evolution. See Cone, *Martin and Malcolm*, pp. 60-63.

41. Ibid., pp. 112-13. Theologian Reinhold Niebuhr's contention that the virulence and intransigence of sin (especially at the level of group relations) must not be underestimated helped to qualify King's own optimism about human potential for good, helping him to take seriously the "reality of sin" (King, *Stride*, p. 99). And yet despite the fact that he had read Niebuhr prior to Montgomery, King's account shows that the Niebuhrian theses didn't quite ring true until tested in the crucible of struggle. King admitted as much when he said that the experience in Montgomery had done more to clarify his thinking about nonviolence than all the books he had read (King, *Stride*, p. 101; *Strength*, pp. 151-52).

42. Washington, *Testament of Hope*, pp. 75-81.

43. A short two years later in 1957, for instance, King began to understand more clearly the connection between racial and economic justice. To attack the "root cause" of racism, King now knew that you had to attack the economic bases of racism simultaneously. Montgomery had proved the power of economic boycott. King now moved to seize the initiative in this area in 1957 when he invited AFL-CIO Unions to participate in a "Prayer Pilgrimage for Freedom" in Washington, D.C., in May. Of course, the AFL-CIO, and most white trade unions, refused to participate (as they did in Montgomery). See Garrow, *Bearing the Cross*, pp. 91-94; and Manning Marable, *Race, Reform, and Rebellion: The Second Reconstruction in Black America, 1945–1982* (Jackson: University Press of Mississippi, 1984), pp. xi-xii, 54-55. King's radical analysis and action also led to an expanded focus (prior to 1963) on voting rights, employment, legislation, and coalition politics. See Washington, *Testament of Hope*, pp. 103-4, 110, 197-99, 201-6.

44. For instance, King's role in the Peace Movement and his critique of the war in Vietnam came about as a result of several factors—his receipt of the Nobel Peace Prize, the voice of James Bevel (a peace activist on King's staff at SCLC), and the Chicago Campaign of 1965–66, which revealed the connection between U.S. domestic and foreign policy. In a similar manner, the influence of the black power philosophy on King came as a result of the Meredith March coalition between SNCC, CORE, and SCLC in 1966. Likewise, King's increasing conscientization around the issue of poverty was certainly helped by the Chicago experience and his contact with the democratic socialist Michael Harrington in 1960. See Garrow, *Bearing the Cross*, pp. 140, 431-74, 475-25, 527-74.

45. See Garrow, *Bearing the Cross,* pp. 278, 288, 326, 340, 344, 353, 358, 364-69, 376.

46. Ibid., pp. 376, 382, 394, 415, 418, 425, 426-27, 428, 430, 431-74.

47. Washington, *Testament of Hope,* pp. 245-52, 394-414.

48. Garrow, *Bearing the Cross,* p. 562.

49. King, *Where Do We Go from Here,* pp. 186-88.

50. The radical elements in King's thinking and activism continued to develop and mature after 1965. Initially in Chicago, for instance, King had come to that city with a naïveté and lack of experience with big city dynamics and "machine" politicians like Mayor Daley. As in the initial stages of the movement in Montgomery in 1955, King had a lot of important lessons to learn and relearn in Chicago. See Garrow, *Bearing the Cross,* pp. 431-525.

51. King, *Trumpet of Conscience,* pp. 53-64.

52. King, *Where Do We Go from Here,* pp. 129, 135-36, 156-57.

53. Ibid., pp. 186-88.

54. Ibid., pp. 182-86.

55. Ibid., pp. 161-66, 196-202.

56. For example, King, prior to 1965, had already begun (as early as 1956) to deal with issues of voting rights, employment, economics and poverty, Vietnam and militarism. See Garrow, *Bearing the Cross,* pp. 61, 77-79, 92-98, 223, 226.

57. Though the fact is not well known, King had paid attention to crises in South Africa, Asia, and other parts of the globe. He recognized America's imperialistic role in global geopolitical affairs. See Washington, *Testament of Hope,* pp. 23-30, 50, 146, 162; Garrow, *Bearing the Cross,* pp. 90-91, 118, 224.

58. King, *Stride,* pp. 216-17; *Trumpet of Conscience,* pp. 48, 53, 74.

59. King, *Stride,* pp. 212-14; King, *Trumpet of Conscience,* pp. 70-75.

60. The conceptual rubric of "radical involvement" provides a way of resolving the tension between Vincent Harding's categorization of "early" and "late" Kings. Harding identifies the King of pre-1965 as the naive ideologue who is enamored with the philosophy of love and the methods of nonviolence and moral suasion. The post-1965 King is labeled as the democratic socialist who is more politically sophisticated and commands a more realistic appraisal of the nature, role, and operation of power in society relative to the politics of race, class, and militarism. Harding is certainly correct in pointing out the developmental aspect of King's thought and action. However, the misappropriation of Harding's typology has, unfortunately, led some to a dismissal of the pre-1965 King as irrelevant to the contemporary struggle for justice. A false choice is thereby induced as to the necessity of a preferential option for the "late" (post-1965) King over the "early" King as a model for liberative thought and action. At the same time, those who are primarily interested in limited, reformist change and quasi-support of the status quo tend to exhibit a decided preference for the "early" King.

While Harding's typology has merit regarding evolution of King's perspective toward radicalism, it tends to obscure the threads of continuity that exist throughout King's developing theological and ethical program. "Radical involvement" allows for the maturation of King's thinking and activism while, at the same time, it gives due credence to those thematics that anchor and guide King throughout his public ministry. It gives proper weight to both the permanency and the change in King. Thus we are able to appreciate both "early" and "late" Kings for their equal concern with radical societal transformation. At the same time, while one might find more of an affinity for either the pre- or post-1965 King, "radical involvement" allows for a more "informed" affinity. It will prevent the tendency to overlook the continuity in King's perspective and methodology while giving due credence to the discontinuous developments.

See several of Harding's articles, "Recalling the Inconvenient Hero: Reflections on the Last Years of Martin Luther King, Jr.," *Union Seminary Quarterly Review* 40 (1/86), pp. 53-68; "Black Radicalism: The Road from Montgomery" in Albert F. Young, ed., *Dissent* (DeKalb: Northern Illinois University Press, 1968), pp. 319-54; "So Much History, So Much Future: Martin Luther King, Jr., and the Second Coming of America" in Michael V. Namorato, ed., *Have We Overcome?* (Jackson: University Press of Mississippi, 1979), pp. 31-78; "The Land Beyond: Reflections on Martin Luther King, Jr.'s, 'Beyond Vietnam' Speech," *Sojourners* (January 1986), pp. 2-9.

61. In the contemporary classic *Suffering* (Philadelphia: Fortress, 1975), pp. 33-61, Dorothy Soelle identifies the major problem of middle-class, capitalistic society in the "post-Christian" era as apathy. Soelle defines apathy as "minimal indifference to the suffering of others . . . toleration of exploitation, oppression, and injustice . . . an unconcern that is incapable of suffering. . . . *Apatheia* is a Greek word that literally means nonsuffering, freedom from suffering, a creature's inability to suffer. . . . Apathy is a form of the inability to suffer. It is understood as a social condition in which people are so dominated by the goal of avoiding suffering that it becomes a goal to avoid human relationships and contacts altogether." This description and critique of apathy represent precisely what King wrestled against throughout his life. His activism and resistance as well as his views on the necessity of suffering in the struggle against suffering aim at a resolution of the problem as illumined by Soelle.

62. King's critique of American culture pointed to what he felt was symptomatic of apathy—conspicuous consumerism, militaristic jingoism, and the exaltation of technology. Through a valorization of these values and objectives, King believed that the society had demonstrated an incapacity "to focus on programs of social uplift," "to make democracy real," "to invest the necessary funds or energies in rehabilitation of the poor." In this way, he linked apathy to a moral crisis not only at the level of individual existence, but at the level of the collective life as well. Thus, King often described apathy as a "malady within the American spirit," "spiritual doom," "spiritual emptiness of contemporary society," "poverty of the spirit," "absence of moral purpose," "soulless society," and "alienation." See King, *Trumpet of Conscience*, pp. 32, 33, 37, 43-44, 64.

63. This may explain, in part, why King's rhetoric contains such picturesque, symbolic military imagery. Notice his descriptive references to "war" and "war against poverty" (King, *Where Do We Go from Here*, pp. 20, 81); "biracial army" and "battle" (Washington, *Testament of Hope*, pp. 218, 229-30); "nonviolent army" and "offensive" (King, *Why We Can't Wait*, pp. 36-38, 62, 123, 116). King often described the methods of the freedom struggle as "weapons" (Washington, *Testament of Hope*, p. 77; and King, *Stride*, pp. 84-85) that are used to "attack" forces of injustice (Washington, *Testament*

*of Hope,* p. 81); nonviolence is the "sword" that heals (King, *Why We Can't Wait,* p. 27).

64. Washington, *Testament of Hope,* p. 257.

65. King, *Stride,* p. 197.

66. King, *Where Do We Go from Here,* pp. 171-72; Washington, *Testament of Hope,* p. 280.

67. The race problem, for King, represented more than a mere social problem. King, in fact, described it as "America's chief moral dilemma." See Washington, *Testament of Hope,* pp. 88, 117.

68. King, *Where Do We Go from Here,* pp. 172-73. Note: The motto of the SCLC was avowedly to "Redeem the Soul of the Nation." King himself frequently used the phrase "to save the soul of the nation." See his sermon, for instance, "What a Mother Should Tell Her Child," delivered at Ebenezer Baptist Church in May 1963 (King Center Transcripts, Number 11, Atlanta).

69. See King, *Stride,* pp. 191, 196-97, 200, 224; *Why We Can't Wait,* pp. 15-26, 115-25, 131-33; and *Where Do We Go from Here,* pp. 16-17, 32-34, 50, 59.

70. In Montgomery in 1955, King asserted that the crisis had become so urgent that blacks had reached the "point of no return" (see Stephen Oates, *Let the Trumpet Sound* [New York: Signet, 1982, p. 67]). In 1961 and 1962 in Nashville, King again warned that "the hour is late . . . the clock of destiny is ticking out; we must act now before it is too late" (Washington, *Testament of Hope,* pp. 117, 209). In the famous "Dream" speech in Washington, D.C., in 1963, King argued that "It would be fatal for the nation to overlook the urgency of the moment. . . . There will be neither rest nor tranquility in America until the Negro is granted full citizenship rights" (Washington, *Testament of Hope,* pp. 217-18). In Chicago in 1965, again King called the nation's attention to the state of siege and crisis gripping the land (Washington, *Testament of Hope,* p. 269). Finally, in 1967 and 1968, at the end of his life, King continued to warn America of the urgent nature of the crisis it faced. "We are now faced with the fierce urgency of now" (King, *Where Do We Go from Here,* pp. 189, 191; Washington, *Testament of Hope,* p. 280).

71. In Montgomery in 1956, King argued that the presence of a revolutionary attitude operating within the collective psyche of black people in America had led to "the extreme tension in race relations in the South today" (Washington, *Testament of Hope,* p. 76). In 1967, King would make the bold claim that the internal, psychological, and spiritual-moral revolution that had occurred in black folks since the late 1950s represented the most profound and enduring accomplishment of the civil rights movement. See King, *Where Do We Go from Here,* chapter 3.

72. King also argued that America had lost its revolutionary spirit, and along with other Western nations, had become an arch antirevolutionary (Washington, *Testament of Hope,* p. 355). King implored America (especially whites) to "recapture the revolutionary spirit" and thereby become liberated from "comfort, complacency, a morbid fear of communism, and [a] proneness to adjust to injustice. . . ." (King, *Where Do We Go from Here,* p. 190).

73. On theological grounds, King argued that the gospel of Jesus Christ was revolutionary in nature. It not only infused the believer with a certain attitudinal perspective, but called for a commensurate lifestyle as well. The apathetic personality

operated in contradistinction to those notions of principled prophetism and social activism inherent in the gospel. See chapter 2 of this work. Also see King, *Strength*, p. 105.

74. King, *Trumpet of Conscience*, pp. 43-44. King's reading of Karl Marx appears to inform his understanding of alienation. In a similar manner, his reading of Paul Tillich appears to inform his notion of separation. King admitted his reading of Marx. Tillich is one of the figures examined in King's doctoral dissertation. It appears reasonable to deduce that King was familiar with the Tillichian corpus. See King's dissertation "Conceptions of God in the Thinking of Paul Tillich and Henry Nelson Wieman," Boston Univ. Press, 1955; *Stride*, pp. 92-95; *Why We Can't Wait*, p. 82; and *Strength*, pp. 103, 149. See also Ansbro, p. 291.

75. King, *Stride*, p. 209.

76. Ibid., p. 90-91.

77. The American dissenting tradition represents that "stubborn tradition of loyal opposition in American history" that is characterized by a "determination to put righteousness, conscience, and morality before social and political expediency." The dissenting tradition of the black religious faith modeled the "determination to resist oppression." See Washington, *Testament of Hope*, pp. xi-xiii.

78. King, *Stride*, pp. 21-22.

79. Ibid., p. 30; Taylor Branch, *Parting the Waters: America in the King Years 1954–63* (New York: Simon & Schuster, 1988), pp. 114-16.

80. King, *Stride*, p. 35.

81. Washington, *Testament of Hope*, p. 89.

82. Ibid., p. 222.

83. Ibid.

84. Ibid., p. 197.

85. Washington, *Testament of Hope*, pp. 213, 296, 354. Two years later, amid the Birmingham Campaign in 1963, King would write a book entitled *Why We Can't Wait*. A major aim of the book was to counter misguided societal positivism with regard to the efficacy of gradualist approaches to social justice. By linking gradualism to antirevolutionary activity, King sought to demonstrate the strategic futility and moral irresponsibility of adopting a slow-paced agenda for change and sought to build national consensus for a consolidated, full-fledged assault on discriminatory policies and practices.

86. Ibid., p. 296. King described the forces of complacency as Negroes who have adjusted to segregation, and of a few Negroes in the middle class who have unconsciously become insensitive to the problems of the masses (ibid., pp. 85, 296). King pushed a notion of nonviolent militancy as a counterposition to the apathy of this group. To the forces of bitterness and violence, King countered with a notion of militant nonviolence based on love. King resisted both counterproductive apathy and xenophobic violence.

87. King asserted that most white Americans thought themselves to be "sincerely committed to justice for the Negro." The majority of whites also felt that America was "essentially hospitable to fair play . . . and racial harmony." King argued that this amounted to "a fantasy of self-deception and comfortable vanity." America was "still struggling with irresolution and contradictions," and while it had been "sincere and

207

even ardent in welcoming some change . . . too quickly apathy and disinterest rise to the surface when the next logical steps are to be taken. . . . " See King, *Where Do We Go from Here*, pp. 4-5, see also pp. 1-12, 67-101; *Trumpet*, pp. 3-10.

88. Washington, *Testament of Hope*, pp. 147-48.

89. King, *Where Do We Go from Here*, pp. 189-90.

90. King, *Stride*, pp. 196, 197; *Strength*, pp. 130-33.

91. Washington, *Testament of Hope*, p. 268; King, *Where Do We Go from Here*, pp. 170-71.

92. Washington, *Testament of Hope*, pp. 91, 94, 160, 167, 176, 231, 354.

93. King, *Where Do We Go from Here*, p. 9.

94. Garber, p. 163.

95. King's activistic focus was understood theocentrically as a choice for God's will for freedom. As early as Montgomery, King had argued that the movement now faced a critical decision: remain shackled to unjust and outdated customs or pledge allegiance to the moral universe's ethical demands. King was clear: the Christian's ultimate allegiance was to God alone. Divine will always took precedence over human convention (King, *Stride*, p. 117). Therefore, human beings must make the ethical choice to join God in the struggle for justice (ibid., pp. 172, 190, 207, 209).

96. King, *Stride*, p. 206; Washington, *Testament of Hope*, p. 10.

97. Washington, *Testament of Hope*, p. 286. Again, King's lifelong quest was to discover God's will and way, and to live in accordance with divine purposiveness ("I just want to do God's will").

98. In this sense, King serves as a kind of precursor to a "theology of liberation." In his classic text, *A Theology of Liberation: History, Salvation, and Politics* (Maryknoll, N.Y.: Orbis Books, 1984), Gustavo Gutierrez (considered the parent of liberation theology) argues that theology (as critical reflection on Christian praxis) involves a two-step process (p. 9). Step one is historical praxis on behalf of justice (p. 5). Step two is critical reflection (p. 9). King's theological perspective appropriated an action-reflection methodology long before the publication of Gutierrez's text in English in 1971.

99. It is not accidental and more than incidental that King's prophetic public utterance and written reflection and analysis always come either *in the midst of* or *after the completion of* particular confrontations in the liberation struggle.

100. Washington, *Testament of Hope*, pp. 82, 87-88.

101. Ibid., pp. 56, 91, 104, 190, 313.

102. King, *Strength*, pp. 131-32; *Trumpet of Conscience*, p. 59

103. This is why the movement as a struggle for liberation began in the black churches and was carried out through black church institutions. Seeing it as a "Christian movement," King appropriated black religious faith to sustain the movement's power. See King, *Stride*, pp. 50, 59-63; and *Trumpet*, pp. 71-75.

104. King, *Stride*, pp. 197-211.

105. Washington, *Testament of Hope*, pp. 33, 34.

106. In the role of public dissenter, King visibly embodied this theological perspective. His prophetic critique and radical praxis made him extremely unpopular with reactionary white elements. At times his public witness carried the threat of death for himself, his family, and others in the movement he led. He

experienced numerous bombings, death threats, jailings, and attempts on his life. In addition, after 1967, King's views on poverty and the Vietnam War made him persona non grata with heretofore friendly forces. King became estranged not only from the Johnson White House, but from other black civil rights leaders as well. See King, *Stride*, pp. 108-50; Garrow, *Bearing the Cross*, pp. 575-624; Howard-Pitney, pp. 175-83.

107. King's position matured over time. In Montgomery, he had great optimism in moral suasion (Washington, *Testament of Hope*, pp. 154-55). By 1967, he had come to see that moral appeal was inadequate. Radical action was necessary (King, *Where Do We Go from Here*, p. 152).

108. King understood the movement for justice as a lifelong commitment to sacrifice. The body came to be understood as an instrument for liberation. King believed that the Christian gospel placed nonnegotiable, moral claims and obligations upon the life of the individual Christian and the church.

109. Again, moral integrity was King's barometer for measuring the health of a society. In this sense, King attempted to alter the moral ethos of the American public. Also see King's discussion of "revolution of values" in *Where Do We Go from Here*, pp. 5, 11, 85, 132-34, 186-91; and Robert Bellah, *Habits of the Heart* (New York: Harper & Row, 1985), pp. 249, 286.

110. In a sermon entitled "The Drum Major Instinct," King asserted that the route to genuine discipleship ran through a service ethic. Jesus Christ had invested greatness with new content. In so doing, he provided a new criteria for determining importance. The hallmark of personal greatness lay in one's capacity to serve humanity. Since this service ethic was accessible to *everyone*, greatness was now achievable by *anyone*. See Washington, *Testament of Hope*, pp. 265-66.

111. Garrow, *Bearing the Cross*, pp. 5, 10. King believed this call was so serious that not even children and youth were exempted from its radical demands. See Washington, *Testament of Hope*, pp. 221-23; and King, *Trumpet of Conscience*, pp. 35-50.

112. King, *Where Do We Go from Here*, pp. 131-32; *Trumpet of Conscience*, pp. 45-47.

113. Washington, *Testament of Hope*, p. 267.

114. See Frederick L. Downing, *To See the Promised Land: The Faith Pilgrimage of Martin Luther King, Jr.* (Macon, Ga.: Mercer Press, 1986), pp. 29-36, 259-64, 279-80.

115. King said that despite the constant "temptation of wanting to retreat to a more quiet and serene life," his faith in God and hope in the future empowered him to embrace a lifestyle in which the servanthood ethic was normatively affirmed.

116. Washington, *Testament of Hope*, p. 179.


## CHAPTER 5


1. Bennie Goodwin observes that King did not necessarily *produce* social change. Describing King as a social educator, Goodwin asserts that "it is not within the province of the social educator to produce social change. It is his task to creatively and persistently present ideas. It is these ideas, effectively presented, which create the pressure which motivates those in power to produce the necessary social changes." See his "Martin Luther King, Jr., American Social Educator," *Journal of the Interdenominational Theological Center* IV (Spring 1977): 42-48.

Goodwin's point is a sobering one. King and other committed civil rights activists were, finally, unable to produce lasting social change for the mass of poor and marginalized people in American society. However, we must not overlook the fact that King and others did manage to produce significant social change in several areas that did benefit many in the culture (e.g., civil rights legislation, dismantling Jim Crow legislation, psychological attitudinal change, and a theological paradigm shift). Further, King not only effectively engaged in the creative presentation of radical ideas in the public domain, he also consistently placed his body on the line with others in active, nonviolent resistance and civil protest in order to place pressure on the prevailing status quo. In this sense, King was more than a social educator; he was also an agent of social change.

2. Contemporary theologies of liberation include African American, womanist, Latin American, feminist, African, Asian, and Native American perspectives.

3. The question of ethics ("What ought I to be or to do?") is answered in the form of a policy, an action, or a judgment. This "answer" is the result of those moral deliberations that are part of any moral argument. Drawing from the work of Ralph Potter, Arthur C. Dyck argues that there are four variables that must be considered in any moral-ethical argument: values, loyalties, anthropological understanding, and situational analysis. See Arthur C. Dyck, *On Human Care: An Introduction to Christian Ethics* (Nashville: Abingdon Press, 1977), pp. 19-21.

4. On the social level, King advocated integrated, intergroup, interpersonal living that transcended the boundaries of race, class, nationality, and religion. In the political arena, King advocated fairness in the use of the franchise vote, democratic participation in electoral politics, shared political power, and coalition politics. On the economic front, King advocated a socially conscious democracy that avoided the excesses and negativities of both capitalism and communism. See Martin Luther King Jr., *Strength to Love* (Philadelphia: Fortress, 1963), pp. 96-105; and *Where Do We Go from Here: Chaos or Community?* (Boston: Beacon, 1967), pp. 139-45, 146-57, 187, 161-91. Also see James Washington, ed., *A Testament of Hope: The Essential Writings of Martin Luther King, Jr.* (San Francisco: Harper & Row, 1986), pp. 117-25, 317.

5. For this reason, King repeatedly stressed the need for values clarification and a recovery of the prophetic, revolutionary spirit. See, for instance, Martin Luther King Jr., *Where Do We Go from Here: Chaos or Community,* pp. 85, 132-34, 186-91; *Trumpet of Conscience* (San Francisco: Harper & Row, 1967), pp. 32-34.

6. King, *Where Do We Go from Here,* pp. 173, 176, 181, 186. King understood the major problematic of humankind to be that of sin, namely alienation or separation from God, and subsequently from self and others. The national and international manifestations of the problem were the "giant triplets" of racism, poverty, and war. However, there were other related problems such as unemployment, crime, lack of quality education and adequate housing. King detailed many of these "spin-off" crises in the Appendix section of *Where Do We Go from Here.*

7. King, *Strength,* pp. 56-66; phonodisc, "A Knock at Midnight" (Detroit: Motown Record Corp., 1968).

8. Martin Luther King Jr., *Why We Can't Wait* (New York: Signet, 1964), pp. 24, 135-36, 141-42, 146.

9. King, *Trumpet of Conscience,* pp. 62-64.

10. Notice King's final "Mountaintop" speech where he described the world as "all messed up" and the nation as "sick." He also made reference to "some of our sick white brothers" in speaking of those who would seek his assassination. See Washington, *Testament of Hope*, p. 280. Also see King, *Where Do We Go from Here*, p. 66, where King described the world as "dark, desperate, confused, and sin-sick."

11. King, *Where Do We Go from Here*, pp. 1-4, 5-8, 13, 19, 80-81, 83, 84, 90-92, 94, 95.

12. Ibid., pp. 132, 172-73, 186-91.

13. Ibid., pp. 85, 132-34, 161-66, 186-91.

14. King, *Trumpet of Conscience*, pp. 21-25, 33-34; Washington, *Testament of Hope*, pp. 232-34, 264-65.

15. Ibid., p. 32.

16. Coretta Scott King, *My Life with Martin Luther King, Jr.* (New York: Holt, Rinehart, and Winston, 1969), pp. 297-317; David Garrow, *The FBI and Martin Luther King, Jr.: From "Solo" to Memphis* (New York: W. W. Norton, 1981), p. 215. Note that King's last Sunday sermon, delivered at Washington National Cathedral on March 31, 1968, dealt with the theme of moral sickness in the society. King again pointed to the gulf between affluence and poverty, resources and distribution, haves and have-nots, conscienceless power and powerless conscience. He identified the vital question as whether or not America had the will to address the rampant social ills of the day. See Washington, *Testament of Hope*, pp. 268-78. King was scheduled to preach on Sunday, April 6. He had intended to deliver a sermon entitled "Why America May Go to Hell," which would deal with more prophetic analysis regarding the dissonance-consonance dialectic. Of course, King was assassinated on April 4, and never lived to give that sermon.

17. King's writings and speeches clearly reflect a concern with the conception of a beloved community. King appropriated the terminology from Josiah Royce, Walter Rauschenbusch, Howard Thurman, and others. He believed that the cosmos and all life processes were moving toward a culminating moment in a just community ordered by agape love (Walter Earl Fluker, "They Looked for a City," *Journal of Religious Ethics* 18 [Fall 1990]: 39). The theme of community would become extremely important for King as a guiding motif throughout his life.

18. King's ethical question, "What is God calling me to be and to do?" is fundamentally driven by the eschatological question of the future, "What may I hope for?" The kingdom of God in the form of the beloved community represented the radical vision that pulled his ethic toward a communitarian thrust.

A commitment to the establishment of a human community characterized by love, justice, and peace marks the core of King's ethic. The ethical perspective may be identified as communitarian in the sense that it concerns itself with restoring broken community. This is what King understood as God's ultimate will for creation—to live in harmony as a loving and just community. The biblical narrative, as well as Bostonian personalism's laws of communitarianism and Rauschenbusch's community-focused social gospel, provided theological and philosophical grounds for King's understanding of God as community-Creator, Sustainer, Redeemer, and Liberator.

That focus led King to engage in acts of nonviolent resistance and emancipatory praxis.

19. For King, Jesus as redemptive reality certainly pointed to the inbreaking rule of God in human affairs. This meant that already, in the present moment, we have been given new possibilities for creating alternative lifestyles, relationships, and institutional arrangements that would reflect more closely the love and justice of Christ.

At the same time, King held that the Niebuhrian analysis of sin must be given due credence. Hence, one must continue to look toward the future for final consummation, culmination, and complete victory of God's sovereign rule. Essentially, King held to the "already-not yet" tension found in the Pauline text of Romans. This approach acted to prevent King from falling victim to a too-easy identification of the kingdom of God with current ecclesial, social, or political structures (a criticism King made against Walter Rauschenbusch).

King's *partially realizable eschatology* led him to believe that the Christian especially had been given the mandate as well as the inner resources to face the crises, ambiguities, and contradictions of life. The present order was to hold no real threat for the believer, since ultimately the present order was being pulled by God's radical vision into a radically new future that was "not yet" fully realized, but "already" operable within human history.

20. King was fond of making use of the dialectics of dissonance versus consonance—the gap between one's professed ideals and one's actual lifestyle. King felt there should be no inconsistency between one's words and one's deeds. Repeatedly, he castigated America for glaring incongruities and contradictions between the ideals of democracy, justice, and freedom and the realities of racism, poverty, and militarism. In the Birmingham Letter of 1963, he chastised the church for failure to act responsibly toward justice, and for its reliance on "pious irrelevancies and sanctimonious trivialities." In 1967, King said that white America was "torn between selves" on the question of race—"a self in which she proudly professed the great principles of democracy and a self in which she sadly practiced the antithesis of democracy." He further called attention to the "tragic gulf between civil rights laws passed and civil rights laws implemented." In 1968, in a speech entitled "Remaining Awake Through a Great Revolution," King urged the nation to "be true to the huge promissory note it signed years ago." King said that the Poor People's Campaign was coming to Washington, to "call attention to the gulf between promise and fulfillment." In the final "Mountaintop" speech of 1968, King again picked up this theme of harmonization between preaching and practice. "All we say to America is be true to what you said on paper." See King, *Where Do We Go from Here,* pp. 68, 76, 82; Washington, *Testament of Hope,* pp. 274, 282.

21. King, *Where Do We Go from Here,* p. 187.

22. Washington, *Testament of Hope,* pp. 118, 119, 120. Note that King sometimes refers to the goal of the movement as *freedom.* A careful reading of King reveals that the content of freedom is essentially that of integration, which in turn is coterminous with that of community. See Washington, *Testament of Hope,* pp. 119-20, 277, and King, *Where Do We Go from Here,* pp. 97-101.

23. King, *Where Do We Go from Here,* pp. 61-62.

24. See King, *Stride*, p. 63; *Why We Can't Wait*, p. 64; *Strength*, p. 114; *Where Do We Go from Here*, pp. 167-73; and *Trumpet of Conscience*, pp. 71-78.

25. Washington, *Testament of Hope*, p. 200. Also King, *Stride*, p. 87.

26. King, *Stride*, pp. 171-72.

27. King's understanding of God is linked to his conception of community. His *"visio Dei"* (conception of God) is, in fact, coterminous with his *"visio communitatis"* (conception of community). In King's thinking, they are as the sound is to the echo one—and the same.

28. Washington, *Testament of Hope*, p. 20. For King, Jesus was the "source of the norm of the beloved community" (Fluker, pp. 42-43). The main point is that King's ethic is derived from a theological position that understands God as radical, agape love in action, while at the same time it understands Jesus Christ to be the very essence of divine activity in history. Therefore, King's search to know what God is up to in the universe is, at the same time, a concern to know who Jesus Christ is, and what Jesus Christ requires of us in the revolutionary situation.

29. King, *Stride*, p. 87; and *Strength*, pp. 35, 45.

30. King, *Stride*, p. 12; and *Where Do We Go from Here*, p. 191.

31. King, *Stride*, pp. 51, 69-70, 105-7.

32. King, *Where Do We Go from Here*, pp. 97, 99, 167.

33. Washington, *Testament of Hope*, pp. 117-25.

34. Thomas J. S. Mikelson, "Cosmic Companionship: The Place of God in the Moral Reasoning of Martin Luther King, Jr.," in *Journal of Religious Ethics* 18 (Fall 1990): 8-9.

35. King, *Where Do We Go from Here*, pp. 167-91; *Trumpet of Conscience*, pp. 68-70.

36. Washington, *Testament of Hope*, pp. 122, 215.

37. King, *Where Do We Go from Here*, pp. 98-99. This is why King so thoroughly condemned segregation as a sociopolitical, legal edifice. It desecrated the image of God in humanity by usurping the individual's capacity to enjoy the fruits of freedom. It "thingified" human beings. See Washington, *Testament of Hope*, p. 119.

38. This phrase, which linked love and justice in King's understanding of community, was adopted as the motto of the week by King and others at the First Annual Institute on Nonviolence and Social Change, December 3, 1956, at the Holt Street Baptist Church in Montgomery, Alabama. Again, King's communitarian ethic stressed a concern for the other. For example, see King, *Where Do We Go from Here*, pp. 85-86, 180.

39. King's doctrine of the Christian life linked personal piety and political praxis at a profound level, and in such a way that his advocacy of nonviolent resistance to collective evil became central to his understanding of Christian discipleship. In this way, King's communitarian ethic was broad enough to legitimate a variety of civil disobedience activities. King believed that this method, which emphasized moral suasion, unearned sacrificial suffering, noncooperation, and massive civil disobedience, was ultimately redemptive in the struggle against evil and injustice. It was the embodiment of the Christian love ethic in action. The individual Christian as well as the church was called upon to follow this path of humility and self-restraint, combining militancy and moderation as modeled by Jesus the Christ. See King, *Stride*, pp. 59-63, 84-89, 101-7, 213-24; *Trumpet of Conscience*, pp. 53-64, 72-75.

40. King, *Where Do We Go from Here,* pp. 172-91.

41. Ibid., pp. 162, 178, 193-202. King's emphasis upon community was especially sensitive to the needs of what he often referred to as "the least of these." King believed that a nation's greatness was ultimately judged by its compassion. He argued that America must rightly use its social, political, and economic power to achieve justice for the truly disadvantaged. Therefore, King advocated and supported specific measures such as a "Bill of Rights for the Disadvantaged" in 1963, a "Freedom Budget for all Americans" in 1967, and a "guaranteed annual income" in 1967. See King, *Why We Can't Wait,* pp. 134-39; keynote address at the National Conference for New Politics, Chicago, Illinois, August 31, 1967, King Center Archives, Atlanta, Georgia. See also Washington, *Testament of Hope,* p. 275.

42. King, *Stride,* p. 99; and *Strength,* pp. 147-48.

43. King, *Where Do We Go from Here,* p. 153.

44. King, *Stride,* p. 63; and *Strength,* p. 91.

45. Preston Williams, "An Analysis of Love and Its Influence on Justice in the Thought of Martin Luther King, Jr.," *Journal of Religious Ethics* 18 (Fall 1990): pp. 21-23.

46. Washington, *Testament of Hope,* pp. 246-47.

47. King, at this point, seemed to be especially influenced by Paul Tillich's *Love, Power, and Justice,* written in 1960. See Williams, "An Analysis of Love and Its Influence on Justice," pp. 19, 21-22, 25-26.

48. King, *Where Do We Go from Here,* pp. 36-38, 66, 128-29, 137-38, 156-57, 190.

49. Note: King's critique of the concept of black power was made precisely on the grounds that black power wrongly stressed nihilistic pessimism, black separatism, and retaliatory violence. King felt that this use of power was severed from its connection with morality or conscience. Consequently, love could not qualify power nor could power be restrained in its use. The end result was not justice and community (which King viewed as the proper end of human action) but rather chaos, fragmentation, and alienation. See King, *Where Do We Go from Here,* pp. 44-66.

50. Washington, *Testament of Hope,* p. 214.

51. King, *Stride,* pp. 50, 96-97.

52. King, *Trumpet of Conscience,* pp. 70-71.

53. King, *Where Do We Go from Here,* p. 171.

54. Washington, *Testament of Hope,* pp. 8, 12, 33, 54-61, 62-72, 365, 390-91.

55. King, *Stride,* p. 213.

56. Ibid., p. 216.

57. Ibid., p. 214. King's final verdict on violence was that it "is the antithesis of creativity and wholeness. It destroys community and makes brotherhood impossible." See King, *Where Do We Go from Here,* p. 61.

58. Washington, *Testament of Hope,* p. 8.

59. King, *Stride,* p. 220.

60. For King, hatred was "just as injurious to the hater as to the hated. Like an unchecked cancer, hate corrodes the personality and eats away its vital unity." See King, *Where Do We Go from Here,* p. 64.

61. Ibid., p. 66.

62. Ibid., pp. 59, 62-63, 65, 66. King's first public speech as president-elect of the Montgomery Improvement Association at the Holt Street Baptist Church in December of 1955 reflected his concern with integrativeness. In King's account, the pivotal question to be faced was "Could the militant and moderate be combined in a single speech?" Derivatively, he understood his task as arousing the people to "positive action and yet devoid of hate and resentment." King wanted the people to be militant ". . . within controllable and Christian bounds." See King, *Stride,* pp. 59-60, 63.

63. King, *Stride,* p. 89; William D. Watley, *Roots of Resistance: The Nonviolent Ethic of Martin Luther King, Jr.* (Valley Forge: Judson, 1985). pp. 111-28.

64. King, *Where Do We Go from Here,* p. 191. King also held to this same point in his final "Mountaintop" speech on the eve of his assassination. See Washington, *Testament of Hope,* pp. 280, 281, 283.

## CHAPTER 6

1. As we have discovered, King himself was no stranger to tension, pressure, and crisis. His own vocational crisis had provided an experiential database as he sought to resolve it. Further, King's philosophy that growth is achieved only through struggle lent itself readily to his pragmatic approach to social change. He never viewed crisis as a negative phenomenon. Rather, King repeatedly sought to generate what he called "creative tension" through nonviolent direct action. In this way, King was eager to precipitate a confrontation of wills and power between the oppositional forces of justice and injustice. Martin Luther King Jr., *Why We Can't Wait* (New York: Signet, 1964), p. 79; James Washington, ed., *A Testament of Hope: The Essential Writings of Martin Luther King, Jr.* (San Francisco: Harper & Row, 1986), pp. 350, 383, 397.

2. *Webster's New Collegiate Dictionary* (G. & C. Merriam Company), pp. 838, 875.

3. Ibid., pp. 345, 875.

4. Richard Mouw, "Faculty as Scholars and Teachers," in *Theological Education* XXVIII (Autumn 1991), p. 76. Also see David Tracy, *The Analogical Imagination: Christian Theology and the Culture of Pluralism* (New York: Crossroad, 1981).

5. Cornel West, *Beyond Eurocentrism and Multiculturalism,* vol. 2 (Monroe, Me.: Common Courage Press, 1993), pp. 37-39. On the postmodern predicament, see also bell hooks and Cornel West, *Breaking Bread: Insurgent Black Intellectual Life* (Boston: South End Press, 1991), pp. 8-19, 44-45, 54-58.

6. See West, *Beyond Eurocentrism and Multiculturalism,* vol. 2, pp. 37-43, 103; *Prophetic Fragments* (Grand Rapids: Eerdmans, 1988), pp. 168-70, 212-16. Jack Solomon, *Signs of Our Time: The Secret Meanings of Everyday Life* (New York: Harper & Row, 1988), pp. 211-30.

7. West, *Beyond Eurocentrism and Multiculturalism, Vol. 2,* pp. 52-54, and *Race Matters* (Boston: Beacon Press, 1993), pp. 5-8, 14-20.

8. Martin Luther King Jr., *Where Do We Go from Here: Chaos or Community?* (Boston: Beacon, 1967), p. 191.

9. For a concise, well-written assessment and critique of the Religious Right, see Gabriel Fackre, *The Religious Right and Christian Faith* (Grand Rapids: Eerdmans, 1982), chapters 1 and 2.

10. King, *Why We Can't Wait,* p. 88.

11. King did not produce a systematic philosophy of statehood, but he did offer clues. In the intimate connection of love with justice, King believed that the state, as a natural creation, derived its existence from the divine mandate. It was subject to the laws of God (namely love and justice). While it should wield the sword and use force, it is to do so with the intent to overcome brokenness and alienation and restore loving community. King supported the notion of separation of church and state, but insisted that religion (in seeking to fulfill its moral obligation as a radically involved community of faith) enjoyed the moral obligation and freedom to seek the construction of laws, policies, and programs in the state that would contribute to the state's operation as a community of love and justice. See Preston Williams, "An Analysis of the Conception of Love and Its Influence on Justice in the Thought of Martin Luther King, Jr.," *Journal of Religious Ethics* 18 (Fall 1990), pp. 18-19, 22-23, 25-26. Also see Hanes Walton, *The Political Philosophy of Martin Luther King, Jr.* (Westport, Conn.: Greenwood Publishing, 1971).

12. Cornel West has argued that contemporary American religious life is experiencing a profound and pervasive crisis in this regard. In fact, "American religious life is losing its prophetic fervor. There is an undeniable decline in the clarity of vision, complexity of understanding, and quality of moral action among religious Americans." West's analysis, hard as it is, speaks to the creative tension that King's theology raises for the present-day church: Is it capable of recovering prophetic and revolutionary elements from its tradition in such a way as to inspire vision, hope, and courageous action toward the actualization of the just community? See West's *Prophetic Fragments*, pp. x-xi.

13. Karl Barth, *Church Dogmatics*, vol. 1, part 1, 2.

14. See Richard Mouw, *Theological Education* XXVIII (Autumn 1991). Also see two texts by Edward Farley that have attempted to deal with the emergent crisis in theological education, *The Fragility of Knowledge: Theological Education in the Church and the University* (Philadelphia: Fortress, 1988), and *Theologia: The Fragmentation and Unity of Theological Education* (Philadelphia: Fortress, 1983).

15. See Cornel West, *Prophetic Fragments*, p. 273 for a provactive and fuller description of the crisis in theological education.

16. Kelsey, "Conjuring Future Faculties" in *Theological Education* XXVIII (Autumn 1991), p. 29.

17. For a particularly helpful discussion on this issue, see Thomas W. Gillespie, "What Is 'Theological' About Theological Education?" *The Princeton Seminary Bulletin* XIV, New Series (1993), pp. 55-63.

18. Dieter T. Hessel, ed., *Theological Education for Social Ministry* (New York: Pilgrim Press, 1988), p. 2.

19. See James Cone, *God of the Oppressed* (New York: Seabury, 1975), pp. 8, 39-45, 53, 82-83, 85-107, 137 for a very helpful discussion of this tension.

20. Paul Tillich, *Systematic Theology, Volume II: Existence and the Christ* (Chicago: University of Chicago Press, 1957), pp. 150-65. See discussion of King's conception of "cross-bearing" in chapter 3 of this work.

21. See King, *Where Do We Go from Here*, appendix.

22. West, *Prophetic Fragments*, p. 277.

23. Richard Niebuhr, *Christ and Culture* (New York: Harper & Row, 1951), pp. 1-44.

24. Ibid., p. 32. Sociologists and anthropologists are virtually unanimous in their defining culture as purposive human activity or "acquired knowledge that people use to interpret experience and generate behavior." See Vine Deloria Jr., "Identity and Culture" in *Daedalus: Journal of the American Academy of Arts and Sciences* 110 (Spring 1981): 13-27.

25. King, *Where Do We Go from Here*, pp. 26-27, 54-66.

26. See "A Letter from H. Rap Brown" in Floyd B. Barbour, ed., *The Black Seventies* (Boston: Porter Sargent Publisher, 1970), pp. 311-13.

27. See Stokely Carmichael and Charles V. Hamilton, *Black Power: The Politics of Liberation in America* (New York: Vintage Books, 1969), pp. 50-53, 82. King also affirmed the presence of systemic violence in the culture, but refused to render the violence-nonviolence question obsolete. See Washington, *Testament of Hope*, p. 327.

28. Washington, *Testament of Hope*, p. 389.

29. In fairness to King, a closer inspection of his thinking about war and the right to self-defense reveals some important distinctions. Although he affirmed their relatedness, King carefully distinguished between personal ethics and social ethics with regard to nonviolence. While holding himself to a strict nonviolent ethic, King differentiated between self-defense in matters of personal safety and self-defense in matters of public safety. "I ain't gon' kill nobody," he said in an interview in the last year of his life (Washington, *Testament of Hope*, pp. 32-33, 334-37, 359-62, 365, 390-91, 589-90). At the same time, King asserted, in response to self-defense advocate Robert Williams, "Nobody argues with self-defense" (ibid., pp. 32-33). King seemed to think it was logically a matter of rational self-interest to expect persons to defend their lives and families.

A careful reading of King's critique against the Vietnam War reveals the basis of that criticism as the unjust nature of U.S. involvement in the war rather than a full-scale critique of war itself (ibid., pp. 231-44, 264-65, 407-8; King, "Declaration of Independence from the War in Vietnam," *A. J. Muste Memorial Institute Essay Series*, Number 1, New York, pp. 35-50). Admittedly, King appeared to be somewhat ambivalent at this point. He conceded that while war may have once served a positive good, it no longer proved efficacious in the settling of human disputes. On the other hand, King seemed to allow for the possibility of "just war" with his critique against the proliferation of nuclear weapons (as opposed to more conventional weapons).

30. For provocative discussions on the issues of violence and peace, see Jürgen Moltmann, *On Human Dignity: Political Theology and Ethics* (Philadelphia: Fortress, 1984), pp. 113-31.

31. James Baldwin, *The Fire Next Time* (New York: Dial, 1963), p. 23. To King's credit, he continued to subject himself to self-criticism as a way of being true to his vocational calling. See Washington, *Testament of Hope*, p. 376. This is why King remained humble in the face of his tremendous responsibility. He reminded us that the vocation to prophetic challenge is not a license for arrogant self-righteousness. The prophet, too, is *one of us*.

32. See Martin E. Marty, *The New Shape of American Religion* (New York: Harper & Row, 1959).

33. See, for instance, Joseph G. Donders, *Non-Bourgeoisie Theology: An African Experience of Jesus* (New York: Orbis Books, 1986).

34. Charles H. Bayer, *A Guide to Liberation Theology for Middle-Class Congregations* (St. Louis: CBP Press, 1986); and Paul G. King, Kent Maynard, and David O. Woodyard, *Risking Liberation: Middle-Class Powerlessness and Social Heroism* (Atlanta: John Knox, 1988). See also Johannes B. Metz's searing critique of middle-class, bourgeois culture in *The Emergent Church* (New York: Crossroad, 1981).

King, of course, addressed this aspect in his critique of white liberals and middle-class blacks, as we have shown in chapter 3 of this work. Other black thinkers have both predated and postdated King in speaking to this issue of apathetic, non-risk-taking lifestyles among black middle-class and the black intelligentsia. See, for instance, E. Franklin Frazier, *Black Bourgeoisie* (New York: Collier Books, 1957); and Harold Cruse, *The Crisis of the Negro Intellectual: A Historical Analysis of the Failure of Black Leadership* (New York: Quill, 1984).

35. C. Eric Lincoln, *Race, Religion, and the Continuing American Dilemma* (New York: Hill & Wang, 1984). King, as we have seen, identified the racial crisis in America as one of its most urgent moral and social problems. See King, *Trumpet of Conscience*, pp. 3-17.

36. See, for instance, Andrew Hacker, *Two Nations: Black and White, Separate, Hostile, Unequal* (New York: Charles Scribner's Sons, 1992); Derrick Bell, *Faces at the Bottom of the Well: The Permanence of Racism* (New York: Basic Books, 1992); Gerald David Jaynes and Robin M. Williams Jr., eds., *A Common Destiny: Blacks and American Society* (Washington, D.C.: National Academy Press, 1989); Cornel West, *Race Matters* (Boston: Beacon, 1993).

When one considers the issue of xenophobic hatred and discrimination with regard to other ethnic groups in the nation—Jews, Native Americans, Hispanics, and so forth—the problem becomes exacerbated to an even greater degree.

37. See Angela Y. Davis, *Women, Culture, and Politics* (New York: Vintage Books, 1990); Barbara H. Andolsen, Christine E. Gudorf, and Mary D. Pellauer, eds., *Women's Consciousness, Women's Conscience: A Reader in Feminist Ethics* (San Francisco: Harper & Row, 1985); Camille Paglia, *Sex, Art, and American Culture* (New York: Vintage Books, 1992); bell hooks, *Black Looks: Race and Representation* (Boston: South End, 1992).

38. See Jaynes and Williams, *A Common Destiny*; and Andrew Hacker, *Two Nations*.

39. Kevin Phillips, *The Politics of Rich and Poor: Wealth and the American Electorate in the Reagan Aftermath* (New York: Random House, 1990).

40. Douglas Sturm, "Martin Luther King, Jr., As Democratic Socialist," in *The Journal of Religious Ethics* 18 (Fall 1992): pp. 79-106.

41. Ibid., pp. 99-103.

42. Systemic elements in King's theology are prominent. Three systemic vectors are clearly discernible in King's theological perspective. The first was a philosophical view of the interrelatedness of existence including affirmations about the sociality, mutuality, and interdependency of human living. The second systemic vector stressed an analytical approach that did not fail to grasp the connection between seemingly disparate aspects of sociopolitical reality. In a word, the interstructuring of oppression. King saw the "triple evils" of racism, poverty, and war as interlocking strands in a web of oppression. The third systemic vector pursued the appropriation

of a method of praxis that affirmed that all emancipatory action (sacrificial suffering, prayer, nonviolent resistance, voting, massive civil disobedience) aimed at the actualization of justice had cosmic implications. That is to say, in a world where God was sovereign, the consequences of human action were always beyond the moment. In this sense, means-ends coherence in the pursuit of community was affirmed, and piecemeal, narrowly circumscribed remedies were rejected.

43. Among the more helpful studies that incorporate class analyses when considering the prospects for societal reconstruction are Michael Harrington, *The Other America: Poverty in the United States* (Middlesex, England: Penguin Books, 1962, 1969, 1981); Manning Marable, *How Capitalism Underdeveloped Black America: Problems in Race, Political Economy, and Society* (Boston: South End, 1983); *The Truly Disadvantaged: The Inner City, the Underclass, and Public Policy* (Chicago: University of Chicago Press, 1987); Sheila Collins, "The Economic Basis of Racism and Sexism" in *Theology in the Americas Documentation Series,* Number 13, November 1980.

44. Among these are economists like Milton Friedman, David Stockman, and Michael Novak; political conservatives like George Will and William F. Buckley; and capitalist business entrepreneurs like T. Boon Pickens, Donald Trump, and H. Ross Perot.

45. For a thorough discussion of the differences between communism and socialism, see Arthur F. McGovern, *Marxism: An American Christian Perspective* (New York: Orbis Books, 1987), pp. 1-8, 49-89, 245-77, 296-308, 309-28.

46. See King, *Stride,* pp. 91-95, and *Where Do We Go from Here,* pp. 161-66, 176-79, 187-89. King was drawing from several streams of tradition in American liberal theology and philosophical pragmatism. We have already alluded to the influence of black religious and critical philosophical thought upon King. In addition, Marx gave King critical analytical tools with which to focus on issues of wealth and poverty. The social gospel movement (especially Walter Rauschenbusch's socialist tendencies) and Paul Tillich's early writings affirming Christian socialism helped predispose King to socialist thinking. As far as the U.S. historical stream is concerned, the tradition of thinking represented by Norman Thomas and Eugene Debs informed King's notions about the need for a "socially conscious democracy." For a discussion of the tradition of socialism in the United States, see McGovern, *Marxism,* pp. 309-28; John C. Cort, *Christian Socialism* (New York: Orbis Books, 1988), pp. 222-81.

47. The public nature of King's perspective concerned itself with the redemption of the collective conscience as well as the salvation of the individual soul. In fact, it was King's affirmation of the sociopolitical dimensions of religion and the gospel that paved the way for a concern with matters of social transformation. Using the language of public discourse, King played in the marketplace of ideas with the intent to shape public ethos and policy, thereby influencing the moral renewal of the society.

Coleman Brown has argued that King is best viewed as public theologian. See his Ph.D. dissertation, "Grounds for American Loyalty in a Prophetic Christian Social Ethic—With Special Attention to Martin Luther King, Jr.," Union Theological Seminary, New York, 1979. While I agree with Brown that King's thought has a definite public emphasis, I see that emphasis as only one aspect of King's overall theological thrust, namely radical involvement.

48. Quoted in Frederick Herzog, *Liberation Theology* (New York: Seabury, 1973), pp. viii, 15.

49. James Cone, *A Black Theology of Liberation* (New York: J. B. Lippincott Company, 1970), pp. 77, 109, 162. By this, Cone means a difference in focus on either doctrinal clarity or justice-oriented praxis.

50. John W. Bowman is helpful in describing prophetic realism as a "type of conversational methodology" that places humanity "in touch with the truth of God." The emphasis is upon the covenantal nature of reality and the notion that humanity can enjoy companionship with God as a normal feature of human living. Bowman argues that prophetic realism promotes a "dialectic" that is threefold. First, God speaks to humanity for its well-being, and humanity is capable of learning God's will for the world. Second, humanity can hear and clearly discern as God speaks to impart divine purposes. Third, humanity can and ought to act resolutely, once it achieves epistemological certainty relative to God's will. See Bowman's *Prophetic Realism and the Gospel: A Preface to Biblical Theology* (Philadelphia: Westminster, 1955), pp. 41-47.

51. Even SCLC, during King's life, contributed to building him in a certain image. See Adam Fairclough, *To Redeem the Soul of America: The Southern Christian Leadership Conference and Martin Luther King, Jr.* (Athens: University of Georgia Press, 1987), pp. 2-3. Today, SCLC has been eclipsed by the more powerful political and business interests in the nation.

52. See C. Eric Lincoln, *Race, Religion, and the Continuing American Dilemma*, pp. 241-48, on King as "paradox par excellence."

53. On the notion of "circles of death," see Jürgen Moltmann, *The Crucified God* (New York: Harper & Row, 1974), pp. 329-32.

54. Several helpful analyses of the postmodern predicament are currently in print. See bell hooks and Cornel West, *Breaking Bread: Insurgent Black Intellectual Life* (Boston: South End, 1991), pp. 8-19, 44-45, 54-58; Frederic Burnham, ed., *Postmodern Theology: Christian Faith in a Pluralist World* (San Francisco: Harper & Row, 1989); Roger Lundin, *The Culture of Interpretation: Christian Faith and the Postmodern World* (Grand Rapids: Eerdmans, 1993).

55. See Henry David Thoreau's book written in 1854 entitled *Walden: Or Life in the Woods* (New York: Harper & Row, 1965), p. 7.

56. bell hooks and Cornel West, *Breaking Bread*, pp. 7-19, 52-58; William J. Wilson, *The Truly Disadvantaged*.

57. Washington, *Testament of Hope*, p. 375.

# BIBLIOGRAPHY

Abernathy, Ralph. *And the Walls Came Tumbling Down: Ralph David Abernathy—An Autobiography.* New York: Harper & Row, 1989.

_____. "Dr. King's Theology in Action." Unpublished paper. n.d.

Albert, Peter J., and Ronald Hoffman, eds. *We Shall Overcome: Martin Luther King, Jr., and the Black Freedom Struggle.* New York: Da Capo Press, 1993.

Alinsky, Saul. *Rules for Radicals.* New York: Vintage Books, 1971.

Allen, Robert. *Black Awakening in Capitalist America.* Trenton, N.J.: Africa World Press, 1990.

Anderson, James Desmond. *The Ministry of the Laity and the Corporate Culture of the Gathered Church.* Washington, D.C.: Mount Saint Alban, 1984.

Anderson, Ralph E., and Irl E. Carter. *Human Behavior in the Social Environment.* Chicago: Aldine Publishing Company, 1974.

Andolsen, Barbara H., and Christine E. Gudorf, eds. *Women's Consciousness, Women's Conscience: A Reader in Feminist Ethics.* San Francisco: Harper & Row, 1985.

Ansbro, John. *Martin Luther King, Jr.: The Making of a Mind.* Maryknoll, N.Y.: Orbis, 1982.

Baer, Hans A. *The Black Spiritual Movement: A Religious Response to Racism.* Knoxville: Univ. of Tennessee Press, 1984.

Baldwin, James. *The Fire Next Time.* New York: Dial Press, 1963.

Baldwin, Lewis V. *There Is a Balm in Gilead: The Cultural Roots of Martin Luther King, Jr.* Minneapolis: Fortress, 1991.

_____. *To Make the Wounded Whole: The Cultural Legacy of Martin Luther King, Jr.* Minneapolis: Fortress, 1992.

Barbour, Floyd B., ed. *The Black Seventies.* Boston: Porter Sargent Publisher, 1970.

Barth, Karl. *Evangelical Theology: An Introduction.* Grand Rapids: Eerdmans, 1963.

Bayer, Charles H. *A Guide to Liberation Theology for Middle-Class Congregations.* St. Louis: CBP Press, 1986.

Beach, Waldo, and H. Richard Niebuhr, eds. *Christian Ethics.* London: Alfred A. Knopf, 1973.

Bell, Derrick. *And We Are Not Saved: The Elusive Quest for Racial Justice.* New York: Basic Books, 1987.

_____. *Faces at the Bottom of the Well: The Permanence of Racism.* New York: Basic Books, 1992.

Bellah, Robert, et al., eds. *Habits of the Heart.* New York: Harper & Row, 1985.

Benne, Robert. *The Ethic of Democratic Capitalism: A Moral Reassessment.* Philadelphia: Fortress, 1981.

Bennett, Lerone. *What Manner of Man.* Chicago: Johnson Publishing, 1976.

Booth, William D. *The Progressive Story: New Baptist Roots.* St. Paul, Minn.: Brown Press, 1981.

Bosmajian, Haigo. "The Inaccuracies of Martin Luther King's 'I Have a Dream' Speech." *Communication Education* 31 (April 1982): 107-14.

Bowman, John W. *Prophetic Realism and the Gospel: A Preface to Biblical Theology.* Philadelphia: Westminster, 1955.

Bowne, Borden Parker. *The Principle of Ethics and Personalism.* New York: Harper & Brothers, 1892.

_____. *Personalism.* Boston: Houghton Mifflin, 1908.

Branch, Taylor. *Parting the Waters: America During the King Years, 1954–1963.* New York: Simon & Schuster, 1988.

Brightman, Edgar S. *Moral Laws.* New York: Abingdon Press, 1933.

Brisbane, Robert. *The Black Vanguard.* Valley Forge: Judson, 1970.

Brown, Coleman B. "Grounds for American Loyalty in a Prophetic Christian Social Ethic—With Special Attention to Martin Luther King, Jr." Ph.D. diss., Union Theological Seminary, 1979.

Brown, H. Rap. *Die Nigger Die.* New York: Dial Press, 1969.

Bruce, Calvin E., and William R. Jones, eds. *Black Theology II.* London: Associated University Press, 1978.

Burnham, Frederic B., ed. *Postmodern Theology: Christian Faith in a Pluralist World.* San Francisco: Harper & Row, 1989.

Cade, Toni, ed. *The Black Woman.* Ontario, Canada: The New American Library, 1970.

Cannon, Katie. *Black Womanist Ethics.* Atlanta: Scholars Press, 1988.

Carmichael, Stokely, and Charles V. Hamilton. *Black Power: The Politics of Liberation in America.* New York: Vintage Books, 1969.

Carr, Carol. *Public Images of Martin Luther King, Jr.* Ph.D. diss., Ohio State Univ., 1977.

Carson, Clayborne, ed. *Papers of Martin Luther King, Jr., Volume I: Called to Serve, January 1929–June 1951.* Berkeley: Univ. of California Press, 1992.

Carter, Stephen L. *The Culture of Disbelief: How American Law and Politics Trivialize Religious Devotion.* New York: Basic Books, 1993.

Chopp, Rebecca. *The Praxis of Suffering.* Maryknoll, N.Y.: Orbis, 1986.

Cleghorn, Reese. "Martin Luther King, Apostle of Crisis." *Saturday Evening Post* 236 (June 15, 1963): 15-19.

Collins, Sheila. "The Economic Basis of Racism and Sexism." *Theology in the Americas Documentation Series.* 1980.

Cone, Cecil W. *Identity Crisis in Black Theology.* Nashville: The African Methodist Episcopal Church, 1975.

Cone, James. *Black Theology and Black Power.* San Francisco: Harper & Row, 1969.

_____. *A Black Theology of Liberation.* Philadelphia: J. B. Lippincott, 1970.

_____. *God of the Oppressed.* New York: Seabury Press, 1975.

_____. *Martin and Malcolm and America: A Dream or a Nightmare.* Maryknoll, N.Y.: Orbis, 1991.

_____. "Martin Luther King, Jr., Black Theology—Black Church." *Theology Today* 41 (January 1986): 409-20.

_____. "The Theology of Martin Luther King, Jr." *Union Seminary Quarterly Review* 40 (January 1986): 21-39.

_____. *Speaking the Truth.* Grand Rapids: Eerdmans, 1986.

Cort, John C. *Christian Socialism.* Maryknoll, N.Y.: Orbis, 1988.

Cox, Harvey. *On Not Leaving It to the Snake.* New York: Macmillan, 1967.

Cruse, Harold. *Crisis of the Negro Intellectual: A Historical Analysis of the Failure of Black Leadership.* New York: Quill, 1967, 1984.

Davis, Angela Y. *Women, Culture, and Politics.* New York: Vintage Books, 1990.

_____. *Women, Race, and Class.* New York: Vintage Books, 1983.

Deloria Jr., Vine. "Identity and Culture." *Daedalus: Journal of the American Academy of Arts and Sciences* 110 (Spring 1981): 13-27.

DeWolf, L. Harold. "Martin Luther King, Jr., As Theologian." *Journal of the Interdenominational Center* 4 (Spring 1977): 1-11.

Donders, Joseph G. *Non-Bourgeoisie Theology: An African Experience of Jesus.* Maryknoll, N.Y.: Orbis, 1986.

Downing, Fred. *To See the Promised Land: The Faith Pilgrimage of Martin Luther King, Jr.* Macon: Mercer Univ. Press, 1986.

DuBois, W. E. B. *The Souls of Black Folk.* Chicago: A. C. McClurg & Co., 1903.

Dyck, Arthur C. *On Human Care: An Introduction to Christian Ethics.* Nashville: Abingdon Press, 1977.

Ellison, Mary. *The Black Experience: American Blacks Since 1865.* New York: Barnes & Nobles, 1974.

Ellul, Jacques. *Jesus and Marx: From Gospel to Ideology.* Grand Rapids: Eerdmans, 1988.

Elshtain, Jean Bethke. *Public Man, Private Woman: Women in Social and Political Thought.* Princeton: Princeton Univ. Press, 1981.

Erskine, Noel. "The Theology of Martin Luther King, Jr." unpublished paper. n.d.

_____. *King Among the Theologians.* Cleveland: Pilgrim Press, 1994.

Evans, James H. "The Graduate Education of Future Theological Faculties." *Theological Education* XXVIII (Autumn 1991): 85 -89.

Fackre, Gabriel. *The Religious Right and Christian Faith*. Grand Rapids: Eerdmans, 1982.

Fairclough, Adam. *To Redeem the Soul of America: The Southern Christian Leadership Conference and Martin Luther King, Jr.* Athens, Ga.: Univ. of Georgia Press, 1987.

Farley, Edward. *Theologia: The Fragmentation and Unity of Theological Education*. Philadelphia: Fortress, 1983.

_____. *The Fragility of Knowledge: Theological Education in the Church and the University*. Philadelphia: Fortress, 1988.

Fluker, Walter Earl. "They Looked for a City." *Journal of Religious Ethics* 18 (Fall 1990): 39.

Foner, Philip S., ed. *Black Socialist Preacher: The Teachings of Reverend George Washington Woodbey and His Disciple Reverend George W. Slater, Jr.* San Francisco: Synthesis Publications, 1983.

Fordham, Monroe. *Major Themes in Northern Black Religious Thought, 1800–1860*. Hicksville, N.Y.: Exposition Press, 1975.

Forell, George W. *Christian Social Teachings*. Minneapolis: Augsburg, 1966.

Fowler, James. *Stages of Faith*. San Francisco: Harper & Row, 1981.

Franklin, Robert M. *Liberating Visions: Human Fulfillment and Social Justice in African-American Thought*. Minneapolis: Fortress, 1990.

Frazier, E. Franklin. *Black Bourgeoisie*. New York: Collier Books, 1957.

_____. *The Negro Church in America*. New York: Schocken, 1964.

Friesen, Duane. *Christian Peacemaking and International Conflict: A Realist Pacifist Perspective*. Scottsdale, Pa.: Herald Press, 1986.

Garber, Paul. "Black Theology: The Latter Day Legacy of Martin Luther King, Jr." *Journal of the Interdenominational Theological Center* 2 (Spring 1975): 100-113.

_____. "Too Much Taming of Martin Luther King?" *Christian Century* XCI (June 5, 1974): 616.

_____. *Martin Luther King, Jr.: Theologian and Precursor of Black Theology*. Ph.D. diss., Florida State Univ., 1973.

_____. "King Was a Black Theologian." *Journal of Religious Thought* 31 (Fall-Winter 1974–75): 16-32.

Garrow, David. *Bearing the Cross: Martin Luther King, Jr., and the Southern Christian Leadership Conference*. New York: William Morrow, 1986.

_____. *The FBI and Martin Luther King, Jr.: From "Solo" to Memphis*. New York: W. W. Norton, 1981.

Gillespie, Thomas W. "What Is 'Theological' About Theological Education?" *The Princeton Seminary Bulletin* XIV (1993): 55-63. New Series.

Goba, Bonganjalo. *An Agenda for Black Theology: Hermeneutics for Social Change*. Johannesburg, South Africa: Skotaville Publishers, 1988.

Goodwin, Bennie. "Martin Luther King, Jr., Social Educator." *Journal of the Interdenominational Theological Center* IV (Spring 1977): 45.

_____. "Martin Luther King, Jr., American Social Educator." *Journal of the Interdenominational Theological Center* IV (Spring 1977): 42-48.

Gustafson, James. *Ethics from a Theocentric Perspective, Volume 2: Ethics and Theology.* Chicago: Univ. of Chicago Press, 1984.

Gutierrez, Gustavo. *A Theology of Liberation: History, Salvation, and Politics.* Maryknoll, N.Y.: Orbis, 1984.

Hacker, Andrew. *Two Nations: Black and White, Separate, Hostile, Unequal.* New York: Charles Scribner's Sons, 1992.

Hampton, Henry, and Steve Fayer. *Voices of Freedom: An Oral History of the Civil Rights Movement from the 1950s through the 1980s.* New York: Bantam, 1990.

Handy, Robert T. *The Social Gospel in America, 1870–1920.* New York: Oxford Univ. Press, 1966.

Hanigan, James P. "Martin Luther King, Jr.: Images of a Man." *Journal of Religious Thought* 31 (Spring-Summer 1974): 68-95.

_____. *Martin Luther King, Jr., and the Foundations of Nonviolence.* Latham, Md.: Univ. Press of America, 1984.

Harding, Vincent. "The Land Beyond: Reflections on Martin Luther King, Jr.'s, 'Beyond Vietnam' Speech." *Sojourners* (January 1986), 2-9.

_____. "Recalling the Inconvenient Hero: Reflections on the Last Years of Martin Luther King, Jr." *Union Seminary Quarterly Review* 40 (January 1986): 53-68.

Harrington, Michael. *The Other America: Poverty in the United States.* Middlesex, England: Penguin Books, 1981.

Harris, John. "The Theology of Martin Luther King, Jr." Ph.D. diss., Duke Univ., 1974.

Harvey, Van A. *A Handbook of Theological Terms.* New York: Macmillan, 1964.

Hauerwas, Stanley. *Should War Be Eliminated?* Milwaukee: Marquette Univ. Press, 1984.

Hessel, Deter T., ed. *Theological Education for Social Ministry.* New York: Pilgrim Press, 1988.

Hodgson, Peter C., and Robert H. King, eds. *Christian Theology.* Philadelphia: Fortress, 1985.

hooks, bell. *Black Looks: Race and Representation.* Boston: South End Press, 1992.

hooks, bell and Cornel West. *Breaking Bread: Insurgent Black Intellectual Life.* Boston: South End Press, 1991.

Howard-Pitney, David. *The Afro-American Jeremiad: Appeals for Justice in America.* Philadelphia: Temple Univ. Press, 1990.

Hoyt Jr., Thomas. "The Biblical Tradition of the Poor and Martin Luther King, Jr." *Journal of the Interdenominational Theological Center* IV (Spring 1977): 12-32.

Ivory, Luther D. "Dr. Martin Luther King, Jr.: More Than a Dream." *Union Theological Seminary Focus* (Spring 1992), 4.

Jaynes, Gerald David and Robin M. Williams Jr., eds. *A Common Destiny: Blacks and American Society.* Washington, D.C.: National Academy Press, 1989.

Jones, William R. "Martin Luther King, Jr.: Black Messiah or White Guardian?" Audiotape of unpublished lecture. Florida A&M Univ., 1973.

Kahane, Howard. *Thinking About Basic Beliefs: An Introduction to Philosophy.* Belmont, Calif.: Wadsworth Publishing, 1983.

Kane, Brian M. "The Influence of Boston Personalism on the Thought of Dr. Martin Luther King, Jr." Master's thesis, Boston Univ., 1983.

Kant, Immanuel. *Foundations of the Metaphysics of Morals.* Translated by Lewis Beck. New York: The Library of Liberal Arts Press, 1959.

Kelsey, David. "Conjuring Future Faculties." *Theological Education* XXVIII (Autumn 1991): 29.

King, Charles H. "Quest and Conflict: The Untold Story of the Power Struggle Between King and Jackson." *Negro Digest,* (May 1967), 6-9, 71-79.

King, Coretta Scott. *My Life with Martin Luther King, Jr.* New York: Holt, Rinehart, & Winston, 1969.

_____, ed. *The Words of Martin Luther King, Jr.* New York: Newmarket Press, 1983, 1987.

King, Jr., Martin L. *Stride Toward Freedom.* San Francisco: Harper & Row, 1958.

_____. *Strength to Love.* Philadelphia: Fortress, 1963.

_____. "Who Is Their God?" *Nation* 195 (October 13, 1952): 209-10.

_____. *Where Do We Go from Here: Chaos or Community?* Boston: Beacon, 1967.

_____. "A Comparison of the Conceptions of God in the Thinking of Paul Tillich and Henry Nelson Wieman." Ph.D. diss., Boston Univ., 1955.

_____. *The Measure of Man.* Philadelphia: Fortress, 1959.

_____. "Action for Interracial Understanding." *Franciscan Herald and Forum* 42 (October 1963): 289.

_____. *Trumpet of Conscience.* San Francisco: Harper & Row, 1967.

_____. "The Negro Is Your Brother." *Atlantic Monthly* 207 (August 12, 1963): 78-81, 86-88.

_____. "Suffering and Faith." *Christian Century* 77 (April 27, 1960).

_____. "Is It All Right to Break the Law?" *U.S. News and World Report* 55 (August 12, 1963), 6.

_____. *Why We Can't Wait.* New York: Signet, 1964.

King, Paul G., and Kent Maynard. *Risking Liberation: Middle-Class Powerlessness and Social Heroism.* Atlanta: John Knox, 1988.

Knudson, Albert C. *The Principles of Christian Ethics.* New York: Abingdon Press, 1943.

Lee, Shin. "Concept of Human Nature, Justice, and Nonviolence in the Political Thinking of Martin Luther King, Jr." Ph.D. diss., New York Univ., 1979.

LeFevre, Perry, ed. *Man: Six Modern Interpretations.* Philadelphia: Geneva Press, 1966.

Leith, John. *John Calvin's Doctrine of the Christian Life.* Louisville: Westminster/John Knox, 1989.

Lincoln, C. Eric, ed. *Martin Luther King, Jr.: A Profile.* New York: Hill & Wang, 1970.

_____. *The Black Experience in Religion.* New York: Doubleday, 1974.

_____. *Race, Religion, and the Continuing American Dilemma.* New York: Hill & Wang, 1984.

Lokos, Lionel L. *A House Divided: The Life and Legacy of Martin Luther King.* New Rochelle, N.Y.: Arlington House, 1968.

Lundin, Roger. *The Culture of Interpretation: Christian Faith and the Postmodern World.* Grand Rapids: Eerdmans, 1993.

McClendon, James W. *Biography as Theology.* Nashville: Abingdon Press, 1974.

McGovern, Arthur F. *Marxism: An American Christian Perspective.* New York: Orbis, 1987.

Mappes, Thomas A. and Jane S. Zembaty. *Social Ethics: Morality and Social Policy.* New York: McGraw-Hill, 1977.

Marable, Manning. *How Capitalism Underdeveloped Black America: Problems in Race, Political Economy, and Society.* Boston: South End Press, 1983.

_____. *Race, Reform, and Rebellion: The Second Reconstruction in Black America, 1945-1982.* Jackson: Univ. Press of Mississippi, 1984.

Meier, August. "On the Role of Martin Luther King." *New Politics* 4 (Winter 1965).

Metz, Johannes B. *The Emergent Church.* New York: Crossroad, 1981.

_____. *Theology of the World.* New York: Seabury Press, 1969.

_____. *Faith in History and Society.* New York: Seabury Press, 1980.

Midgely, Mary, and Judith Hughes. *Women's Choices: Philosophical Problems Facing Feminism.* New York: St. Martin's, 1983.

Mikelson, Thomas J. S. "Cosmic Companionship: The Place of God in the Moral Reasoning of Martin Luther King, Jr." *Journal of Religious Ethics* 18 (Fall 1990): 8-9.

Miller, Keith D. *Voice of Deliverance: The Language of Martin Luther King, Jr., and Its Sources.* New York: Free Press, 1992.

Miller, Larry. "King's Liberating Theology." *Thought* 23 (January 1988): 5-24.

_____. "King's Liberating Theology." *Quaker Religious Thought* 23 (January 1988): 5-24.

Mitchell, Henry. *Black Belief.* New York: Harper & Row, 1975.

Moltmann, Jürgen. *The Crucified God.* New York: Harper & Row, 1974.

_____. *On Human Dignity: Political Theology and Ethics.* Philadelphia: Fortress, 1977.

Morris, Aldon. *Origins of the Civil Rights Movement.* New York: Free Press, 1984.

Morris, Calvin. "Martin Luther King, Jr., Exemplary Preacher." *The Journal of the Interdenominational Theological Center* IV (Spring 1976): 61-66.

Mouw, Richard. "Faculty as Scholars and Teachers." *Theological Education* XXVIII (Autumn 1991): 76.

Namorato, Michael V., ed. *Have We Overcome?* Jackson: Univ. Press of Mississippi, 1979.

Nash, Arnold, ed. *Protestant Thought in the Twentieth Century.* New York: Macmillan, 1951.

Newbigin, Lesslie. *Truth to Tell: The Gospel as Public Truth.* New York: Eerdmans, 1991.

Niebuhr, H. Richard. *Christ and Culture.* New York: Harper & Row, 1951.

Oates, Stephen. *Let the Trumpet Sound.* New York: Signet, 1982.

Oglesby, Enoch. "The Theology of Martin Luther King, Jr." unpublished paper. n.d.

Paglia, Camille. *Sex, Art, and American Culture.* New York: Vintage Books, 1992.

_____. *Sexual Personae: Art and Decadence from Nefertiti to Emily Dickinson.* New York: Vintage Books, 1990.

Paris, Peter. *Black Religious Leaders: Conflict in Unity.* Louisville: Westminster/John Knox, 1991.

_____. *Social Teachings of the Black Churches.* Philadelphia: Fortress, 1985.

Phillips, Kevin. *The Politics of Rich and Poor: Wealth and the American Electorate in the Reagan Aftermath.* New York: Random House, 1990.

Rathbun, John. "Martin Luther King: The Theology of Social Action." *American Quarterly* 20 (Spring 1968): 38-53.

Rauschenbusch, Walter. *A Theology for the Social Gospel.* New York: Macmillan, 1917.

_____. *Christianity and the Social Crisis.* New York: Harper & Row, 1907.

Reist, Benjamin. *Toward a Theology of Involvement: The Thought of Ernsth Troeltsch.* Philadelphia: Westminster, 1966.

Richardson, Herbert, "Martin Luther King, Jr.: Unsung Theologian." *New Theology Number 6.* New York: Macmillan, 1969.

_____. "Martin Luther King—Unsung Theologian." *Commonwealth* 89 (May 3, 1968): 201-2.

Riddick, Lawrence. *Crusader Without Violence: A Biography of Martin Luther King, Jr.* New York: Harper & Brothers, 1959.

Runyon, Theodore. "Tillich's Understanding of Revolution." *Theonomy and Autonomy,* Atlanta: Mercer Univ. Press, 1984.

Scott, Robert L. and Wayne Brockriede, eds. *The Rhetoric of Black Power.* New York: Harper & Row, 1969.

Smith, Ervin. "The Role of Personalism in the Development of the Social Ethics of Martin Luther King, Jr." Ph.D. diss., Northwestern Univ., 1976.

Smylie, James H. "On Jesus, Pharaohs, and the Chosen People: Martin Luther King as Biblical Interpreter and Humanist." *Interpretation* 24 (January 1970): 74-90.

Soelle, Dorothy. *Suffering*. Philadelphia: Fortress, 1975.

Sowell, Thomas. *A Conflict of Visions: Ideological Origins of Political Struggles*. New York: William Morrow, 1987.

Stackhouse, Max. *Public Theology and Political Economy*. New York: Univ. Press of America, 1991.

Stang, Alan. *It's Very Simple—The True Story of Civil Rights*. Belmont: Western Islands Publishers, 1965.

Stringfellow, William. *Dissenter in a Great Society*. New York: Holt, Rinehart & Winston, 1966.

Sturm, Douglas. "Martin Luther King, Jr., as Democratic Socialist." *Journal of Religious Ethics* 18 (Fall 1990): 79-106.

Tillich, Paul. *Systematic Theology*. Chicago: Univ. of Chicago Press, 1951.

_____. *Systematic Theology*, Vol. 2, *Existence and the Christ*. Chicago: Univ. of Chicago Press, 1957.

Tracy, David. *The Analogical Imagination: Christian Theology and the Culture of Pluralism*. New York: Crossroad, 1981.

Turkel, Studs. *Race: How Blacks and Whites Think and Feel About the American Obsession*. New York: New Press, 1992.

Turner, Jonathan H. *Patterns of Social Organization*. New York: McGraw-Hill, 1972.

vanDijk, Tuen A. *Communicating Racism: Ethnic Prejudice in Thought and Talk*. Newbury Park, Calif.: Sage, 1987.

Walker, Theodore. *Empower the People: Social Ethics for the African-American Church*. Maryknoll, N.Y.: Orbis, 1991.

Walton, Hanes. *The Political Philosophy of Martin Luther King, Jr*. Westport, Conn: Greenwood Publishing, 1971.

Washington, James. *Frustrated Fellowships: The Black Baptist Quest for Social Power*. Athens: Univ. of Georgia Press, 1986.

_____, ed. *A Testament of Hope: The Essential Writings of Martin Luther King, Jr*. San Francisco: Harper & Row, 1986.

Washington, Joseph. *Black Religion*. Boston: Beacon, 1964.

_____. *Black Sects and Cults*. Garden City, N.Y.: Doubleday/Anchor, 1973.

_____. *The Politics of God*. Boston: Beacon, 1967.

_____, ed. *Black Religion and Public Policy*. Philadelphia: Univ. of Pennsylvania Press, 1978.

Watley, William D. *Roots of Resistance*. Valley Forge: Judson, 1985.

West, Cornel. *Race Matters*. Boston: Beacon, 1993.

_____. *Prophetic Fragments*. Grand Rapids: Eerdmans, 1988.

Williams, Preston. "An Analysis of the Conception of Love and Its Influence on Justice in the Thought of Martin Luther King, Jr." *Journal of Religious Ethics* 18 (Fall 1990): 18-19, 21-23, 25.

Wilmore, Gayraud. *Black and Presbyterian: The Heritage and the Hope.* Philadelphia: Geneva, 1983.

_____. *Black Religion and Black Radicalism.* Maryknoll, N.Y.: Orbis, 1984.

Wilson, William J. *The Truly Disadvantaged: The Inner City, the Underclass, and Public Policy.* Chicago: Univ. of Chicago Press, 1987.

_____. *The Declining Significance of Race: Blacks and Changing American Institutions.* Second edition. Chicago: Univ. of Chicago Press, 1980.

Wolfenstein, Eugene Victor. *The Victims of Democracy: Malcolm X and the Black Revolution.* New York: Guilford, 1993.

Wright, Anthony. *Socialisms: Theories and Practices.* New York: Oxford Univ. Press, 1986.

Young, Alfred F., ed. *Dissent.* DeKalb: Northern Illinois Univ. Press, 1968.

Zepp, Ira, and Kenneth Smith. *Search for the Beloved Community: The Thinking of Martin Luther King, Jr.* Valley Forge: Judson, 1974.

Printed in the United States
74983LV00003B/98